As a Fire by Burning

Mission as the Life of the
Local Congregation

Roger Standing

scm press

Published in 2013 by SCM Press
Editorial office
3rd Floor Invicta House
108–114 Golden Lane,
London
EC1Y 0TG

SCM Press is an imprint of Hymns Ancient & Modern Ltd
(a registered charity)
13A Hellesdon Park Road
Norwich NR6 5DR, UK

www.scmpress.co.uk

British Library Cataloguing in Publication data

A catalogue record for this book is available
from the British Library

978-0-334-04370-6
Kindle edition 978-0-334-04461-1

Typeset by Regent Typesetting, London
Printed and bound by
CPI Group (UK) Ltd, Croydon

Contents

Contributors

Pete Atkins leads a church called Threshold in rural Lincolnshire, which he and others planted in 1995. Threshold has members in many villages, where they seek to live missionally. Pete is a Director of Ground Level – a UK-based 'new church' network with partner networks in South Africa and the USA. Pete and his wife Kath are both members of the national Fresh Expressions team, where they work within the training hub. Pete also has the brief within the team for rural fresh expressions of church.

Terry Drummond is the Bishop of Southwark's Adviser on Urban and Public Policy. With nearly forty years' experience in ministry, he has worked as an adviser on mission in the local economy, advised on the contribution of the local churches on combating social need and inequality and on good practice in supporting individuals and families who live on the fringes of society. Previous publications have been essays published on Christianity and poverty, Christian responses to the market economy, and the local churches' contribution to working to create healthier communities.

Clare Hooper is a Baptist minister (youth specialist). She has served in the same church and community since 1997 and loves the people with whom she works. During this time, she has been involved in church-based youth work, street work, council youth clubs, drop-ins, schools work, mentoring, residentials, youth exchanges, project work, small groups and other bits and pieces. In all of these things, she seeks to help people connect with God and his Kingdom. Clare trained with the Oxford Centre for Youth Ministry.

Simon Jones is the ministry team leader at Bromley Baptist Church and an associate tutor in New Testament at Spurgeon's College. He is the author of nine books, including *The World of the Early Church: A Social History* (Lion Hudson, 2011), *Building a Better Body: The Good Church Guide* (Authentic, 2007), *Discovering Galatians* (Crossway, 2007) and

Discovering Luke (Crossway, 1999). A former financial journalist, he was minister of Peckham Park Baptist Church, launch editor of *Christianity* magazine and co-ordinator for London and the South East for BMS World Mission. Simon is married to Linda with two grown-up daughters and two granddaughters.

David Kerrigan is General Director of BMS World Mission. David first served with BMS in the 1980s in Bangladesh and later in Sri Lanka, where he operated as BMS Team Leader for Asia, with responsibility for work in Nepal, Thailand, Indonesia, India and Afghanistan. During this time, he served as President of the United Mission to Nepal, before returning to the UK in 1999. For ten years David was responsible for oversight of BMS overseas ministries, before being appointed as General Director in January 2009.

Juliet Kilpin helps to co-ordinate an urban mission agency called Urban Expression and co-runs the Crucible Course, which equips those seeking to follow Jesus on the margins. She co-led the first Urban Expression team, which went on the adventure of forming a church in Shadwell, Tower Hamlets, London. Juliet is also a Baptist minister involved in local creative ministry and is a freelance consultant, development worker and trainer. Her previous publications include *Church Planting in the Inner City: The Urban Expression Story* (Grove Books, 2007).

Cid Latty worked in worship ministry for ten years before two successive ministries leading Baptist churches and then founding the Cafechurch Network (www.cafechurch.net). He now regularly runs training days, produces cafechurch resources and helps churches start cafechurches. Cid is also the Director of Living Well, a renewal agency that works with churches in decline, to experience turnaround. He has written about worship in *Many Nations One Church*, a Christian Aid publication.

Samantha Mail is a Baptist minister in a small church in Berkshire. Together with her husband Sam, she made the transition from a large pioneer church to a small Baptist church over five years ago. Originally from Berlin, she is passionate about the local church and bringing people to a place where they are actively engaging in God's mission.

David Male is an Anglican minister and is Director of the Centre for Pioneer Learning based in Cambridge and Tutor in Pioneer Mission Training at Ridley Hall and Westcott House, Cambridge. He previously helped to plant the Net Church in Huddersfield, a 'network type' church, which was one of the first Anglican fresh expressions of church. His previous publications include *Church Unplugged: Remodelling Church without Losing Your Soul* (Authentic, 2008) and he has edited *Pioneers 4 Life: Explorations in Theology and Wisdom for Pioneering Leaders* (BRF, 2011).

Martyn Percy is Principal of Ripon College, Cuddesdon, the Oxford Ministry Course and the West of England Ministerial Training Course. He is also Professor of Theological Education at King's College, London, and Professorial Research Fellow at Heythrop College, London. An Honorary Canon of Salisbury Cathedral, he has served as curate at St Andrew's, Bedford, and Chaplain and Director of Studies at Christ's College, Cambridge, before being appointed as Director of the Lincoln Theological Institute in 1997. He was a Canon of Sheffield Cathedral from 1997 to 2004, and Canon Theologian of Sheffield Cathedral from 2004 to 2010. He moved to Oxford in 2004 to take up his current position at Cuddesdon. He writes on Christianity and contemporary culture, modern ecclesiology and practical theology.

Yvonne Richmond Tulloch, an Anglican priest and consultant in mission and ministry, is a leading thinker in contemporary forms of mission. As a minister in the Coventry diocese, she spearheaded 'Beyond the Fringe' (research into spirituality outside of church), which led to the groundbreaking publications *Evangelism in a Spiritual Age* (Church House Publishing, 2005) and *Equipping Your Church in a Spiritual Age* (Churches Together in England, 2005). In this book, Yvonne writes from her experience of cathedral ministry from being a canon at Coventry Cathedral and then Birmingham.

Roger Standing is a Baptist minister and Deputy Principal (Principal from September 2013) of Spurgeon's College, London, where he teaches mission, evangelism and pioneer ministry. Previously, he was the Regional Minister/Team Leader for the Southern Counties Baptist Association. With over thirty years of experience in ministry, he worked as an evangelist in Liverpool before pastoring churches in Leeds and South London. His previous publications include *Finding the Plot: Preaching in a Narrative Style* (Paternoster, 2004) and *Re-emerging Church: Strategies for Reaching a Returning Generation* (BRF, 2008).

David Shosanya is a regional minister with the London Baptist Association (LBA), where he has responsibility for the care of ministers and encouraging churches in their mission. David is also a co-founder of the nationally acclaimed Street Pastors Initiative, the State of Black Britain Symposium, the National Leadership Summit and the National Black History Month

(BHM) Civic Service of Celebration. David writes a monthly column for *Keep the Faith* magazine and is a regular contributor to 'Word for the Day' on Premier Radio and speaks at many of their conferences.

Susan Stevenson is a Baptist minister and a Director of Ascension Trust/ Street Pastors. Over the last twenty years, she has provided leadership to diverse multi-cultural churches in London, initially in West Norwood and more recently in Greenwich. That experience is reflected in the article 'A Journey of Dis-Empowerment: The Challenge of Multi-Cultural Church' (*Ministry Today* 40, 2007).

Tom Stuckey was President of the Methodist Conference in 2005, Chair of the Southampton Methodist District, and is a former Canon of Salisbury Cathedral. He has ministered over the past thirty-six years in a variety of appointments in Britain and taught and lectured in mission both in this country and overseas. He is author of *Into the Far Country: Mission in an Age of Violence* (Epworth, 2001), *Beyond the Box: Mission Challenges from John's Gospel* (Inspire, 2005) and *On the Edge of Pentecost: A Theological Journey of Transformation* (Inspire, 2007). He is at present visiting scholar at Sarum College and writing a book on atonement and the wrath of God.

Martin Turner has been a Methodist minister for thirty-five years, serving in Bradford Mission, Halifax and Hertfordshire, before moving ten years ago to be the Superintendent Minister and Team Leader at the Methodist Central Hall, Westminster. He led the evangelical grouping within Methodism (now Methodist Evangelicals Together) for six years, sits on the co-ordinating group of the Methodist City Centre Network and has served on the Methodist Conference for many years. He is widely travelled as a preacher and Methodist leader. He was co-author of *Digging for Treasure* (MET Publications).

Michael Volland is an Anglican priest and is presently the Director of Mission and Pioneer Ministry at Cranmer Hall, Durham. Prior to this Michael worked as an Ordained Pioneer Minister on the staff of Gloucester Cathedral, where he pioneered and led a fresh expression of church. Michael's previous publications include *God on the Beach* (Survivor, 2005) and *Through the Pilgrim Door: Pioneering a Fresh Expression of Church* (Survivor, 2009). He is also a co-author of *Fresh!: An Introduction to Fresh Expressions of Church and Pioneer Ministry* (SCM Press, 2012). Michael is on the worship planning team for Greenbelt festival and facilitates a monthly worship gathering at Durham Cathedral.

Introduction

Mission work does not arise from any arrogance in the Christian Church; mission is its cause and its life. The Church exists by mission, just as a fire exists by burning. Where there is no mission, there is no Church; and where there is neither Church nor mission, there is no faith.[1]

Emil Brunner's famous articulation of the priority of mission was first delivered as part of a series of lectures given at King's College, London, in March 1931. Interest had been rising in the dialectical theology, or neo-orthodoxy, of which the Swiss theologians Barth and Brunner were key leading thinkers. Brunner may have seen mission primarily in terms of gospel preaching – the reciprocal act of receiving and giving of the Word of God in Jesus Christ upon which everything Christian depends, 'the spreading out of the fire which Christ has thrown upon the earth' – yet, with Barth, his ideas about the missionary nature of the Church were to provide a robust theological basis for the development of missiological understanding through the rest of the century and into the next. The impact of their ideas must not be underestimated.

When I first encountered Brunner, the simplicity of his image fixed itself in my imagination. His expression of the experimental priority of mission was clear, unequivocal and passionate. Reading further, I discovered that he continued to work with the metaphor, picturing the believer, burning with the gospel, propagating the fire wherever they went. This burning, a Wesleyan-like image of the inner person on fire and passionate for mission, is fuelled by both 'urge' and 'command'. The 'urge' is the necessity of compulsion, 'Woe is unto me, if I preach not the gospel.' Having received the amazing gift of God's grace and benefited from the expression of his love expressed through mercy, kindness and generosity, it is of the nature of the 'fire' that it self-propagates. But to this 'urge' is added a 'command', 'Go ye into all the world and preach the gospel.' Jesus commands that the

---

1 Emil Brunner, *The Word and the World*, London: SCM Press, 1931, p. 108.

good news of the Kingdom is made available to all, that is, the good news of the rule and reign of the heavenly King and of the accessibility of the divine remedy for everyone.[2]

While Brunner's language may sound a little dated, his ideas remain as pertinent as they did at the beginning of the 1930s. For all of the progress in mission thinking over the years, there is frequently a discrepancy between this missiological reading of the Scriptures, formulation of theology and revision of ecclesiology, and the lived experience of the local congregation. Almost twenty years ago, Robert Warren wrote of his concern that '[l]ittle attention has been paid to the church as the primary agent of mission'.[3] While this is less the case now, what is written often falls into one of three unhelpfully deficient categories. First are those expositions of biblical and theological ideas that lack the lived reality of day-to-day church life. Second, by contrast, are those that are much more practically earthed, but are inspirational in tone and aspirational of what 'ought to' or 'could' be possible and yet still present unrealizable goals that are soon abandoned. Third are the 'how to' manuals and strategies for church life that advocate an approach to mission that has worked somewhere else, helpfully broken down into implementable stepped programmes but that, in practice, do not really fit.

In this book, my concern is that mission is firmly rooted in the life of the local church. However, in contemporary Britain the context of the local church is far from uniform. Large church, small church, urban church, rural church, cathedral, fresh expression, black majority ethnic church, multi-cultural church – the range of situations in which local communities of believers live the life of faith within these shores is vast. This variety of contexts requires far more than just nuanced variations in missional living. The differences between them are often far more substantive. So in giving attention to the local church as the primary agent in mission, we will begin with the experience of the local church itself. As few individuals have the first-hand and in-depth knowledge of ministering within such a wide range of situations, I am grateful to those practitioners who have spent time reflecting on their experience of mission and committing it to the chapters that follow. Then, in the latter part of the book, I will explore some of the issues that are integral to the ongoing life of a local congregation, with which they will need to wrestle as they seek to embody the missional DNA of the Kingdom of God in their life of witness and service. What are the issues that surround our conduct of worship, our practice of

2 Brunner, *Word*, p. 109.

3 Robert Warren, *Building Missionary Congregations*, London: Church House Publishing, 1995, p. 1.

leadership, how we effectively engage in forming missionary disciples and how we participate in and form partnerships with our local community?

Brunner is nothing if not straightforward: 'Where there is no mission, there is no Church.' As Charles Wesley wrote in what was to become an iconic Methodist hymn:

O Thou who camest from above
The pure celestial fire to impart,
Kindle a flame of sacred love
On the mean altar of my heart!

There let it for thy glory burn
With inextinguishable blaze,
And trembling to its source return,
In humble prayer and fervent praise.

Jesus, confirm my heart's desire
To work, and speak, and think for Thee;
Still let me guard the holy fire,
And still stir up thy gift in me –

Ready for all thy perfect will,
My acts of faith and love repeat,
Till death thy endless mercies seal,
And make the sacrifice complete.

Missional Church

One of the great things about teaching in a theological college is to see students beginning to grapple with the dance of ideas that flow from the Bible, their experience of Christianity and the Church and their developing theological awareness. It is the breakthrough moments that are really delightful. Jody was wrestling with the dilemma posed by an assignment asking the question, 'mission-shaped church or church-shaped mission?' Half-way through she declared, 'it is a tautology for us to speak of a missional church; a church which is not missional is not a church'. She had understood.

Working with a new intake of students each year is instructive for other reasons too. For all of the books, conferences, strategies and initiatives in mission that there have been over the last half-century, fundamental misunderstandings about mission continue to sit in the consciousness of many of our students and the churches from which they have come. 'Missionary work' is still primarily conceived as happening overseas in exotic and distant locations. Indeed, for many churches this dimension of mission still accounts for a considerable, if not complete, focus for their missionary support and giving. Or again, in general day-to-day language mission and evangelism are commonly used interchangeably as synonyms with no comprehension of the substantive difference in meaning between the two words. Perhaps most worrying of all is the conviction that mission is something that the Church 'does'; an activity that sits alongside all of the other elements of church life and against which it must compete for time, energy and resources. Of course, a congregation can also choose that it is something that they do not do, and mission becomes merely an optional add-on, a programme choice alongside many others.

The meaning of mission

The twentieth century witnessed great strides forward in missiological understanding, bringing a renewed focus on mission with increasing clarity and perception that rooted mission in the nature of God himself. At the Brandenburg Missionary Conference of 1932, Karl Barth observed that historically the word *missio* had originally been an expression relating to the Trinity and of the divine sending forth of self in sending the Son and Holy Spirit to the world. This sending then embraces the Church, as it is drawn up to be a partner in the divine mission of making known the definitive work of reconciliation accomplished in the cross and resurrection of Jesus Christ. Barth's work on the Church's mission is contained in the fourth volume of his *Church Dogmatics*, which addresses the doctrine of reconciliation. God in Christ lowers himself to become partner with humanity, while at the same time lifting humanity to partner with himself.[1]

It was at the Willingen Conference of the International Missionary Council in 1952 that these ideas and the influence of Barth matured further with what was to become known as the *missio Dei* (literally the mission or sending of God). A third movement was added to the classical statement of the Father sending the Son, and the Father and Son sending the Holy Spirit. The third movement saw the Father, the Son and the Holy Spirit sending the Church into the world. As David Bosch sagely notes, mission is thus placed within the doctrine of the Trinity, and not ecclesiology or soteriology.[2]

Mission is therefore hard-wired into the nature of the Church. According to Barth's scheme, mission is essential to its existence. The Church was born of mission and is called by God to participate in his mission. Indeed, the New Testament itself can be viewed as a series of missionary documents, the Gospels being the record of the Father's sending of the Son, and the Acts of the Apostles of the Father and the Son sending the Holy Spirit, and the Father, the Son and the Spirit's sending of the Church. The letters are then first-hand records and reflections on the dynamic missionary life of the early Church. In so far as theology itself is rooted in the Bible, it too can legitimately be said to be a missionary reflection. Out of this growing body of missiological thinking emerges the ecclesiological realization that the Church is missional by its very nature.

All of this might sound a little esoteric; however, it has profound implications for the life and ministry of a local congregation. The American Lutheran missiologist Craig Van Gelder sees this dynamic of the Church being missional by nature working itself out in a clear progression. First, if the Church is, of its essence, missional, then that is its identity, its

---

1 Waldron Scott, *Karl Barth's Theology of Mission*, Downers Grove: InterVarsity Press, 1978, pp. 10–11.
2 David Bosch, *Transforming Mission*, Maryknoll: Orbis Books, 1996, p. 390.

character and what makes it what it is. Second, the fundamental nature of the Church then determines what it does. It gives the Church its purpose, its direction and the scope of its work. Doing flows out of being: 'The Church does what it is.' Third, 'the Church organizes what it does': its administration and governance, the strategies it adopts and the organizational superstructure that support and facilitate its work then sit at the end of the process. Thus the organization of a congregation's shared life is shaped by its missional identity and the practical demands of the day-to-day living that are the expression of its identity. Van Gelder stresses how crucial it is for the proper sequence of these three to be maintained.[3]

> The premise ... is that the missional church is missionary by nature – *the church is*. In living in the world, the missional church engages in ministry that is consistent with its nature – *the church does what it is*. Finally, the missional church seeks to bring order and organization to these activities – *the church organizes what it does*.[4]

Nineteenth century: urban mission innovators

For all of the developments in missiological thinking in the twentieth century, what we understand to be mission practice in the UK has its roots in the nineteenth century and the response of the churches to urbanization. With the growth of the Victorian city, the churches became increasingly concerned that the urban working class were not attending church.

One of the earliest and most effective attempts to address this situation was the emergence of non-denominational town and city missions across the country. David Nasmith is looked upon as the founder of the movement, having been the moving force behind the Glasgow Mission in 1826 and the London City Mission at Hoxton in 1835. Nasmith was a personal evangelist who was anxious not to create a new denomination either. His vision was to bring into being a society whose missionaries could be the servants of all evangelical churches. The Missions flourished as the century progressed, and by 1850, the London City Mission alone was employing 235 lay agents.[5] Based on a strategy of house-to-house visitation, the assumption that the Church must go to the masses, rather than

---

3 Craig Van Gelder, *The Ministry of the Missional Church*, Grand Rapids: Baker, 2007, pp. 17–18.

4 Van Gelder, *Ministry*, p. 122.

5 John Kent, *Holding the Fort: Studies in Victorian Revivalism*, London: SCM Press, 1978, pp. 101–2.

expecting the masses to come to church, their work was almost wholly evangelistic in nature.

The dire nature of the situation in the country's rapidly growing cities was confirmed by the 1851 Religious Census, and this resulted in a great upsurge of activity across the whole spectrum of churches for the rest of the century as resources were made available to build churches, appoint clergy and engage in evangelism.

Coming face to face with extreme poverty, disease and insanitary housing, these churches first became engaged in establishing social provision in an attempt to alleviate the suffering they encountered. Beyond this they began to involve themselves in local and national politics as they sought to address the wider issues that sat behind the frontline conditions they had become involved with. In 1883, a penny tract, *The Bitter Cry of Outcast London*, was published. Some consider it the single most influential piece of writing on the poor in English history.

> Whilst we have been building our churches and solacing ourselves with our religion and dreaming that the millennium was coming, the poor have been growing poorer, the wretched more miserable, and the immoral more corrupt; the gulf has been daily widening which separates the lowest classes of the community from our churches and chapels, and from all decency and civilization.[6]

Charles Garrett and Hugh Price Hughes among the Wesleyans, the Baptists John Clifford, F. B. Meyer and C. H. Spurgeon, with R. W. Dale and Silvester Horne from the Congregationalists, and Anglicans like Wilson Carlisle and Robert Dolling, increasingly embraced what, a century later, would come to be called 'holistic mission'. They established children's homes, employment exchanges, penny banks, poor man's doctors and lawyers, basic employment schemes, aiding striking workers and a plethora of other initiatives to attempt to meet the needs that were presented to them in the poorest areas. Alongside these activities of practical service, they also began to get involved in civic life and politics to help address the problems from a different angle. In many ways, the rise of the fabled 'Nonconformist Conscience' in national life is not unrelated to the development of a political dimension in British church life.

It is no coincidence that many of these initiatives carried the title 'Mission' in their name. Indeed, the Wesleyans had been explicitly talking

---

6 Anthony S. Wohl, *The Bitter Cry of Outcast London by Andrew Mearns with Other Selections and an Introduction by Anthony S. Wohl*, Leicester: Leicester University Press, 1970, p. 55.

about 'Home Mission', as opposed to 'foreign mission', from the 1850s, and had set up a fund to finance it. Rather late in the day, but nonetheless capturing the mood of British Christianity, General Booth of the Salvation Army launched his grand scheme, *In Darkest England and the Way Out*, which gave birth to the Army's involvement in social work with the poorest in communities throughout the world.

As these activists responded to the needs of the cities it is interesting to listen to them reflecting biblically and theologically on what they were doing. A common connection roots their social and political work in an understanding of the nature of God, often expressed in the phrase, 'the Fatherhood of God and the brotherhood of man'. This is fascinating in that, at least implicitly, it is far more egalitarian in outlook than popular stereotypes of Victorian paternalism portray. R. W. Dale, the Congregationalist from Birmingham, suggested a different line for theological reflection among the Wesleyans. Addressing their annual conference in 1879, he suggested that the doctrine of perfect sanctification ought to have led to ethical developments in the practical social and political questions of the day.[7] Hugh Price Hughes, minister of the West London Mission and editor of *The Methodist Times*, attempted to do exactly that.

> During the fifteen years which have elapsed since those words were uttered there has been a great change, and Methodism has done much to redeem herself from the reproach of ethical sterility. We no longer shrink ... from the discharge of our political duties. We are beginning to apply our ethical conceptions to business, to literature, and to art.[8]

Using his editorial columns in the 1890s, he regularly called for the denomination to add 'social holiness' to their teaching on 'personal holiness' and a Pentecostal outpouring of the Holy Spirit to empower and embolden God's people to this end. It is interesting to note that Hughes believed that an understanding of the Kingdom of God would become a distinctive note of Christianity in the twentieth century.[9]

---

7 *The Methodist Times*, 4 February 1886, p. 1.
8 *The Methodist Times*, 20 December 1894, p. 1.
9 *The Methodist Times*, 12 April 1900, p. 1.

Twentieth century: an integrated vision of mission lost and found

The first half of the twentieth century largely witnessed the separation of evangelism from social concern, in what the American historian Timothy L. Smith called 'the great reversal'.[10] The 'social gospel' was seen to be a reductionist retreat from biblical faith of those who espoused a liberal approach to theology, whereas evangelism was the preserve of evangelicals who remained faithful to the Christian tradition, and for whom this was synonymous with mission. While this response was never absolute on either side of the theological divide, it was the prevailing mood through the middle decades of the century. However, the rise of thinking in terms of the *missio Dei* and the Kingdom of God began to erode this dichotomy in mission understanding by the 1970s–80s, and to filter down into the life of mainstream denominations through national mission programmes like the Methodists' 'Sharing in God's Mission' (1985) and the Baptists' 'Action in Mission (AiM)' (1988).

The Lambeth Conference of the Anglican Church in 1988 was also a landmark event in restating the priority of mission across the Communion. 'This conference calls for a shift to a dynamic missionary emphasis going beyond care and nurture to proclamation and service.'[11] The Conference was also the first body to endorse the Five Marks of Mission, which are now widely adopted and used:

1   To proclaim the Good News of the Kingdom
2   to teach, baptize and nurture new believers
3   to respond to human need by loving service
4   to seek to transform unjust structures of society
5   to strive to safeguard the integrity of creation and sustain and renew the life of the earth.[12]

Indeed, in the final pastoral letter from the conference, they maintained, 'In many parts of the world, Anglicans have emphasized the pastoral model of ministry at the expense of mission. We believe that the Holy Spirit is now leading us to become a movement for Mission.'[13]

---

10 David O. Moberg, *The Great Reversal: Evangelism versus Social Concern*, London: Scripture Union, 1973.

11 Graham Cray, *Mission-Shaped Church: Church Planting and Fresh Expressions of Church in a Changing Context*, London: Church House Publishing, 2004, p. 36.

12 These were adopted by the General Synod of the Church of England in 1996 and Churches Together in England in 1997.

13 Michael Nazir-Ali and Derek Pattinson (eds), *The Truth Should Make You*

For all of the reflection, conferences and denominational strategies, the Anglican Robert Warren observed in 1995 that '[l]ittle attention has been paid to the Church as the primary agent of mission'.[14] He explores why historically the Church has slipped into 'pastoral mode' and how it is both desirable and necessary for a 'missionary mode' to be recaptured, where '[a] missionary congregation is a church which takes its identity, priorities, and agenda, from participating in God's mission in the world'.[15] To accomplish this, he advocates a model where worship, community and mission form three interlocking circles of a self-sustaining congregational life with spirituality at the heart.

Another classic exploration of the missionary vocation of a local church was put forward by Raymond Fung, Secretary for Evangelism at the World Council of Churches in the early 1990s. *The Isaiah Vision: An Ecumenical Strategy for Congregational Evangelism*[16] has proved itself to be an influential and inspirational consideration on the missional shape of church life. Fung developed a three-dimensional model of partnership, worship and discipleship, based on Isaiah 65.20–23, upon his conviction that the local church was the key element at the heart of Christian mission.

> But at the end of the day, it is the local congregation, in its life and ministry, that must address the task of witnessing to Jesus Christ before every person and in every neighbourhood, day in and day out, year in and year out.[17]

In a *partnership* approach to local needs, the local church engages with individuals, voluntary or governmental groups around the concerns of the Isaiah passage itself:

- Children do not die.
- Old people live in dignity.
- People who build houses live in them.
- Those who plant vineyards eat the fruit.

Free: The Lambeth Conference 1988, the Reports, Resolutions and Pastoral Letters of the Bishops, London: Anglican Consultative Council, p. 327.

14 Robert Warren, *Building Missionary Congregations*, London: Church House Publishing, 1995, p. 1.

15 Warren, *Missionary Congregations*, p. 4.

16 Raymond Fung, *The Isaiah Vision: An Ecumenical Strategy for Congregational Evangelism*, Geneva: WCC, 1992.

17 Fung, *Isaiah Vision*, p. vii.

Partners are then invited to share *worship*, as this provides the opportunity to celebrate what has happened, and to stop and reflect on the shared journey, as celebration is a deep human instinct, and church worship can provide a unique opportunity for this to happen. The third stage of the invitation to *discipleship* arises naturally out of shared partnership and moments of celebration and reflection.

Twenty-first century: a mission-shaped missional church

The publication of the *Mission-Shaped Church* report in the Church of England in 2004 was to prove to be a highly significant moment, as its impact rapidly spread out, touching vast numbers of parishes with new mission initiatives experimenting in 'fresh expressions of church', instigating a new category of 'Ordained Pioneer Minister', establishing a highly regarded 'Mission-Shaped Ministry Course' for lay training and even modifying ecclesiastical law through the drawing up of 'Bishops' Mission Orders'. Ostensibly a report about church planting, the response across the board was to help stimulate new initiatives across the whole range of missional engagement. The Anglicans were soon joined by the Methodist and United Reformed churches in the 'Fresh Expressions' initiative.

The report proposed that alongside the 'five marks of mission' there should be a framework of 'five values of mission', which could be applied to help shape initiatives in fresh expressions of church. First should be a focus on God the Trinity, nourishing spiritual life prayerfully and in the worship and service of the missionary God. Second, the incarnational nature of mission recognized that this means being responsive to the activity of the Spirit already at work in the community. Third, a missionary church is transformational in that it seeks the transformation of its community through the power of the gospel and the Holy Spirit, as it is true to its nature as a servant and sign of God's Kingdom. Fourth, it is a disciple-making community as it calls people to faith in Christ, and, fifth, it is a relational community characterized by welcome and hospitality.[18]

The first ever statistical mapping of the Fresh Expressions movement within the Church of England during 2010 recorded at least a thousand examples of new congregations with an overall attendance of thirty thousand, who would not be otherwise attending other forms of more traditional worship. Graham Cray estimated a further one thousand could

18 Graham Cray et al., *Mission-Shaped Church*, London: Church House Publishing, 2004, pp. 81–2.

be found within the Methodist Connexion.[19] The shape and contexts of these fresh expressions of church have varied greatly according to their context, from the more common experiments with cafechurch and Messy Church, to work with the surfing community at Tubestation, Polzeath in Cornwall, or in exploring contemplative outreach at the Norwich Meditation Centre, or by being church in clubland at Church for the Night in Bournemouth.

The great strength of the Fresh Expressions movement is its emphasis on being a genuinely local church, listening for God in the local community and shaping church to fit; a three-way engagement between a local congregation, the gospel, and the community of which it is a part. In this sense, it fits well into what has become known as the missional church conversation. It emerges in the United States from a group of younger educators and leaders wrestling with Lesslie Newbigin's question of what a genuine missionary engagement of the gospel with contemporary Western culture would look like in the late 1980s. While the word 'missional' has earlier uses, it is from the work of this group and a collaborative book of essays, edited by Darrell Guder, *Missional Church: A Vision for the Sending of the Church in North America*, that its present common usage originates.[20] While the term is used in very many different ways, Roxburgh contends that it is more elusive as it is actually a coming together of three powerful currents of mystery, memory and mission – the mystery of the existence of the Church as a strange, mixed, social community; the memory of the life, death and resurrection of Jesus Christ and the outpouring of the Holy Spirit; the outgrowth of being a missionary Church participating in Christ as it participates in God's mission in the world.[21]

The missional church conversation

This missional church conversation has released a passionate and dynamic, outward focus and inward critique. The introduction of the word by the team who wrote *Missional Church* was intentional as, with a new word, an adjective, not laden with the past history of missionary, missions or mission, there was a chance to create a real opportunity to consider a new way of being church. They were clear that it was not just a new

---

19 Church of England Press Release, 'Provisional attendance figures for 2010 released', 19 January 2012.

20 See Alan J. Roxburgh and M. Scott Boren, *Introducing the Missional Church*, Grand Rapids: Baker, 2009, pp. 9–11, 31; and Alan J. Roxburgh, *Missional: Joining God in the Neighborhood*, Grand Rapids: Baker, 2011, pp. 49–54.

21 Roxburgh and Boren, *Missional Church*, pp. 39–45.

label for what the Church had always done, nor was it a new strategy or programmatic approach of a new format to connect with those who have no interest in traditional church. However, in the passion of committed dialogue and the rhetoric that freely flows from it, the conversation often runs the risk of warping its understanding by overstatement and historical amnesia.

'Moving from maintenance to mission' may be appropriately descriptive of a local church that has been inwardly focused on itself and merely oiling the wheels to keep going. However, it runs the risk of creating a false juxtaposition, if maintenance and mission are seen to be two ends of a continuum. Maintenance is a necessary component of life. It can no more be avoided or dismissed with impunity in the Church than in any other area of life or experience. Those practices that maintain vitality of life and effectiveness of action enable long-term sustainability.

The contrast between the Church in 'pastoral mode' and 'mission mode' carries a similar danger. While the two modes in missional thinking have precise and legitimate definitions relating to the cultural context of a local congregation – being at least nominally Christian because of the legacy of Christendom, or being of alien or competing value systems – the apparent pitting of 'pastoral' over against 'mission' is fraught with potential misinterpretation. So the focus on the outward directed life of a congregation is prioritized and maximized, and the inward responsibility to be in relationships of love, trust and care is minimized and disparaged.

The focus on 'inherited' and 'emerging' forms of church is a third example of this false dichotomy. Leaving aside the culturally conditioned enthralment with the 'new' in a consumer society all too easily conditioned to discard that which is old and beyond its 'use by date', any newly emerged form of church will only be recognized as such because of its conformity to our inherited understanding of the ecclesial minimum that makes an expression of church a genuine church. Of course, the reality of the cultural diversity in contemporary Britain means a wide variety of received forms of church remains culturally appropriate. What all local churches must do is understand their missional identity and find ways to live and express discipleship to Jesus in their corporate and individual lives. From his time as a bishop in Wales, Rowan Williams has spoken about the need for a 'mixed economy' of churches in this regard, and this seems to be a wise observation.

A further nuance on these ideas sits with the missional call to depart from being an 'institutional church' to become a 'missional movement'. In an age that is deeply suspicious of institutions in general and the hidden use of power, along with the prevailing cultural preference for new

over old, informality over formality and freedom to act over the con-
straints of responsibility, it is clear where the rhetorical force lies. In so
far as the structures of institutionalized expressions of church carry the
dead weight of lifeless ways of doing things that sap energy and resources,
they are justifiably objects of criticism in need of reformation or abol-
ition. However, such institutional expressions of life have been shaped by
the gospel tradition and provide the structure and accountability that can
often be missing from an informal movement. The real challenge is how a
missional movement might flourish in the inherited institution of which a
local church is a part.

A final victim in the war of rhetoric is the relationship between what are
stereotyped as 'incarnational' and 'attractional' models of church, unhelpfully stylized as fidelity to the gospel injunction to 'go' and a programmatic
invitation to 'come'. But this is a rhetorical set-up. In the ministry of Jesus,
there is both a sending out of the disciples and a coming to Jesus of the
crowds. Sometimes they came from all over Galilee, Jerusalem and Judea
(Luke 5.17). There is something deeply attractive about Jesus that leads
the crowds to respond to his invitation to 'come'. Likewise, this attractive-
ness is also seen in the life of the early Christian community that led them
to be held in the favour of all the people (Acts 2.47). Incarnational mission
and attraction are clearly both biblically and missiologically compatible
and have a complex relationship. For example, many congregations use
their premises for incarnationally inspired programmes to serve their
communities who come to them for youth clubs, luncheon clubs, parenting courses and mums and toddler groups. Or again, off-site missional
initiatives in pubs and coffee shops still entail a 'coming' to the half-way
house or 'third space'.

Ultimately, when it comes down to it, what really matters is the lived
life of the local church. As Lesslie Newbigin famously said, 'The only
hermeneutic of the gospel, is a congregation of men and women who
believe it and live by it.'[22]

---

22 Lesslie Newbigin, *The Gospel in a Pluralist Society*, Grand Rapids: Eerdmans,
1990, p. 227.

PART I

Mission in Context

2

Mission and Locality

Every congregation has a postcode, a place in which they locate themselves, a locality to which they belong. The reasons behind location can have a surprisingly large range, the most common, of course, is residential, as a church serves a community of people within its immediate vicinity. Of course, patterns of residence change, and the nature of a local neighbourhood can evolve to be something quite different from what it was. However, patterns of belonging can continue, and a 'commuter church' is born, where those who formerly lived near to the church continue to travel back to be a part of the congregation. Historical factors can also go much further back over centuries, reflecting social and physical geography that has long disappeared. Contemporary geographical concerns can also be influential: a city-centre church will reflect the gravitational pull of the urban context across the whole of life, while a rural community in a larger village draws from neighbouring communities to cross the threshold of social viability. Ecclesiological, relational and recreational issues also have a part to play in where congregations are located, as can something as simple as the availability of an appropriate venue to hire or affordable land on which to build. So while every local church has a locality, the reasons can vary widely. As we will see, this is not unimportant in helping to understand the dynamics and implications of sharing in God's mission.

Locality and mission engagement

Locality is important for another reason too. Our missional identity always expresses itself in a locality. To add to Van Gelder's phrase, 'the church does what it is … where it is'. The first focus of locality will be the immediate vicinity of the congregation, however that is determined. A congregation in the heart of a large town, drawing people from all parts of the community, may have a town-wide vision. By contrast, a back-street mission hall or a congregation meeting in a suburban estate may have a readily identifiable neighbourhood, which is measured in walking distance.

A second dimension of locality may take other factors into consideration. In addition to thinking of the congregation in terms of a gathered community, thought is given to its shape and reach when it is dispersed. In this regard, issues of relational networks, recreational activities and patterns of work become insightful access points to understanding a congregation's missional influence.

A final contribution of locality to a church's missional engagement relates to the potential co-conspirators in missional action. Location is determinative of who these will be. Who are the other Christian communities, who are our partners in the gospel? Who are the voluntary organizations and other faith groups, with whom we have a mutual concern or shared agenda? Where is civil authority located and who has responsibility for our neighbourhood? How a church understands its location immediately identifies those with whom it may make common cause.

Understanding the nature of the locality in which a congregation is rooted, and why it is rooted there, is vitally important for the strategic dimension of its engagement in mission. Some baulk at the seeming discrepancy between an intentional and strategic approach to mission in contemporary life and the seemingly unplanned peripatetic ministry of Jesus as a first-century travelling preacher. However, this is to misread the Gospels. Jesus' choice of Capernaum as his base of operations was no accident. As a thriving lively community situated on the trade route known as the Via Maris, it had a small Roman garrison, because of the customs post – hence the presence of tax collectors – as well as good transport links by road and the Sea of Galilee, and was a local centre for trade. These are strategic considerations, if you want to maximize the speed with which the news and content of your message is circulated and the ease with which people can come and see for themselves. Capernaum was no accident on Jesus' part. Neither were his forays into the Greek-speaking cities of the Decapolis or Caesarea Philippi (Matt. 16.13; Mark 7.31), which would not have been obvious choices for a Jewish rabbi and his disciples. His decisions to visit Jerusalem, when there were the maximum number of people present at pilgrimage festivals, or his advice to the disciples to wait in Jerusalem until what turned out to be the feast of Pentecost, also fall into this strategic category (John 4.45; 7.2). Given the importance of locality, it is highly significant that Jesus did not just stick with the familiarity of his home neighbourhood, but he also intentionally pushed on elsewhere too, at times to locations that were not like home at all. Of course, the spontaneous and unplanned incidents, as he travelled and taught, were an integral part of daily life with him, but in dealing with the gospel narrative one story at a time there is a danger of missing the more strategic dimension that informs and shapes it.

This strategic dimension is also reflected in the much overlooked accounts in Luke's Gospel of Jesus' mission strategy and missional formation of the disciples. First, with the Twelve in 9.1–6 and then the Seventy-two in 10.12, Jesus sends them off in pairs to preach the good news of the Kingdom, heal the sick and drive out demons. In what clearly resembles a training strategy with a strategic dimension of preparing the ground for his own arrival, Jesus does not expect his disciples merely to breeze in and out of the villages they are going to. Building relationships through consistent hospitality and table fellowship, Chorazin, Bethsaida and the other places were to be given the opportunity to see and hear of the proximity of the reign of God and have the opportunity to turn around and embrace.

The apostle Paul reveals similar thinking in his letter to the Corinthians, explaining how he 'became all things to all people so that by all possible means I might save some' (1 Cor. 9.22b, TNIV). Respecting who people were and where they were coming from was of critical importance for him. Building on existing local communities within the synagogues or establishing new networks of relationships as with Lydia at Philippi or Dionysius and Damaris in Athens, he then went on to appoint indigenous leaders and thus affirmed the significance of locality in his missionary journeys.

Missional intelligence

As a congregation seeks to live out its identity in the light of the New Testament narrative, it is perhaps helpful to talk about its 'missional intelligence'. This is the degree to which it perceives its internal and external context in missional terms, allows that to initiate prayerful and reflective thinking in the light of the *missio Dei*, resulting in a deeper missional understanding that leads to appropriate praxis.[1] This missional intelligence is undergirded by three questions:

---

1 I have transposed these ideas directly from the thinking that arose in the 1990s about emotional intelligence (EI). Mayer and Salovey, who began this area of thinking, speak of four branches of EI: perception, appraisal and expression of emotion; emotional facilitation of thinking; understanding and analysing emotion – employing emotional knowledge; reflective regulation of emotion to promote emotional and intellectual growth. See John D. Mayer and Peter Salovey, 'What is Emotional Intelligence?', in Peter Salovey and D. Sluyter (eds), *Emotional Development and Emotional Intelligence: Educational Implications*, New York: Basic Books, 1997, pp. 3–31.

- How do we understand ourselves?
- How do we understand our neighbourhood?
- What do we sense God is saying to us?

How do we understand ourselves?

At a really basic level this involves identifying what kind of church we are. In the evolving discipline of congregational studies, there are a variety of tools and frameworks that can assist a congregation in their self-understanding. Helen Cameron helpfully talks about five different cultural forms of church in contemporary Britain, which have their mirror in the wider life of the country.[2] These are not exhaustive, and some churches will find that they either do not fit, or that they are some form of hybrid. However, it does affect the style, ethos and internal culture of the church, how it engages with the wider community and how it is perceived by those from outside of itself.

The parish church

Acting as a public utility like the water and electricity supply, it has complete territorial coverage of the country through the parish system, and has a legal status and responsibility to provide services, which it does through public worship, baptisms, weddings and funerals. Emerging in the medieval period, Cameron sees it as transitioning to a model of a private utility company as its formal links with the state and public life are eroded.

The gathered congregation

This is very similar in nature to a voluntary association. Formally organized with office holders, a constitution and a registered membership, voluntary associations can be inwardly focused for 'member benefit' or outwardly facing for 'public benefit'. Self-financing, members are expected not only to pay for the church through their contributions, but also to give their time and energy in working for the stated aims of the association and participating in its democratic processes.

---

2 Helen Cameron, *Resourcing Mission: Practical Theology for Changing Churches*, London: SCM Press, 2010, pp. 24–39.

Small group church

This model has a long history from New Testament churches meeting in people's homes, through the early Methodist class meetings, the base ecclesial communities of Latin America of the 1960s, the Restorationist House Churches of the 1970s and the more recent Cell Church movement. The parallel here in wider culture would be the social homogeneity of a book club or party plan. It is fascinating to note the parallels with the book club, where people wish to meet with those with whom they are socially at ease for stimulating conversation, or with the party plan, where Cameron notes the parallels between the literature of the Ann Summers organization and the Cell Church movement.

Third-place churches

These mirror the third-place concept of finding neutral venues, where guests and host experience a greater degree of social equality. Coffee shops, pubs, bookshops, school halls, gyms and leisure centres are classic examples of third-place venues. Cameron notes that some churches experiment in making their own premises into quasi-third-place spaces in activities like the Alpha meal or through turning a worship space into a temporary cafe.

The magnet church

Magnet churches parallel how parents choose their children's school. Research indicates that the categories of local school, right school and good school tend to determine the choice of parents. Locality is the preference of working-class families, a 'right' school, that is, ethos, fit and pedagogical style, for middle-class parents, and a 'good' school as determined by league tables for those with a managerial background. Cameron notes from her research that tentative connections can be made between this analysis and families' choice of church.

While understanding what kind of sociological community a church is can be really helpful, there are other questions of self-understanding that can be more revealing. These relate to the areas of identity, composition, dynamics and resources.

Identity is found in history. How was the church founded and why? What is the denomination affiliation or theological orientation of the congregation and how widely is this known and embraced? What are the defining moments in its corporate life, for good or ill? What are the high spots in living memory and what do they say about the church and its present aspirations? How has the church played a part in the wider life of the local community and how does that shape present perceptions of it by those outside the congregation?

Composition is clearly about who is a part of the congregation. What is the social profile of the church by age, residence, gender, place of origin, educational achievement and occupation? What are their interests and passions? Where are their responsibilities and commitments located?

Dynamics is about the nature of church life – is participation growing or declining? If it is growing, who is joining and why? Classic church growth theory identifies the differences between transfer, biological and conversion growth. Francis and Richter, by contrast, have differentiated between fringe worshippers, the open and closed dechurched and the open and closed unchurched. Their research has also identified a framework of fifteen broad categories of reasons why people leave the church and how likely they are to return.[3] Clearly reaching out to those who have, through their life experience, become dislocated from church is easier through an invitation to a 'back to church Sunday', as opposed to someone who has found the atmosphere of church too conservative and restrictive and has left as a matter of principle. Francis' and Richter's categories can also give insight to a church that is in a numerical decline not substantially attributable to death and members moving away.

Further questions on the dynamics of church life might include whether it is programme-driven or relationally based. More outward facing in outreach and service, or inwardly focused in pastoral care and spiritual growth? Or what an audit of how it uses its finances says about the priorities of the church, the nature of its community and the shape and scope of is missional engagement.

The resources available to a local congregation may seem obvious – the people, the finances, its property and any staff it may employ. However, there is more to be said here, particularly in regard to people. It is not unusual for audits of spiritual gifts to be undertaken to identify how someone might be best used and most fulfilled in their service to Christ within the church. But what about doing an audit of where people work, what organizations they belong to, what family and friendship networks they are a part of, and how they might be more fully equipped to serve the *missio Dei* in the vast array of contexts in which they find themselves during any given week. In the wider perspective of civic life, sociologists

3 Leslie J. Francis and Philip J. Richter, *Gone But Not Forgotten*, London: Darton, Longman & Todd, 1998; Leslie J. Francis and Philip J. Richter, *Gone for Good? Church Leaving and Returning in the 21st Century*, Peterborough: Epworth, 2007.

like to talk about the 'social capital' that is derived from the involvement and co-operation between individuals and groups. This has real collective and economic benefits, and Christian communities have this in abundance. In the late 1990s, a South London borough commissioned a survey of community life and provision and was staggered by how far the well-being of the borough rested on the community engagement of the churches. They concluded that the total value of this, in terms of social capital, was beyond their ability as local government ever to finance or provide. A leading borough officer observed how effective local clergy were as social entrepreneurs.[4]

How do we understand our neighbourhood?

For almost a whole generation, various models, schemes and programmes of local community or mission audit have been available to a local church to help it understand its local context better.[5] While there are a variety of potential approaches, the common denominator is the desire to help build a three-dimensional picture of the community of which a church is a part. The following seven-step approach against the acronym 'MISSION' can help to form the basis of discerning and compiling such a picture.

M – members' knowledge and experience
Providing a forum for members of the congregation to share their knowledge of local history, the dynamics of the present community, identifying key local opinion-makers and gate-keepers to resources and other networks, alongside naming local concerns and perceived needs.

I – information and data sources
Mining information on the local community from the data available via the internet through the Office of National Statistics, who also publish census data, and organizations like ACORN (A Classification Of Residential Neighbourhoods), which have pioneered the compiling of geo-demographic data against UK postcodes, census returns and other

---

4 Stewart Worden, *The Church in Croydon's Community: The Role of the Church in Local Economic and Community Development*, Croydon: CTBC/London Borough of Croydon, 1998.

5 Some of the most recent UK-based material includes Jim Curren, *How to Develop a Mission Strategy*, Cambridge: Grove Evangelism Series, 2004; Stephen Croft, Freddy Hedley and Bob Hoskins, *Listening for Mission: Mission Audit for Fresh Expressions*, London: Church House Publishing, 2006; Mike Chew and Mark Ireland, *Mission Action Planning*, London: SPCK, 2009.

information such as lifestyle surveys. Other local data may also be available through the local council.[6]

S – strategic interviews

Having identified key opinion-formers and gatekeepers in the community, to these can be added other important community figures such as headteachers, senior police officers, local politicians, leaders of voluntary groups, local journalists. Care needs to be taken in identifying exactly what you want to learn and framing a list of questions around that.

S – surveys and questionnaires

These are best completed by an interviewer rather than through a letter drop and also need to be carefully thought through. They can be completed on the street or in a shopping centre (be sure to obtain the appropriate permission) or by door-to-door visitation.

I – informal conversations

Having begun to form impressions of potentially important missional issues in the community, members of the congregation can be briefed so that they can explore these further on an informal basis with their friends, neighbours and colleagues. This should not have to be forced, and it is always better for the questions to be framed with transparency: 'At our church we're doing some research into our community, we thought ... what do you think ... ?'

O – Outsider feedback

As the picture gets clearer, it can be a helpful and insightful experience to seek a more structured feedback from those outside the church. A focus group over a meal in the function room of a local pub is an excellent way of setting up such a session.

N – neighbourhood prayer initiatives

Throughout a mission audit process like this the fundamental question that is being asked is how do we join God in his mission in our community? So throughout the various steps it is equally important to maintain a prayer focus. Having teams prayer-walking with their eyes open to observe what they see and hear can provide unexpected shafts of insight and observation. Some have found it particularly appropriate

---

6 www.ons.gov.uk; www.caci.co.uk/acorn.

to provide the opportunity for local residents to make prayer requests. A leaflet drop one week explains the invitation to make prayer requests to a follow-up visit the next week. Others have used the Yellow Pages to write systematically to all local groups and firms in turn asking them to make prayer requests for their community and enclosing a SAE.

What do we sense God is saying to us?

This raises questions of spiritual discernment and guidance. How do we hear God's voice and how can we distinguish between alternative and competing pathways? A congregation's ongoing devotional life together provides the essential environment for this task of spiritual perception. Study of the Scriptures alongside the celebration of God's acts of grace and deliverance establishes the boundaries of who God is, what he is like and what he does. The focus of this defining dimension of a congregation's corporate life provides a consistent bench-marking process in this regard. Indeed, for a church's missional engagement to be part of its intercessory prayer, biblical study and theological reflection establishes its spiritual nature.

The simple question, 'What does God want?' remains the most significant. Answering it is not simple and should draw on a number of factors that help mutually to triangulate or corroborate one another. The inner witness of the Spirit is most often the lynchpin of these elements. This can be expressed in a variety of ways, from the oft quoted 'it just seemed right', through a passion and excitement that is generated among those involved, to a more considered, prayerful conviction. To all intents and purposes it is a kind of 'spiritual intuition'. However, because such intuition, even if genuinely felt and well intended, can be influenced by so many other factors, other dimensions of discernment also need to play their part.

Of first importance is the bringing to bear of the Christian tradition in which we stand, and specifically in asking biblical and theological questions. What does our knowledge of the Bible contribute to our understanding in this? What are its theological implications and what would such a course of action say about God? Then there are questions of circumstance. Does this marry up with what we know about ourselves and the neighbourhood to which we belong? To these must be added issues of resources and God's provision. Do we have the people, the access to facilities and the funds that may be required? It is true that God's people do need to travel light and step out in faith that God will provide when the resources are needed, as with the sending out of both the Twelve and the Seventy-two. However, just a few chapters later in Luke's Gospel, Jesus also addresses the need to understand the implications of discipleship by comparing it to being a construction project with insufficient funds available (Luke 14.25–30).

Our knowledge of the limitation of our understanding, the fallible nature of our interpretation and the deceitful fallenness of our hearts means that humility is essential. Our comprehension of God's will, purpose and guidance is at best partial, so the expression of what we 'believe' to be God's will and direction needs to be both understood and expressed in those terms. It is therefore open to revision, correction or the learning experience of having missed the mark.

Also fundamental to an understanding of missional intelligence is the objective of drawing together God's will and purpose and a specific group of gathered believers in a particular geographical context. This is both difficult to do and to maintain. For some, it is far easier to focus on the apparently more objective sociological and contextual elements of the task. In the extreme, a merely nominal acknowledgement of the faith base of the activity makes it no different from other examples of community-based action and is missiologically reductionist both theologically and spiritually. For others, the consuming focus on the devotional dimension of the task leads to an over-spiritualized emphasis completely disconnected from lived reality. It is not an easy task for a local church to hold these elements together, but to be held together they must maintain the integrity of a congregation's involvement in the *missio Dei*.

The Refugee Day Centre, West Croydon: a case study

The church of which I was the minister during the 1990s had traditionally been gathered from all over South London as a significant preaching centre. It had been initially led by James Archer Spurgeon, the brother and colleague of the great Victorian preacher Charles Haddon Spurgeon. By his death at the turn of the twentieth century, over 1,200 attended worship each Sunday. A slow decline during the century was initially offset by the arrival of the West Indian community from the 1960s, and, by the end of the century, modest growth was being maintained and a congregation comprising of over thirty nationalities was 40 per cent black.

The congregation was keen to be outwardly focused towards its neighbourhood and began to explore what that might mean. Given it had a healthy children's and youth ministry, it was a short step to see this as the potential focus of serving our local community and seeking to meet perceived local needs. Over a period of months, a community survey was undertaken to assess the nature of those needs, statutory and voluntary youth work providers were consulted and the possibility of funding streams explored. The outcome of a considerable investment of time and energy was to conclude that there was already sufficient alternative provision that was planned and in place for the needs we had identified. Disappointed and a little disheartened, the church continued to pray for discernment about how the evangelical gospel it proclaimed could be more explicitly and intentionally demonstrated in Kingdom action and service within its locality.

At about this time, during 1996, the controversial Asylum and Immigration Act of July 1996 removed state benefits from most asylum seekers. A Churches Together in Croydon forum addressed the anticipated avalanche of need. Recognizing that the Home Office's national office of immigration, Lunar House, was only 300 yards away, the church thought it might open a drop-in centre on a Tuesday. A relatively recent arrival in the church's worshipping community, who had a background in leading community provision through the Co-operative Movement, agreed to head up the initiative, seeing it as an expression of Jesus' teaching to clothe the naked and feed the hungry from the parable of the sheep and the goats in Matthew 25.

Over the next two years, a clothing store, food bank and access to white goods were established alongside links with health, housing and advice services to make the Day Centre a one-stop shop. In 1998, there were 1,588 new registrations, and the Centre had effectively become too big for one local congregation to service. First, the other churches of the borough started providing willing helpers, then other local volunteer organizations. The Refugee Day Centre, West Croydon, became a charity in its own right with key individuals joining its list of patrons, including the Mayor of Croydon and the Chairman of the Council of Mosques and Imams in Great Britain, the late Dr Zaki Badawi.

While the Day Centre grew up to be an independent body in its own right, it was birthed out of a local congregation seeking to participate in the *missio Dei* in their own locality. Its buildings still provide the home of the Centre, and its members still provide the core volunteer support, the international origin of a large part of its membership reflected in the international scope of those served by the Centre.

3

Mission in an Urban Context

Urban Expression

JULIET KILPIN

Urban Expression is a small mission agency deploying teams in inner-city communities. It began in 1997, and at the time of writing there are Urban Expression teams creating relevant expressions of church in Birmingham, Bristol, Glasgow, London, Manchester and Stoke. The Netherlands and some parts of North America have initiated their own Urban Expression teams in partnership with us, and conversations are underway with friends in Sweden – between us, there have been around twenty-five teams deployed so far. Over these fourteen years, around eighty adults have committed a minimum of three years to urban mission in Britain – most have given substantially more than this. We also host the Crucible training course in Birmingham with several partner agencies, which seeks to equip people for mission in an urban, post-Christendom context.[1]

Urban Expression started as an idea of Stuart Murray Williams, who still co-ordinates the work alongside my husband Jim and myself, each on a part-time basis. We also currently have two one-day-per-week regional co-ordinators across England and a one-day-per-week administrator, meaning that Urban Expression currently employs the equivalent of only two full-time workers.

Urban Expression is not a success story and is barely scratching the surface of urban mission. We probably fail to incarnate the values and practices we advocate as fully as we would like, but our story thus far earths the values and illustrates the practices that we hold dear.

---

1 See www.cruciblecourse.org.uk.

Why *Urban* Expression?

Urban Expression was born in the mid-1990s out of frustration. One key irritant was that in an era when church planting was high on the Church's agenda, many new congregations were simply replicating failing forms of church. Why, we wondered, were church planters not taking the opportunity to experiment with different ways of being church, when existing forms of church were so obviously haemorrhaging? Einstein famously said that '[s]tupidity is doing the same thing over and over again and expecting different results', yet church planters didn't seem to be heeding this advice!

This frustration was obviously becoming shared by others, as shortly after Urban Expression began, the British 'emerging church' conversation became more vocal, and later the Fresh Expressions initiative was pioneered by the Church of England and the Methodist Church. This was all encouraging and welcome missional thinking, but one key distinctive of Urban Expression was born out of another irritation, that church planting was often having little impact on the inner city. New churches were mostly being planted in communities where there were already many churches, rather than on huge inner-city housing estates with minimal Christian presence. This commitment has only deepened over the years, as the theory of urbanization has been replaced by the undeniable fact that more people in the world live in urban communities than don't,[2] and so Christian denominations, agencies and networks that are prioritizing non-urban contexts are focusing resources on a decreasing percentage of our population. People in non-urban contexts are unquestionably equally important, but the danger is that the balance of our activity and investment is not shifting in response to massive contextual changes.

A further frustration was that, although students training for ministerial leadership were embarking on innovative church-planting courses,[3] relatively few ended up putting this training into practice. Why might this have been the case? Maybe because the theory of planting churches is

---

2 'In 2008, the world reaches an invisible but momentous milestone: For the first time in history, more than half its human population, 3.3 billion people, will be living in urban areas. By 2030, this is expected to swell to almost 5 billion. Many of the new urbanites will be poor. Their future, the future of cities in developing countries, the future of humanity itself, all depend very much on decisions made now in preparation for this growth.' United Nations Population Fund, *State of World Population 2007*, http://www.unfpa.org/swp/2007/english/introduction.html. See also http://news.bbc.co.uk/1/shared/spl/hi/world/06/urbanisation/html/urbanisation.stm.

3 Especially the Oasis/Spurgeon's church planting and evangelism course (which Stuart directed and on which I trained).

easier than the reality; there are few paid opportunities for new ministers in such ventures (most posts are for ministers, associates or youth workers, rather than church planters); and the lure of a secure, predictable and quantifiable role is often more attractive than risky, experimental and difficult-to-explain church planting.

So Urban Expression began with an unshakable commitment to 'recruit, equip, deploy and network self-financing teams pioneering creative and relevant expressions of the Christian church in under-churched areas of the inner city'.

Risk-taking

We started Urban Expression because we wanted to challenge Christians about the vast mission gap in the inner cities and to encourage people to take risks and experiment with new expressions of church. We decided to recruit teams who would move into inner-city communities and work together to create relevant forms of church. These teams would be incarnational and become part of their communities, working *with* and not simply doing things *for* them. They would try not to impose culturally irrelevant forms of church and would listen to their communities to understand their character, culture and needs. They would operate as teams, harnessing their creative thinking and different gifts to create churches, and the teams would ideally be placed near each other so they might escape the isolation so often experienced by inner-city ministers.

It was clear that the teams would need to be self-funding. Between them, team members would need to raise their own support. Some would need to find paid jobs (full- or part-time); others might raise support from friends or suburban churches. Some might get funding through their denominations, but this was unlikely as few denominations have structures that prioritize pioneers. Teams might need to be very open about money and radical about how they shared their resources together. They might need to go without things many expect in Christian ministry, like a manse, expenses or subsidized telephone bills. So much for the theory – but would anyone respond to this risky challenge?

My husband Jim and I were certainly up for it! We had spent almost ten years living and ministering in inner-city London and Birmingham and had learnt much from our involvement in various multi-cultural established urban churches. But we knew we were pioneers and were desperate to rise to the challenge of starting new expressions of church in inner-city communities. So in March 1997, Jim was appointed to lead the first team in Shadwell, East London, and I began to work for Urban Expression as a co-ordinator to recruit future teams. Miraculously, we managed to find six others who were crazy enough to join this adventure – and so began the most exciting, heart-in-the-mouth, exhilarating, heartbreaking, fulfilling, nail-biting ride of our lives!

For all we knew at that time, we might be the only team ever. Although we were intent on seeking out others to initiate and join further teams, there certainly wasn't confidence that this would be inevitable, but there are obviously a few more Jesus followers than we thought, who share the same passions! We don't keep a close track on numbers and statistics, but for the purpose of this chapter I decided to do a little maths. From 1997 to 2010, in Britain there have been seventeen church-planting teams initiated. These teams have been made up of around seventy volunteers, each of whom have given a minimum of three years and many of whom have given far more than that (over two hundred years' worth of urban investment). Interestingly, there are barely any who have not completed this minimum commitment, which is surprising and reassuring. Of these volunteers, twenty have been denominationally trained leaders (sixteen Baptist ministers, two Salvation Army officers, two Assembly of God pastors).

There have also been team leaders of no denominational allegiance, although, because Urban Expression is not and has no plans to become a denomination or formal network of churches, those leaders or teams with no allegiance have often ended up deciding which wider network is most suitable for them to link with. The decision was made early on that to become a network of churches would mean an inevitable shift towards maintenance. It was felt that there were sufficient denominations, who manage the maintaining of churches quite adequately, and there was no point reinventing the wheel – but there was a need for mission agencies that are freed up from those demands in order to pioneer.

Foundations

At the outset, before the first team had even moved in, it seemed important to think through the values that would undergird this initiative. This felt like a good place, and a somewhat counter-cultural place, to start. In the mid-1990s, we were surrounded by many projects, programmes, strategies and models that promised much yet delivered little, so we steered away from a purpose-driven, goals-orientated or model-led initiative and chose to be guided instead by core values,[4] which would express who

---

4 See www.urbanexpression.org.uk/convictions/values.

we were rather than what we might do and would encourage freedom of expression by different teams in varying locations. One distinctive of urban mission is that one neighbourhood can be vastly different from another, even if it is only a quarter of a mile away. This brings about a vibrancy and diversity rarely seen in suburban locations, but also raises challenges for those trying to discern an appropriate way of developing church and mission in a place that may have so many distinguishing characteristics. Values, rather than models, give freedom for contextualization to take place.

We had no idea then what impact these values would have, but most people have joined Urban Expression teams, become associates or mission partners because they have been enthused by something in the values. People frequently say things like 'Your values just sum up everything I am feeling about what I am called to' or 'Your values seem to make so much sense'.

It seems strange now that something that began as an informal discussion has become meaningful to so many others, but we are pleased that these values are offering people a framework for mission and ministry. And we are convinced that core values are more foundational than purposes, strategies, models or goals. They have become so foundational to us that we have since devised a daily liturgy, which enables us to reflect regularly on these biblically based values, ensuring they don't become a dusty document kept in a filing cabinet but a living covenant that inspires, challenges and shapes our mission. There is also an Urban Expression values game, developed by the teams in the Netherlands, which helps teams to engage with the values and reflect on their impact in day-to-day life.

The values are drawn around three core principles – relationship, creativity and humility – and also embrace some core commitments. These express much of our theological, missiological and ecclesiological emphases.

Our commitments

We are committed to following God on the margins and in the gaps, expecting to discover God at work among powerless people and in places of weakness. We are committed to being Jesus-centred in our view of the Bible, our understanding of mission and all aspects of discipleship. We are committed to seeking God's Kingdom in the inner city, both by planting churches and by working in partnership with others in mission. We are committed to a vision of justice, peace and human flourishing for the city and all its inhabitants. We are committed to uncluttered church, focused on mission, rooted in local culture and equipping all to develop and use their God-given gifts. We are committed to unconditional service, holistic ministry, bold proclamation, prioritizing the poor and being a voice for the voiceless. We are committed to respecting and building relationship with other faiths.

Our values

Relationship

We believe that, in Jesus, God is revealed locally, and that we should be committed to our local community or relational network and active members of it. We believe that the gospel works through relationships and that serving God consists largely in building life-giving relationships with others. We recognize that Christian faith is a journey, and we are committed to helping people move forward, wherever they are at present. We focus on under-churched areas and neglected people, trying to find ways of communicating Jesus appropriately to those most frequently marginalized, condemned and abused by society. We challenge the trend of some Christians moving out of the cities and encourage Christians to relocate to the inner cities. We believe in doing things with and not just for communities, sharing our lives with others and learning from others who share their lives with us. We see teamwork, networking and mutual accountability as vital, recognizing that individuals and churches need each other.

Creativity

We recognize the importance of taking risks and the demands of mission in the inner city, and we believe that it is acceptable to fail. We value courage, creativity and diversity, as we try to discover relevant ways of being church in different contexts. We believe that questions and theological reflection are important, as we learn together and so discern the way forward. We aim to be catalysts, encouraging and releasing creativity in both church and community, as we seek and share God in the inner city. We believe in discouraging dependency and developing indigenous leadership within maturing churches, which will have the capacity to sustain and reproduce themselves. We are excited that God can be discovered in the heart of the city and commit ourselves to explore various forms of prayer and worship that are appropriate here. However, we also realize that we cannot assume that our work will continue indefinitely.

Humility

We acknowledge our dependence on God's empowering Spirit. We believe that all people are loved by God, regardless of age, gender, education, ethnicity, class or sexuality and that God works through all believers and others besides. We respect others working alongside us in the inner city and are grateful for the foundations laid by the many who have gone before us. We want to learn from others, seeking to shape what we do in light of the experiences, discoveries, successes and mistakes of fellow-workers. We are careful not to drain other local churches of their often limited resources, but hope to be an encouragement and support to them. We realize the importance of living uncluttered lives, holding possessions lightly, and we know we are not indispensable and that what we attempt to do is part of a much bigger picture, so will try to keep ourselves in perspective.

Reflections

As well as providing a permission-giving culture for developing contextual mission in urban communities, the values also highlight some emphases Urban Expression has towards mission that are perhaps worth highlighting here.

Mission is incarnational

While much of British culture operates along networks of relationships, we believe strongly that many inner-city and more deprived communities are still inherently locational. People who rarely travel, work or study outside their estate, don't own cars and don't own a second home in the country have a very limited network of relationships. For these people to encounter a Jesus-follower, that follower needs to incarnate these limited networks. For this reason, we ask all our teams to live within the community they are seeking to impact.

Mission is God's

While in our research we may have discerned a neighbourhood that is under-churched and has very little Christian presence (Shadwell, at the time we moved in, had an estimated Christian presence of 0.5 per cent), we do not presume that we are bringing God with us. We honour the work of Christ's followers who have preceded us and those who may already be there but hidden and marginal, but we also honour a God who is perfectly able to reveal his presence to people in that neighbourhood without our interference! Therefore we go with eyes open to see what God is already doing (God's mission) and join in, to find people of peace who sense something of God but need it explained, and to discern creatively what partnerships can be formed to further God's work in that place. Too many urban neighbourhoods have been 'targeted' by short-term Christian mission groups who have not consulted and have not honoured the work already there. Put this alongside the experience of short-term government initiatives that run out of money after three years, and it is not surprising that there is often a legacy of doubt and distrust resulting in people not welcoming 'another bloody project'. Remembering that it is primarily God's mission helps keep our perspective.

Mission is church

The relationship between mission and church in our experience is always fluid. When does team become church? When does a team meeting become a church gathering? When has a church been planted? Stuart Murray Williams has written extensively on these important questions.[5] However, they can sometimes be a distraction from the core task, which is seeking the Kingdom of God. Depending on your definitions, it would appear that churches can no doubt exist without mission, and there are certainly mission organizations determined to exist without stepping on the toes of church. But I would suggest that wherever the Kingdom of God is sought – that is mission; and wherever there is a community of people seeking that Kingdom, church is inevitable.

Mission is glocal

One key point from Brunner's quote that raises questions especially in an urban context is the idea that 'where there is neither Church nor mission, there is no faith'. Many inner-city communities are 'glocal' and are indeed richer for having the world on their doorstep. In these neighbourhoods, there is very often faith, even if there is no obvious Christian mission activity or church presence. The faith exhibited may not be in the Triune God, but it is a genuine starting point, which must be honoured, and to assume that without a church people are unable to explore faith is somewhat presumptuous.

---

5 Most recently in Stuart Murray, *Planting Churches: A Framework for Practitioners*, Carlisle: Paternoster, 2008.

Mission is messy

Discipleship in Britain is becoming more and more of a challenge, as people begin their faith journey further back than they used to. Most cultural shifts are experienced in the inner city first, and this is true of the post-Christendom trends too. The discipleship adventure, which sees the heartbreak of watching someone take one step forward and two steps back, has been the experience of many an urban church for years. This is compounded by higher-than-average rates of mental health illness and a range of addictions, which often play a high part in the chaotic path of discipleship. Perhaps urban churches have learnt to cope in this context and might be looked to for help by the wider Church. Perhaps urban churches have learnt to live with the mess and glorify God in the unpredictability of life.

Mission is transforming

While mission is about the lifelong transformation of individual lives into the people God made us to be, it is also about the transformation of all of creation. Urban Expression teams seek out opportunities to achieve this and have seen wonderfully creative opportunities to be part of God's transformative hope for neighbourhoods. One example is the reopening of Glamis Adventure Playground in Shadwell, brought about by a local management group spearheaded by Urban Expression team members.[6] Another example is the annual 'Deal with It' festival in Stepney, set up by the Drug Action Forum, a partnership of local groups concerned about the effect of drugs in their community, pioneered by Urban Expression team members.[7]

Mission is vast

While the place of mission is ideally within the local church, there are clearly limits to what the established pattern of local church in the UK can achieve. Urban Expression was initiated in response to the limits of the British suburban church, which can be marvellously effective in local mission initiatives but delightfully ignorant of the enormous missional needs just a few miles away on these small islands of ours. With information and partnership, church congregations and mission agencies can work together to complement and support one another in these tasks.

---

6 See www.glamisadventure.org.uk.

7 See www.ashes2asha.blogspot.com.

Mission is risky

In our increasingly risk-averse society, my final reflection is that mission from the margins and to the margins entails many hazards, and success (whatever that may mean) is not guaranteed. An inherent feature of experimentation is failure, and some of our efforts at being incarnationally missional have not worked as well as we had hoped. Others have worked far better than we dared dream. Some of the initiatives pioneered have become strong and sustainable, others will remain fragile and indeed find their identity in being delicate. We are grateful that we find each of these attributes in our God, and we commit ourselves to dwelling within the tension that is found in the midst of both transformation and brokenness, overcoming powerlessness, certainty and confusion.

4

Mission in a Rural Context

Threshold

PETE ATKINS

I'm not a theologian; rather I'm primarily a practitioner. For us, the vision and the call to pursue it, to see it earthed in our experience, came first – guided by prayer, reflection on the Scriptures and the experience of others. Theological reflection in a more focused and structured fashion began some time into our story – this may not have been the best way, but this is our journey!

I will start with a brief description of Threshold, as it is at the time of writing, to provide a frame of reference. Then, starting from different parts of our story, I will weave in some of the key theological insights that have shaped us and continue to 'power' the main thrust of our current approach and the shape of the fabric of our life together – albeit this was sometimes more unconscious at first.

An overview of Threshold

Threshold began in 1995 in Nettleham, Lincolnshire – three to four miles outside the city of Lincoln, so commuter land really. Nettleham is a village of 3,400 or so people; it has an old centre with typical 'halo' development of new housing as well as new infill around the centre. From the beginning, we have had a vision to see the Church re-established in rural areas.

We began with a roomful of people in our lounge and, by the grace of God, have grown to a community of two hundred or so people from fifteen different villages and the city. We now have three congregations, two village-based and one in the city, who meet most weeks in their locations. We also have three couples who have intentionally moved to particular villages to co-operate with God in his mission there – whatever that might mean in those places. Currently, all of us meet together every month for a celebration.

There are leadership teams in place for each congregation and an overall church leadership team of six. We have a youth team working across the whole church. Threshold is part of Ground Level Network – a Lincolnshire-originated 'new church' network of eighty or so churches led by Stuart Bell.

Our story: its theological insights and practical implications

It all began with a death. In 1993 and 1994, I had been leading a church plant/fresh expression from a local village church with a number of others. This came to a traumatic end after two years for a variety of reasons, mostly to do with national church 'politics'.

It felt like a death, as we stopped meeting and ceased all our other activities. We advised people to seek another home and go back to their sending congregation or somewhere else. It was also the death of a dream, with all we had invested in it, our hopes and aspirations over the previous three years. There was another kind of death too: a death to a sense of self-sufficiency and the independence from God flowing from it. Not that this doesn't try to resurrect itself at times, but this death was crucial for the future.

It was a very difficult time; one of the Scriptures I hung on to at the time was 1 Corinthians 15.37–38:

> And what you sow is not the body that is to be, but a bare kernel, perhaps of wheat or of some other grain. But God gives it a body as he has chosen, and to each kind of seed its own body. (ESV)

It seemed to give me perspective; a making sense of what was happening. It seemed to me that just a seed was left of the congregation of forty plus, which had died. That seed was a dozen or so folk, and I had no real idea of how God would keep us together. These were the few who didn't move back into the main church, and they, some principles we had learnt, the relationships we had built and a vague sense of calling was the seed that remained. This seed needed to be buried for a while, for the outer husk to come off and for something new to grow with the shape God had determined.

A few of us started meeting weekly on a weekday evening, mainly for prayer and worship. One of the main elements of what I now think God was doing in us was to reorientate us to a focus on relationship with him

37

rather than the completion of tasks 'for' him – he is the foundation of his Church, and we need to be joined to him, through the atonement and resurrection. We came to him – to know, love and worship him in our weakness.

In our times together, we studied the Bible and in time started seeking vision for the future, but we would still focus mainly on prayer and worship. At weekends, we would go to other churches and not have a public accessibility of our own – this continued for the best part of a year. In a sense, we remained hidden for that time, in much the same way as a seed when planted.

Looking back, I can see now that what subsequently emerged was shaped by the particular outworking of some foundational theological truths, although I don't know if I understood that at the time.

Theological insight: Jesus – the foundation and cornerstone upon which we build, the head of the body that is his church

We had to relearn the need to stay close and dependent on him. He is the point of it all; he is the 'joy waiting at the end'. Within this truth lies the death and resurrection of Jesus, which makes possible the establishment of his body here on earth, which makes relationship with the Father through him possible, which sets a pattern for our lives and is the basis for the fact that we live rather than perish. In terms of the establishment of the Church, this principle is what mission-shaped church refers to as 'dying to live' – which at one stage was going to be the name of that report.

Personal implications

This was something I felt acutely over many months as God shaped me – causing me to be utterly dependent upon him in a time of conflict and doubt. The resurrection became the focus of my hope for the future. For us, it all began with a death, but in the midst of that dying, in the heart of times of grief and anxiety, came a renewed closeness to God. From that place arose the first sense of vision and hope for the future, a stirring of calling to the rural areas of Lincolnshire, a desire to plant again and the regaining of courage to consider leading again. I learnt the hard way that God is more important than the vision or the people. Here is something I wrote as we contemplated the birth of something new:

Let the foundations of each community and team be love for you and for your word.

Let them be the recognition of and gratitude for your immense grace and mercy given to us through Jesus.

Let them be a desire to know you, to love you and be loved by you in holiness and truth.

Jesus, build your Church, beautiful and holy, according to your word.

Corporate implications

In our life together now, we seek to maintain above all our relationship with God, to seek him for every development. We seek always to be a prayerful people, to worship him ás we meet together and to remind ourselves that but for his presence with us we would be no different from any local club other than having a religious *raison d'être*. We acknowledge our dependence on God by his Holy Spirit to see anything change; we seek to be empowered by him, filled with him and led by him. 'Dying to live' is a theme we return to from time to time, especially when we are changing structures, and people may need to sacrifice convenience, the familiar or regular contact with Christian friends within the church for the sake of pursuing our vision for those who are outside it.

I guess a close identification with the death and resurrection of Jesus should birth in us a security that enables him to express more fully his generosity through us. His incarnation and death were ultimately acts of extreme generosity and self-giving, ensuring for us a certain future in him. We can trust all to him 'against that day'. This early breaking experience has built into us a sense of trusting God with all that we are and have and not needing to hold on tightly to people, ideas or structures.

I believe that generosity is a key value for a church that is to be mission shaped: generosity is birthed in us through a knowledge of and security in the generosity of God, and allows him to reshape his body for purpose, realigning his resources as his mission requires and always blessing the givers – 'For it is more blessed to give ...'.

Those of us who are now engaged in starting work in other villages cannot overstate the importance of personal and corporate prayer and worship and maintaining a closeness and dependence on God as we navigate the way ahead.

Story

As vision was birthed again it was entirely missional in thrust, and this in time began powerfully to shape our life together. Throughout the difficult time described briefly above, we maintained our friendships with non-church folk and had one or two events – usually parties – and expeditions together, like the memorable sailing weekend we held. In the autumn of 1995, we came to a point where we believed it right to embark upon an Alpha course with our non-church friends. As we experienced the Alpha course together, we saw several folk come to faith, and by the end of the course we were a community of forty or so people of all ages. Up to that point, we had not yet met in public, but now it seemed right to become more visible in that sense. This eventually came about because we found that through Alpha a community had been birthed who felt it was right to worship together regularly. We began worshipping in a local school every other week.

Now, fifteen years on, both of our rural congregations are defined by their heart for God's mission. They remain immersed in the life of their villages and seek to walk alongside others exploring faith in Jesus. One congregation has recently stopped its mid-week small group meetings and has encouraged its members to become involved in some aspect of village life or to start something where there is interest or need. The result is involvement in a range of activities, from leading uniformed organizations for young people or participating in walking clubs, to reading groups, cycling, sports spectating and an old car club. All those involved are also encouraged to meet with three others for an hour of prayer each week, focusing on their area of activity and their relationships in that sphere. The mission of God is central to our being as a church.

Theological insight: the mission of God

Our key understanding is that the purpose of the Church[1] is to see everyone reconciled to God through Jesus. We have come to understand that our life together needs to be shaped by God in alignment with his mission to humanity. This arises from his love for all and his desire that 'none should perish'. One implication of the breaking time we experienced and our shift towards dependency was to follow the leading of the Holy Spirit – seeking to co-operate with the mission of God to humankind rather than 'doing our thing' and asking God to co-operate. The name of our church, Threshold, comes from a version of Psalm 84.10: 'I would rather stand at the *threshold* of the house of my God than dwell in the tents of wickedness' (New American Standard Bible, updated version). About halfway through the first year, for a variety of reasons, we believed that this should

---

1 Which itself should be a community of people restored to relationship with God and expressing that in worship – in the sense of putting him first in the whole of life.

be our name. The sense of the name in our understanding is that we are very much part of God's house but are to be near or even among the 'tents of wickedness' – so that we make it easy for people to cross the threshold into God's house.

Implications

Our self-understanding is that we were born for mission; we understand that our focus is to be on non-church people, that the purpose of the Church, and one aspect of truly worshipping God, is to co-operate with him towards seeing all people reconciled to him.

We are not primarily interested in building church with migrants and disaffected Christians from other churches. The point of planting is to reach those outside the boundaries of the Church with the gospel.

We want to exercise 'go, not come' ministry in terms of our approach, reflecting the apostolic nature of Jesus as the one who was sent.

Following the insights of John V. Taylor,[2] as we begin work in new communities one primary task is to discover what God is already doing and then join in. We ask God to lead us as to how best to pursue his mission in that place – including the support of existing Christians and churches and the establishment of relationships with those currently outside the Church's doors.

We know that as we co-operate with God in his mission the church will be birthed and established.

The call to mission is something we feel every Christian has, and it is to be lived out individually and corporately.

Story

As we came to the end of that first Alpha course, many significant issues needed to be considered in a short space of time:

1 We felt the prompting of God to be visible and accessible in our community and to serve our community – this also had the benefit of providing open, public accountability. Apart from individual friendships, this has meant involvement in parish councils, retail, uniformed organizations, health care, school governorships, carnival committees, heritage groups and many other community organizations.

---

2 John V. Taylor, *The Go-Between God: The Holy Spirit and the Christian Mission*, London: SCM Press, 1975.

2 We embarked on a study of the Scriptures and other material as to how to be church in the community and how to include children, establish leadership patterns, incorporate communion and baptism, sort out giving and financial matters, consider overseas mission activity and seek accountability.

3 We knew we needed to establish good relationships with the other churches who didn't necessarily think we were a 'proper' church.

4 We came to feel that we were called to a wider area and understood that we had a specific call to plant into a village eight miles away.

Theological insight: incarnation – following Jesus meant we had to be rooted in the life and culture of these communities

Nothing new here for the established rural church, but for us a challenge! 'Visible and accessible' was our phrase. We were not to be hidden, but accessible with the right values, a willingness to serve and to demonstrate love and care for people.

Implications

This has always meant lots of hospitality and food for us. It has also meant a focus on creativity.

As we share this aspect of church planting we teach our leaders:

We are here to serve, love, be generous, be happy, be visible (but not pushy), be appropriate, be prayerful, be creative, exercise 'go' not 'come', be genuinely interested (no place for ecclesiastical scalp-hunting), be human, be ourselves, be with each other but be inclusive not inaccessible. Teach and model these attitudes to the church/team.

Be visible as a group of people with the right message – non-church friendly, preferably happy, clear about your vision but in terms the community can understand.

Engage with others in the things that you are interested in and enjoy – be it a craft, a sport, walking, pub quizzes, music, eating (!), computing or more or less anything. Most people become Christians through the influence of a friend(s) or family member. NB: Other dynamics have been observed in history and may yet be observed again!

The incarnation is our model for engagement – real, earthy and earthly, weddings, funerals, harvest, fishing, self-giving and love among the business of life in the power of the Spirit.

For us at this time, and in every community we live in, this primarily means establishing relationships at individual and village levels – including with other Christians and churches. We know that being seen together in our relationships is important.

Story

Early on in the first few months, as hope returned, we tried to articulate the vision God was giving us. Already we were conscious of the closing chapels across the rural scene; we believed the vision was for beyond our village. As we sought to understand, we eventually articulated the vision for Threshold as: 'To see the Kingdom of God further established in Lincolnshire'.

Theological insight: the Kingdom of God became a key theological understanding for us

We believe that as we focus on the coming of the Kingdom the Church will arise. We hold a high value on local church, but believe our focus should be on God and the coming of his Kingdom – he then shapes church as it is born and established to further co-operate with his mission purpose. Our rather simple description of this to the Church has become:

To see the Kingdom of God further established means
- people entering the Kingdom and joining Kingdom community
- to see communities of the Kingdom set within the communities of our area living out Kingdom values
- to see the values of the Kingdom becoming the foundations of society thus seeing the culture change.

This demands an understanding of how we can all grow to become mature disciples of Jesus, and we have had to identify principles that will help us do this in each context in which we are active.

Implications

Working with others

Our purpose is to see the Kingdom of God established – not build a big church, 'empire' or organization called Threshold. This encourages us to work alongside other Christians and churches with a sense of generosity in joint prayer for each community, mission activities, financial support, joint Alpha courses, worshipping together and a whole range of other initiatives.

Serving a bigger vision

Our vision is for a wide area not just one village. We believe that we need to seek to see the Kingdom come throughout Lincolnshire, and this can only be done by serving a bigger vision, contributing who we are to a wider scene. This has implications not just for Threshold, but has led to the development of a Church Planting Strategy for the region.

Church planting

Church planting is one vital reflection of this for us. We had a second church plant in mind, before we started regular public worship at all. We have had families move to locations in which they feel called to begin Christian community. We currently have congregations in two villages and one inner-city area, with further missional activity in several other villages begun by folk who feel called to this and who have some entrepreneurial giftedness. They are at least prepared to begin with a blank sheet and follow God in a missional adventure.

Our understanding of mission

We understand that mission includes but is not confined to evangelism. Prayer and action for road safety, school meals in a deprived area, supporting a girls' football team, funding for swimming pool/play groups are examples of this. We provide part-time chaplaincy to a local Church of England secondary school, have folk involved as village-based parish councillors; some run quilting groups, others work as Street Pastors or with their prayer teams in the city. We also encourage Threshold to be involved in societal issues such as the G8 summits, UK Parliamentary issues and the Micah Challenge. We have seen the Kingdom extend through individuals coming to faith, through the establishment of new Christian communities and through impact on our surrounding communities.

Mission and worship

We believe that mission and our commitment to it is part of our worship – part of a life set apart for God, lived for him, reflecting his love for all and his mission to all peoples. Our times of gathered worship need to be flexible in different ways, as we discern God's leading in a changing, mobile culture and take opportunities that may be time limited.

Worship takes place in a variety of settings and in a variety of ways: this reflects our missional vision and the need to be flexible according to purpose and context.

Contexts

Small groups, a congregation or the gathering of the whole church. Any could be focused on the needs of Christians or non-churched-people friendly. We have found that reflecting the Christian seasons in our worship – especially Christmas and Easter – resonates with the communities in which we are set.

Venues

School halls, village halls, YMCA facilities, community centres, homes, church buildings, open air.

Styles

These vary from 'front led' to participative, contemplative to expressive, cafe arrangement to rows or zoned, kids in or out, limited interactivity to all playing games. Worship can be silent, said, sung, CD-enabled or led by one musician, a choir, a band or a big band.

Creative input

This includes use of DVD, dance, sketches, quizzes, fry-ups, food before, during or after, or all of them.

Teaching

This can be 'live' with application, vision-casting or expository, on CD with application.

Prayer activities

These include 24/7 prayer, prayer triplets, prayer in cells, 'transformation prayer' – praying in a village with other Christians from that location, prayer-walks and men's prayer.

This is where we have got to so far on our journey. There is much yet we do not understand – we are on a journey and will need much help on the way. I also suspect that as we go on, our theological understanding will become fuller and deeper – and yet simpler at the same time.

5

Mission in a Large-Church Context

Park Road Baptist Church, Bromley

SIMON JONES

I'm an inner-city minister exiled in the 'burbs; a small-church guy involved in leadership of a stalled supertanker. I'm a ministry team leader trying to make sense of who I am and who we are in the turmoil of significant cultural change – and offer some direction to the troops.[1]

This is the context in which I am thinking about mission; in particular about how I can help our church discern where God is and what he is doing, so that we can get on board.

Microcosm of the English church

I lead a 360-member suburban/town-centre church, which is, in so many ways, a microcosm of the Church in these islands.

First, it has a conservative ethos, where people trust what they have known, where they have been. The church was full within living memory, so the feeling is that if we do what we did then, we'll be OK, the church will fill up again.

Second, therefore, we spend a lot of time converting the convinced. In the good old days, evangelism was about calling people to commit to a story we all knew – hence the success of Billy Graham in the 1950s. Long-standing church members tend not to believe that people in their neighbourhood don't know the Christian story any more. But it is true; they don't.

---

1 I have reflected on this in an article in the magazine *Ministry Today*. Simon Jones, 'The Half-Life of Exiles: Reflections on Ministry from the Margins', *Ministry Today*, Spring 2009; available online at http://www.ministrytoday.org.uk/article.php?id=662.

Third, we spend a good deal of time concentrating on caring for the baffled. So many in the church have found the social changes and upheavals of the past forty years too much to bear; they cling to a changeless church – except, it isn't changeless, much to their chagrin.

Finally, like so many churches, we are anxiously counting the faithful. We have been in gentle decline over the past twenty years. But this gradual change masks the seismic shifts in demographics from builders to boomers and busters; from the richest UK generation ever to one that's increasingly struggling to make ends meet in London's second most expensive borough.

Moving from maintenance to mission

As I have sought to lead the church through these choppy waters, I have operated by two basic principles.

The first is that it's best to start any journey from where we are, not where we wish we were. This is pretty obvious but not acknowledged by lots of churches. So many people ask me to do things, initiate things – indeed I have tried to launch things (as I'll outline in a moment) – that require us to be in a very different place from where we currently find ourselves.

But it is possible to engage significantly in mission, starting from where we are, that subtly shifts the location of the church. We have tried to do this in three ways.

The first is that we have tried to see ourselves as a resource church. Many of our members are busy people with complex lives, who need help to be disciples where they are; they don't need me laying a heap of guilt on them that they're not supporting my programme.

This is a product of the significant demographic change in our congregation from the builder generation – retired for a considerable period of time – to young professionals with demanding jobs, which they see as 'vocations'. I firmly believe that disciples make disciples (Matt. 28.16–20), so our weekly teaching programme needs to help everyone earth their faith in lives lived for Jesus at work, home, in the voting booth, at neighbourhood BBQs, and so forth. Many of our best and most committed people are unavailable for 'church' activities – whether those are mission events or maintenance groups.

Many of our good people are just passing through – social mobility is an increasing feature of a town, which once had a very settled population. Our aim is to be an effective motorway service station on their journey, to provide nourishment and refreshment while they are with us, fuel for the rest of their journey.

Increasing numbers of those we resource are not PLUs (people like us). For years, Park Road has been a church bursting at the seams with white, aspiring middle-class folk, focused on educational achievement, career progression and supporting the structures of the church. Recently, that has begun to change, as Bromley has begun to change. In 2007–08, of 126 newcomers, 78 were from minority ethnic groups – many didn't stick around for long, but it's indicative of how things are changing. Those who are sticking tend to be people from the poorer parts of the community with multiple issues and needs.

Not only do we find ourselves needing to recruit seven or eight new financial givers to replace one member of the builder generation going to glory or Eastbourne, we also need to rethink the whole chunk of church life that their volunteering maintained as no one steps in to fill their shoes.

The second is by rewiring our offer. We can make these tensions work in our favour not only to build the body but also, and crucially, to do mission. So we have revamped our evening offer by creating two new evening services – Sunday Break, a classic mix of hymns and inspiration; and the Later Service, a contemporary and interactive gathering. Both these offer mission opportunities to identified cultures. Those comfortable with what we offer – either at 5 p.m. or at 7 p.m. – will feel confident to invite their friends.

In some senses this is what Francis and Richter identify as Multiplex Church (nice phrase) – an offering that they claim is more ambitious than the mission-shaped church model and that 'consists of many elements in a complex relationship'.[2]

What we are finding as a result is that there is a complete absence of tension at the evening services, as everyone coming along knows what to expect and has opted for the service they are most comfortable with. Over time, we will see if our folk will rise to the challenge of inviting their friends to the service of their choice. Our hopes are high, in part helped by the success of our summer outreach to older people, called 'Holiday at Home', the audience for which is the obvious mission-field for Sunday Break, though three years in, the results are less than spectacular.

Finally, we are trying to re-imagine church for the unchurched. In common with lots of large churches, we have a bustling mid-week programme aimed at people in our community – toddler groups, senior citizens drop-in and leisure club, and the like.

---

2 Leslie Francis and Philip Richter, *Gone for Good? Church Leaving and Returning in the Twenty-First Century*, Peterborough: Epworth, 2007.

A dads' pop-in (a Saturday morning, once a month spin-off from Contact, our Wednesday parent and toddler group) led us to set up pop-in at the pub, exploring what church might be like if ... well, if those who don't come to church had a say in creating something that enabled them to explore what faith might be about. It didn't take off, but the conversations have led to some other creative thinking.

We set up a Sunday morning Messy Church[3] – an hour of arts, crafts, stories, songs and breakfast – two years ago. An average of fifty folk, a mixture of some churched but mostly non-church families, gather once a month. I view this as a new congregation to add to the three we already have on a Sunday.

Now, we are not Kendal; there is not a thriving New Age subculture creating a group of people ready to engage in spiritual conversations. Rather, we are a conservative London suburb with a significant number of late family formation couples struggling to juggle the demands of careers and young children, as they reach the big four-o. In many ways, they are not looking for abstract and spiritual answers; they certainly appear to have no needs. Discovering what the gospel might be for this group of people is making Sunday evenings at the pub and Messy Church really quite interesting.

The challenge for us is how to build on the success of Messy Church and provide a forum where the adult attendees can raise adult responses to and questions about faith and meaning. In January 2011, we started Messy Talk, using the resource *Table Talk*[4] from the Ugly Duckling Company to stimulate conversation among the adults attending Messy Church. Six months in, this has proved to be pretty successful, and we're exploring how to build on it.

A big challenge in all this is simply: Will our people bring their friends to anything we organize? And the jury is out. Some have said flatly that they won't – either because they don't have any friends or because they don't think their friends come to meetings!

We are tackling the former through offering some training events on making friends, sharing our faith and how to have conversations with people, which give us opportunities of talking about issues of faith and meaning.

The latter issue – that our friends don't want to come to meetings – really illustrates a deeply ingrained mindset: everything the church does is a 'meeting', and no one wants to come to those – especially when they've

---

3 Lucy Moore, *Messy Church*, Oxford: Barnabas, 2006.
4 See http:/www.table-talk.org/.

spent the week at them at work or live lives that don't include meetings or keeping to a schedule of any kind.

Part of the solution to this, it seems to me, is to have more parties! We need to change people's perception that when we are doing events, we are doing meetings. People will often come to gatherings with food, where there'll be a chance to chill and chat, where there's no pressure to decide anything or achieve anything. Messy Church illustrates this wonderfully. I think we need to get better at hosting informal gatherings that involve food, fun and conversation.

The other part of the solution is to use the teaching programme to educate committed members about the nature of the church and resource them to know and have confidence in their Christian knowledge, when they are in conversation with friends, neighbours and work colleagues. This is not just about preaching (though that remains important) but about home groups and how we use our website (notes, study guides and MP3s of sermons, for example). This sounds pretty obvious, of course; but six years in, it does seem to be beginning to yield encouraging results.

One missional challenge we face is that the inherited church is uncertain about whether mission is a desirable thing at all. It's not that they are not hugely supportive of sending people overseas to share the Christian faith – we support half a dozen such people and their families. It's that they have grown up in a church that didn't have to do mission. They grew up in an age when people went to church, where even those who didn't knew the Christian story and reckoned that it was the best way of making sense of the world. They remember when the church was full; and when it was full, we sang traditional hymns and had 45-minute sermons and read from the Authorized Version of the Bible. Decline in numbers has coincided in their mind with changes in worship style and sermon content. A return to tried and tested forms will see the numbers swell again.

It is very difficult to help them see that the changes that have happened in the culture over the past generation or two have rendered that way of doing church irrelevant to large sections of the population. I have been saying for quite a while that the traditional attractional model of mission – where we invite people to come to us – no longer works. This is why we are doing Messy Talk, and I'm encouraging people to throw more parties.

Unfortunately, Messy Church suggests that I am wrong! People do come to that. But I think they are coming to a space they visit during the week, when it is used for a parent and toddler group, to do a very similar activity with people they are already familiar with. It just happens that the hall we meet in is part of a complex of church buildings. So we are not really inviting these folk to come to church as we currently practise it at

10:30 a.m., 5 p.m. and 7 p.m. Rather, we're inviting them to come to their parent and toddler group on a Sunday morning.

A key part of the teaching challenge is helping the inherited core of the congregation to see the implications of the rapid social change we've experienced over the past twenty-five years for the way we express our discipleship and organize ourselves as a community of Jesus followers.

We are beginning to explore a more radically decentralized model of church, where neighbourhood-based home groups become the focus of mission in our community. Using material by Alan Roxburgh, a few of us are looking at how we can move back into our neighbourhoods and discover what God is up to there and how we can get involved. I guess the ideal would be that the ministry team gets invited to activities that members are involved in in their homes and gardens – that is to say, they're having more parties and want us to come and join the conversation going on there.

Such activity could also significantly shape the teaching programme happening at the centre of the church – the Sunday morning gathering in particular. Questions that arise as small groups seek to embody the gospel for their neighbours could be tackled and help offered to enable people to live more intentionally as disciples. Eventually this would result in a significant change in the flavour of our Sunday gatherings. But it is unlikely that a recognizable Sunday morning service will disappear any time soon.

The second principle that I have been working from is that of seeking connection in the wider world. This is the whole area of what are sometimes called social ministries or community involvement.

I struggle with the invisibility of our church. We have regular users of the building who do not know we are a 'church'. Why should they? They come for an activity with their kids, for example. I remember a conversation I had in the Welcome area of our church (the part people access from the street) with a mum, who had been coming to Contact, our midweek parent and toddler group, for years and didn't know that if she turned right through the doors, she'd end up in 'a church'. I have frequently suggested to our folk that people outside the church do not see us as irrelevant, they do not see us! And until recently, I thought this was unequivocally a bad thing.

I have to say that more recently I've been wondering whether invisibility or anonymity is not something to aim for. I began to ponder this when Brodie, a Scottish blogger, asked what single word would sum up the post-Christendom Church, if power summed up Christendom. Here's what I suggested:

I think 'anonymous' is a possible way of contrasting Christendom and post-Christendom. The Church under Christendom was all about profile as well as power, it's about seeking attention from the world, the Church has a 'look at me' mentality, because it believes that if the world looks at the Church, it will believe its message. This is nonsense, of course, in our changed world. Anonymity provides us with the opportunity to live our lives as followers of Jesus without that living being distorted by the thought of having an audience. It gives us the possibility of being stumbled over by those who didn't know they were looking for us and who in finding us enter a conversation of equals. Maybe I'm just being optimistic and maybe I'm feeling the pressure of feeling constantly in a goldfish bowl in the church I lead! I also don't think it contradicts Jesus' calling us the salt of the earth and light of the world because I'm not sure that our being these things ought to be a self-conscious act on our part that invites attention being paid to us. After all, a candle does not sit on the table saying 'look at me', it provides light so that we can see other things. Likewise salt preserves or makes things grow (whichever interpretation we go for) and doesn't draw attention to itself – unless there's so much of it that it swamps every other flavour (hardly what Jesus had in mind).

I quite like the thought that people coming into our building for a parent and toddler group don't know we're a church. It means that conversations start on a slightly more level playing field – neither side is feeling defensive. It also means that they don't have all sorts of preconceptions about what I believe about life and its meaning before we've actually got into a conversation.

This doesn't mean, however, that as a church we don't do things in our community. We do – it just means that we go about those things in a particular way.

First, it means responding to community-identified needs in partnership with other providers. There are a whole load of things that need doing in our communities; people need help, and churches are ideally placed to get involved. So we have Friends International, a project meeting the needs of refugees, asylum seekers and other migrants, and we are involved in the Street Pastors initiative.

I have a simple, single rule of thumb in approaching these ministries: I will not do on my own what I can do better in partnership with others. I think for too long churches have looked for social projects they can handle alone because they see them as a means to an end – that of recruiting new members.

Working with others – churches, voluntary organizations, the statutory sector – means that genuine partnerships are formed and genuinely new services can be created out of those partnerships. We bring our skills, insights, contacts, workforce to the table and can quickly establish ourselves as equals in the provision of a range of services. My model and mentor in all this is Raymond Fung and his important book, *The Isaiah Vision*.[5]

Second, this is about renewing our mandate: Jeremiah 29.7 – it called me into ministry, and it defines all we do. Why am I in exile in the 'burbs? It seems me that it's to bless the community I've pitched up in. Why's the church here? To do the same! At its core, mission is very simple – we've been blessed, we pass it on; we are beggars telling other beggars where we have found bread for ourselves and to share.

---

5 Raymond Fung, *The Isaiah Vision: An Ecumenical Strategy for Congregational Evangelism*, Geneva: WCC, 1992.

6

Mission in a Small-Church Context

Sandhurst Baptist Church

SAMANTHA MAIL

In 2005, my husband and I moved from one Berkshire town to another. Not a significant demographical change at all, merely a move from one predominantly white middle-class town to another in the South East of England. However, it was a considerable change in our experience of church. We moved from a large, thriving charismatic congregation in one of the new-church streams to a small somewhat struggling Baptist chapel, where I was inducted to be the sole minister. This church has now been our home for the past five years and has provided the context for a huge learning curve for me. Looking back, I can't quite remember what I pictured being a Baptist minister would be all about but, if I am honest, images of transforming this small church into a large church were certainly somewhere in the back of my mind. I guess with our Free Church background we were used to thinking that being in a large church meant being in a 'successful' church, a church that 'got it right'. Suffice to say that this is not how things have turned out to be at all. Instead of now being the minister of a 'large, successful' church, I find myself five years on still to be the minister of a small somewhat struggling Baptist church. Yet the church and its outlook on mission and its engagement with the community around it have dramatically changed.

Defining mission

Before I reflect upon how we as a church are trying to join in with God's mission in our local context, I want to begin by defining what I perceive mission to be. After all it can get a bit confusing, since so much has been written and talked about mission generally and specifically in recent years, with people trying to determine what it means to be a Christian presence within a society that seems more and more uninterested in the message of Christ. Books upon books have been written with well-meaning analyses, models on how to be successful, and, of course, new ideas have been generated from those in the pioneering ministries on what 'mission-shaped church', 'liquid church' or a 'new kind of Christian' could look like. As a minister in a small church in a middle-class setting in the South of England, I find all these books and discussions on the one hand very interesting and challenging but also overwhelming and destructive at times. There always seems to be someone who 'has worked it all out', but it somehow never quite seems to translate into my own personal experience. Furthermore, I find that if I am not careful with these 'experts' behind the books, as a minister I can become disempowered and forget to trust my own ability to listen to the voice of God for the people among whom he has placed me. So with an openness to new ideas and input from the outside, I feel more often than not that I am 'making it up' as I go along, desperately trying to figure what the next step for us a church community ought to be. At the same time, with humility and a deep longing to discern the mind of Christ for his church and the people he has entrusted to me, I am taking one step at a time on this road of discipleship.

So what is mission for me? I have found Peskett's and Ramachandra's definition to be helpful.

> Christian mission is *integral and universal* ... 'There is not a square inch, in the whole domain of our human existence over which Christ, who is Sovereign over *all*, does not say: "Mine".' God's concern embraces not only all individual men, women and children, but also the physical and biological environment which sustain their lives, and the social, economic, political and intellectual structures that shape the forms of their existence. Mission, then, is primarily God's activity. God is reaching out to his world through Christ and his Spirit.[1]

To me the fact that everything around us – whether Christian or not – belongs to God and that God is forever searching to find ways of bringing people and creation into a wholesome and healing relationship with him is the overriding paradigm when it comes to mission. I find that believing wholeheartedly in the *missio Dei*[2] takes the pressure off believing 'it is all down to me'. Instead, it requires faith in God's unconditional love and his

---

1 H. Peskett and V. Ramachandra, *The Message of Mission*, Leicester: Inter-Varsity Press, 2003, pp. 28–9, quoting Abraham Kuyper.

2 Literally, 'the mission of God'.

commitment to the redemption of all of creation. In believing that, it shifts our perspective from a church-centred approach to an approach that is life affirming and kingdom-focused. Vinoth Ramachandra puts it like this:

> The emphasis on the triune God as the subject of mission delivers the church from both an idolatrous self-centredness and also a narrowing of the scope of mission. The *missio Dei* embraces both the church and the world, and the church is called to the privilege of participation in this divine mission.[3]

It is important that we as Christians never become church-focused, believing that it is the church through which salvation comes to the world. We need to remain Kingdom-focused, believing in God's mission and accepting the privilege to work alongside him as his people here on earth. The challenge lies therein for a church not to become preoccupied with growing the church but with advancing the Kingdom of God. And these two – while they are clearly linked – are intrinsically not the same.

> The church [can] neither be the starting point nor the goal of mission. God's salvific work precedes both church and mission. We should not subordinate mission to the church nor the church to mission; both should rather, be taken up into the *missio Dei*, which now becomes the overarching concept. The *missio Dei* institutes the *missio ecclesiae*. The church changes from being the sender to being the sent one.[4]

Once we understand that the Christian world mission is Christ's, not ours, and that mission is not optional, but that it is God's mission, and we as the church – no matter what size – are invited to join in, then we have a pretty good starting point. What remains is our need to discern the framework in which we outwork God's mission in the places he has called us to. Such an understanding is hugely liberating when you work in a small church context. It is the constant reminder that being faithful to God's calling does not mean automatically being a large church as a result. It is also the challenge not to become complacent, taking God's grace for granted, making excuses and becoming inward-focused. This after all is not a message of cheap grace.

Personally, I find I am motivated in my endeavours by the fact that I believe God to be a missionary God, which in turn means that we as God's people are called to be a missionary people. This, together with the fact

---

3 Peskett and Ramachandra, *Message of Mission*, pp. 28–9.
4 David Bosch, *Transforming Mission*, Maryknoll: Orbis Books, 1992, p. 370.

that Jesus himself has promised life to the full for everyone (John 10.10), and the belief that human life has eternal value because we are loved and accepted by God, inspires me to bring this life-giving message of hope and new beginnings to those I encounter around me.

What kind of church?

One of the most important questions any church needs to ask itself on a regular basis is 'What kind of church are we called to be?' That is, we need to consider whether we are in fact called to be a small church. Most people probably struggle to believe that being a small expression of church could be a calling rather than an indication of a lack of growth. However, the truth is that there are real advantages in being small. After all, the majority of big churches break down into small groups because they understand that there is something about being in a smaller, more intimate context, where people have a real chance to get to know one another and journey with one another on the road of discipleship. I believe that it is possible that once you seek to determine what kind of church you are called to be, you can arrive at the outcome that it may be a small church expression; yet still to be a church, where people come and find faith, a church where people find healing and restoration, a church where people are committed to mission. The challenge therefore for any small church is to utilize these advantages of being small. Here are a few of the most common advantages we have discovered in our church setting:

- everyone knows one another.
- strong relationships and friendships
- support network for the individual
- hospitality, food and socials.

Of course, these advantages need to be held in a balance, so that they never become an exclusive form of church that is inward-looking and not welcoming to newcomers. We find that these strengths have opened up many doors for us into the community and also have enabled us to minister to people who have come to us from other, larger churches, where it is much easier for the individual to be overlooked.

On being a small church

The challenges and disadvantages of a small church are of course well known and easily spotted:

- resource issues, such as time, finance, people power
- not being 'taken seriously'
- unfavourable comparisons with bigger churches
- always thinking of what could be or what we don't have.

We discovered that if we want to be an active and healthy small church, we need to accept that we cannot do everything that a large church can do. We also need to acknowledge the natural limitations, which are given due to the size of the congregation. Yet at the same time, we found that once we embraced the possibility that our size as a church may be our calling, it set us free and enabled us to work within our limitations. It completely shifted our perspective and instead of feeling a sense of disappointment and resentment, we are now able to use the strengths we possess and experience a freedom and peace that only God can bring.

When I began my post in 2005, people struggled to believe that God could 'properly' use them as a small church. It has taken a number of years – and, if I am honest, it is still an ongoing process – for people not to discount themselves, to truly believe that God has a plan for this church as partners in his *missio Dei*. However, it really shouldn't come as a surprise to us that God uses and deliberately chooses the small expressions; after all, that's the model we can see right from the outset in Scripture (1 Sam. 9.21; Isa. 60.22).

As a minister at a small church over the last five years, I have found that it is important to invest in one form or another in each member, to get to know them, to spot their talents and their gifts and through encourage-ment release and empower them into exercising the God-given gifts that they possess. The thinking behind that is to move away from a model of church where the minister ministers and the congregation simply congre-gates, or, to put it differently, to move every member into ministry and to minimize the number of people who just sit and do nothing.

As we moved people into an active expression of their discipleship, at a corporate level, we also began to ask, 'What *can* we do?' instead of, 'What *should* we do?' as a church community. The difference is that we deliber-ately choose not to put pressure on ourselves to do things that are beyond our capabilities, but rather to make good use of the gifts and talents that are present within our congregation. This approach has led to a variety of different expressions of mission, and it has resulted now in at least 80 per cent of people being actively involved in the life of the fellowship in one way or another. Unfortunately, this kind of change also meant that we lost a number of people over the years, who felt that they would rather just observe than participate. This has been a great sadness to us. The pain of this is felt all the more intensely because we are a small church, where people know each other well and where every person counts.

Sunday morning isn't everything

The second biggest mind-shift for us as a church was to understand and wholeheartedly believe that 'Sunday morning isn't everything', in other words, to be aware of the numbers game, in which the health of a church is purely determined by the number of people who attend the Sunday morning service. This is an ongoing journey for the church, since every-thing around us seems to promote the idea that 'the more people you have on a Sunday morning, the more successful you are as a church'. Our church regularly has about twenty-five to thirty out of a possible forty to fifty on any one given Sunday morning in the service. Sometimes the num-bers can drop as low as ten people. To conclude from this lack of service attendance that we are a struggling and failing church would be a com-pletely wrong conclusion. The truth is we have a very high involvement rate by the church congregation in all sorts of aspects of the fellowship's life, anything from serving teas and coffees, cutting the grass, decorating the church, to running a communal cafe, the Activity Club, a tap-dancing class, mums and babies groups, a lunch club for the elderly, supporting two orphanages, actively engaging with the Trussell Trust, employing a joint youth worker with one of the local Anglican churches and exploring the potential of a possible partnership (LEP) with the Methodist Church with a view to building a new purpose-built church in the heart of the town.

The Coffee Spot is a cafe in the centre of our town, which we started running five years ago on behalf of the Council. We worked hard in getting the support from all the other local churches, and today the cafe is run by five churches. Together we employ two members of staff. The Coffee Spot is used by regular customers, such as mums and toddlers, the disabled and their carers, members of a walking group, business people, who spend their lunch hour there. We hold monthly ecumenical services; the ministers from all the churches are available for one lunchtime a week for conversation and prayer; we have volunteers working in the cafe, both from the churches and from the local community; we have youth work happening from there and it is home to the Activity Club.

The Activity Club is a group that was established in 2005 for single, divorced and widowed people, particularly in their fifties and sixties, which aims to provide a support network of friendship and activities. This group started with three people five years ago and now has over sixty members, who get together once a week to plan their respective activities and then spend the weekends together. Out of this group, we have five people who now regularly attend our church.

We support two orphanages, one in India and one in Kenya. Both have been visited by various church members. As a church, we also sponsor one child in Kenya and support an overseas mission organization and our local secondary school, which is working with orphans in Rwanda.

The Trussell Trust is a local charity that collects and redistributes food to local families in need. We collect food on an ongoing basis and deliver it to our nearest branch.

Our youth worker does church-based youth work, but he also works extensively in the local schools, working in partnership with the Council in after-school projects, and is involved in the preaching of our church. We wanted to give him a voice to shape us as a church that is more than just youth-work based.

We are currently exploring whether our church and the local Methodist church are called to become a Local Ecumenical Partnership. Not because our aim is finally to have a large church, but because our heart is to determine whether by pooling our resources, we can become even more effective in participating in God's mission.

All these activities and many more are delivered by one small church. And while we may not have a full church on a Sunday, and we struggle to get attendance to midweek evening meetings, there is a commitment and passion within the church to see our locality impacted with the good news of Jesus Christ in very practical ways. We have built many good relationships with people in the community and with the local Council. The challenge is to maintain these relationships and for us to be the people God has called us to be. No one knows whether any of these people will ever come to faith and attend our church. However, they have encountered something of the values of the Kingdom of God through who we are and what we do. In the end, we need to remain faithful to the calling that Jesus placed upon his disciples to seek first the Kingdom of God (Luke 9.2f.) and to trust that he himself will build his church (Matt. 16.18).

It has been, and still is, a tough challenge to create a sense of self-belief in this small church and to help its members not to discount themselves, but rather to take themselves seriously and believe that God can use them and that this church has something to offer to the wider community in our locality. From a church that was fairly insecure, and identified on its mission statement that its only point of outreach was letting the church hall, we have come a long way. Of course, the challenge is to keep going and trust that the Holy Spirit will lead us on further; to pace ourselves so that we do not burn out and to remain open-minded about where God is taking us. As a minister – in tough times – I take comfort from the fact that the little chapel in which we meet was established in 1881. This serves as a constant reminder that this church was here before me, and it will definitely be here after me.

7

Mission in a Black Majority
Church Context

DAVID SHOSANYA

Introduction

It is said that 11 a.m. on a Sunday morning is the most segregated time in America. Regretfully, the same sentiment is increasingly true of the UK. Like our American cousins, Sunday services have become an opportunity for us to retreat from the world, the 'other', and into the comfort of being with our own kind. By occupying separate spaces for worship, we simultaneously conceal the latent prejudices that cultural groups within society – black and white Christians included – secretly harbour against one another, but that are unwittingly but profoundly displayed through this passive – and in some cases active – act of tribalism. This is in spite of being the body of Christ and being called to be God's agents of reconciliation in the world (2 Cor. 5.19).

The truth is that the complexities we are forced to negotiate – issues of race and the practical reality of racial politics – can and do manifest themselves in the visible separation of the races for the act of Christian worship, and by extension into mission and ministry. While there are individual churches that buck this trend, they are few and far between and need to be multiplied if the eschatological vision of a multi-ethnic heaven in Revelation 4 and 5 is to begin to be realized here on earth. In other words, this vision of the Church united in worship before the throne of God is the fruit of the practical outworking of this vision for unity between the divided and diverse Christian communities with differing and conflicting cultures in the here and now.

Purpose

My aim in this brief account is to outline the distinctive culturally specific perspectives that inform and shape an African and Caribbean missiological praxis, and to posit the argument that the increasing numbers of African and Caribbean Christians in the UK at this time might be an expression of God's providence and provision to his Church in the UK for such a time as this, when it is increasingly difficult to reach white British communities with the gospel. I will argue that given the exponential growth of Christians of African and Caribbean heritage, the rapid decline in the numbers of white British people attending church and the incremental substitution of social action for evangelism, African and Caribbean Christians have a unique opportunity, if so minded, to be at the very epicentre of a much needed impetus for evangelistic outreach here in the UK.

The facts

According to research carried out by the Christian Research Agency (CRA), faith in the UK has continued to decline over the past 31 years from 5.4 million church attendees in 1979 to number 4.7 million in 1989, 3.7 million in 1998 and 3.2 million in 2005. However, the rate of decline is slowing down from 1 million in 9 years to 500, 000 in 7 years. Of the population, 6.3 per cent attend church on a Sunday, with a further 0.6 per cent attending at some other time in the week. Therefore, a total of 6.9 per cent of the population either attend church on a Sunday or during the week.[1]

A number of reasons have been suggested for this decline. First, we are not evangelizing as much as we used to; second, the Church in the UK is ageing; third, the Church is not attracting men and is losing women. We can add to this the fact that young people are haemorrhaging from the Church, a lack of relevance of church to real life, the relaxation of Sunday trading laws, with Sundays being increasingly viewed as a recreational day, and changing patterns of family life.

What is interesting is that many of the reasons suggested for the decline in church attendance among white communities in the UK are not applicable to African and Caribbean Christian communities. The research evidence indicates that African and Caribbean churches continue to place a high premium on evangelistic activities, including proclamation evangelism, a trend that has all but disappeared from white British churches. They are also continuing to retain and attract young people, although these young people will be forced to face the challenges that emerge from being a part of two cultures as young black people and the inevitable

---

1 Peter Brierley, *Pulling Out of the Nosedive*, London: Christian Research, 2006.

renegotiation of their identities that will follow. These churches are also retaining and attracting men; many have even devised special outreach strategies specifically designed to reach men. Although they are facing the challenges of contemporary life that other sectors of society have to navigate, African families are maintaining a reasonable level of stability, while some Caribbean communities are mirroring the experience of the wider society with many of the issues affecting family life.

African and Caribbean Christian communities: an exception

The figures for the growth of the Church on the African continent and in the African diaspora are nothing but astounding. Phillips Jenkins, drawing on figures from the Centre for the Study of Global Christianity, has pointed out that in 2005 there were 2.5 billion Christians on the planet – 531 million in Europe, 511 million in Latin America, 389 million in Africa, 344 million Asians and 226 million in North America. Statisticians have projected the rate of growth of African Christians to be approximately 2.36 per cent per annum, which will result in a 50 per cent growth in 30 years. By 2025, it is projected that 595 million Christians will live on the African continent.[2]

Here in the UK, the exponential growth of Christian communities largely constituted of Africans and Caribbeans was not something that would have been foreseen when immigrants from the then colonies began to arrive on British shores. Neither would one have been able to have conceived that these communities, small as they were, in just over sixty or so years would be an integral part of God's strategy to reach the UK with the gospel of Jesus Christ. But this is now a very real possibility. Jenkins' observation that 'the numerical changes in Christianity are striking enough, but beyond the simple demographic transition, there are countless implications for theology and religious practice'[3] is an insightful and perceptive comment. One of those 'implications for theology and religious practice' is a radically different missiology from the one adopted by the Church in the West. I will briefly highlight five characteristics of an African and Caribbean missiology before exploring the role that African and Caribbean Christians might play in reaching white communities with the gospel.

---

2 P. Jenkins, *The Next Christendom*, Oxford: Oxford University Press, 2007, pp. 2–3.

3 Jenkins, *Next Christendom*, p. 6.

Hallmarks of African and Caribbean missiological praxis

Prayer

Prayer is the cornerstone of African and Caribbean Christianity and spirituality. At the heart of this spirituality is the belief that the spiritual world interacts with the human world in a very real way. It is therefore critical that any attempt at evangelism is predicated upon a recognition of the need to draw near to God for protection and power to overcome and subdue the works of the devil. Prayer therefore becomes the neutralizing force against the power of evil and has the potential to free the human mind from deception (2 Cor. 4.3–4), to resource the individual with the supernatural power of God (Mark 16.15–18; Acts 1.8) and to give power to the words spoken in the name of Christ (Acts 2). Prayer is the 'powerhouse' through which individuals can tap into the finished work of the cross (Col. 1.15–19) and cause it to have a positive effect here on earth.

An African missiological praxis therefore places a very high premium on being prepared through prayer for battle as modelled by Christ (Luke 4.1–15), encouraged by the apostle Paul (Eph. 6.10–18), taking time to anticipate and prepare for/against the inevitable backlash of confronting the spiritual forces that control human beings and communities (Eph. 2.1–5), to bind the strong man – the spiritual power over a physical location or territory that can, according to Walter Wink, be represented by the civic and other infrastructures in a locality – prayerfully neutralize pride-filled thoughts and cleverly devised arguments (2 Cor. 10.1–5), to receive power to be insulated from intimidation and threats (Acts 4.29–31), to speak boldly for Christ (Acts 1.8) and to demonstrate the power of God over human disease and sickness (Matt. 10.1).

Given this world-view, it is not be unusual for Christians of African and Caribbean heritage to engage in a substantial time of prayer prior to any personal or corporate evangelistic outreach being embarked upon. This makes sense in that, as in the times of Jesus, the proclamation of the gospel as the arrival as the Kingdom of God is seen as a direct challenge to the kingdom of darkness – and potentially civic authorities – and any attempt to free human beings from bondage will inevitably be resisted directly or indirectly by the powers (Acts 4). It is also worth noting that the African and Caribbean world-view takes seriously the demonic – spiritual powers that possess, influence and manipulate the human will and consequently the behaviour of an individual under their control – and often see it as the root of physical, psychological and emotional illnesses. Therefore, if one of the manifestations of the Kingdom of God is the removal of such human maladies through the appropriation of the atoning work of Christ to the circumstance at hand, then one must be adequately filled with the power of God through the Holy Spirit (1 Cor. 4.20) in order to be used by God to bring about such change.

Proclamation

Both Africa and the Caribbean enjoy a rich oral tradition, where great pride is taken in the spoken word. Oratory is therefore taken very seriously and frequently deployed to create rich pictorial images to reinforce what is being said. *The UNESCO General History of Africa* suggests oral tradition is 'a testimony transmitted verbally from one generation to another'.[4] This corresponds well with the observation of the Psalmist: 'we will tell the next generation the praiseworthy deeds of the LORD, his power, and the wonders he has done' (Psalm 78.4, NIV).

Understanding the importance of oral history to African and Caribbean people is important, in that it provides an insight into the significance placed on proclamation and the manner in which the gospel is communicated. In the African tradition, the orator does not speak for himself but on behalf of, or to, the village elders and other villagers. The orator therefore occupies a critically important position that is invested with mystic significance. One can see then why the preacher of the gospel in the wider Christian community is held in the highest esteem and why proclamation is such an important part of an African and Caribbean missiological praxis. The emphasis placed on the importance of living together and being community also explains the predisposition towards focusing on a single person speaking from the front when an important, life-changing message is being delivered.

This contrasts with the highly individualized notion of existence that is increasingly characterizing Western living, and is a radical departure from the missional methodologies being employed by European sisters and brothers, who are increasingly moving away from proclamation evangelism as an effective way of communicating the gospel, in favour of relational and informal ways of sharing the Christian gospel of hope. Africans, steeped in and appreciative of a rich oral tradition, continue to see *preaching* the gospel, from the pulpit or on the streets, as a key role of the Church.

But there is more than historical conditioning or learnt behaviour that informs this particular methodology and preference for sharing the gospel

---

4 J. Ki-Zerbo, *The UNESCO General History of Africa: Vol. 1, Methodology and African Prehistory*, Paris: UNESCO, 1981, p. 142.

in African and Caribbean Christian communities. Preaching in this context requires that one has an unwavering confidence in God, his Word and in the Holy Spirit's capacity to confirm God's Word with signs and wonders. This is not such a priority in Western cultures, where a premium is placed on a cognitive rather than an experiential understanding of the faith. The emphasis placed on preaching the gospel is therefore much more than a confidence in one's oratorical skills, a preference of one style over another, but rather an expression of confidence in a God that backs up his Word with his power when it is preached.

Power

This leads naturally to another characteristic of an African and Caribbean missiology: power. The strong belief held by Africans and Caribbeans in the supernatural – which is arrived at by a close study of Scripture – means that they are keen to exercise faith to see God's power through healings, deliverance and other supernatural expressions of power. The fact that God is all-powerful means that '[t]he reason the Son of God appeared was to destroy the devil's work' (1 John 3.8, NIV). More than that, a refusal to believe that God will exercise supernatural power through his agents of change on the earth is to deny what has been made plain in and through Scripture and to be disobedient to God's commands to subdue the works of the devil (Matt. 10; Luke 4; Mark 16).

What needs to be understood is that power does not carry the same connotation in the African and Caribbean psyche as it may do in a Western or European understanding, given the hostile environments in which many African and Caribbean Christians have grown up.

Expectancy

Expectancy is another key feature or characteristic of African and Caribbean spirituality. Expectancy is based on a strong belief that God has made his word plain and clear and that he is only restricted by the degree of faith we choose to exercise. Therefore, the bigger the faith we exercise the greater the outpouring of God's power and presence that is expected. Expectancy is a natural extension of the strong belief in prayer and power. Having prayed according to the Word of God (John 14.12–14), waited on the Holy Spirit (Acts 1.8) and with an unshakable confidence in God's power to do anything, the failure to expect God to work is unacceptable. Expectancy is therefore the combination of a strong belief in prayer, a strong conviction in the power of God that results in active faith (Heb.

11.1). Faith is another key feature or characteristic of African and Caribbean Christianity.

Faith

Faith is taken very seriously in African and Caribbean Christian communities. The statement found in Hebrews 'that without faith it is impossible to please God' (Heb. 11.6, NIV) is taken literally and as an indicator of the priority that God places in believing that he can and does do things that contradict human wisdom and overthrow human power.

Added to this faith in God is a strong self-belief that is the result of what many African and Caribbean Christians call 'redemptive uplift', the new-found sense of confidence that invades the psyche and informs the actions of individuals who have discovered faith in Christ and inspires a deep sense of self-belief. Many African and Caribbean Christians would point to and quote Scriptures, such as Ephesians 3.19–21, which speaks of God being 'able to do exceedingly abundantly above all that we ask or think ... according to the power that works in us' (NKJV). Scriptures like these are used to encourage Christians to have a sense of confidence in their potential in and through Christ and to dare to believe that God is able and willing to use them. In order to be used, they are encouraged to have a strong sense of expectancy, which they are taught to believe that God will honour.

Strategic planning

Strategic planning may seem to be out of line with the other characteristics of an African and Caribbean missiological praxis, which I have outlined above. However, the fact that strategic planning plays a significant role makes sense when ones considers more closely what African and Caribbean Christians expect from prayer. Let me illustrate this with a brief story.

I was attending a National Teams Day meeting for Baptist Union staff and regional ministers, when the issue of hospitality to congregations from other cultures was being discussed. Jonathan Edwards, then the Senior Regional Minister/Team Leader of the South West Baptist Association, told a story of talking with the leaders of an African congregation who wanted to join them. He recounted how he was struck silent when the African minister asked him what the Association strategy was to reach Plymouth with the gospel. They didn't have one. But this single-congregation church did! Whether the strategy worked was effectively immaterial. The important thing was that they had a strategy.

This church is not unique. Soon after coming to Christ in 1983 under the ministry of Les Isaac, I was quickly made a member of the evangelism team. Our task was to co-ordinate the evangelistic activity of the church. We quickly set about developing a strategic plan, implementing and modifying it where necessary. The plan consisted of a systematic process of visiting every home within a specified catchment area around the church, carefully recording the details of conversations and prayers with residents, responding to prayer requests, recording and ensuring that individuals were prayed for as requested and that they were informed of that fact; organizing 'follow-up' of individuals and teams to revisit over time so that links were maintained, and ensuring that the whole process was covered in prayer, even to the extent that when a team was out, that team was covered in prayer for as long as they were out. That was 1983. The church was 99.9 per cent African with a few white English and Caribbean attendees. African and Caribbean leaders were responsible for all the planning. Strategic planning has always been a critical component of an African and Caribbean missiological praxis for as far back as I can remember and continues to be today.

The challenge: reaching white communities with the gospel

At present, the relationship of the majority of African and Caribbean Christians to white British communities is comparable to a powerful boiler, which has the mechanical capacity to power the radiation system in a cold house but remains disconnected from the radiation system. What is needed is for a plumber to connect the two systems so that the potential of both the boiler and the radiators are realized.

As part of a sabbatical study in 2009, I was keen to explore if I could measure, or at least get a fairly accurate sense of, what appetite existed among African and Caribbean leaders to rise to the challenge of reaching white British communities with the gospel. What I discovered was that many African and Caribbean church leaders have become convinced through prayer and hearing from God that part of the reason for them being in the UK at this time in history is for them to be instrumental in bringing revival to the UK through sharing the gospel with indigenous communities.

Some might consider the fact that African and Caribbean Christians place a strong emphasis on the supernatural would be problematic in that both communities have radically differing world-views. The fact remains that despite the historical tendency, even predisposition, for the Western world-view to fail to take significant notice of the spiritual world, it still remains and interfaces with the human experience on a personal and communal level. Indeed, this is not just an African and Caribbean world-view but one that is reflective of a biblical world-view too.

It may even be argued that the African and Caribbean world-view is increasingly relevant to a postmodern, post-Christian society, which has jettisoned historic representations and expressions of the Christian faith in favour of a variety of alternative spiritualities including New Age, Paganism, Eastern religions and so forth. The advantage that African and Caribbean Christians have over and above the majority of their white British sisters and brothers in Christ, particularly those that stand outside of the Pentecostal and charismatic traditions, is that their experience and interpretation of spirituality offers a very unique insight into the spiritual rhetoric that is increasingly becoming normative in Western culture. In other words, the Pentecostal and charismatic tradition and experience has inadvertently equipped African and Caribbean Christians with the spiritual insights and vocabulary to dialogue with individuals who are increasingly embracing alternative spiritualities. The challenge is whether Christians of African and Caribbean heritage are willing and able to undertake the journey that will allow them to contextualize their inherited faith perspectives so that they are meaningful to white British people.

8

Mission in a Multi-Cultural
Church Context

SUSAN STEVENSON

All we know of God we know in mission. Our entire knowledge of God comes through God's self-revelation in creation and redemption. We would have no life without the mission of God. It is no surprise, therefore, that any reflection on mission leads into an exploration of many other facets of life and of Christian discipleship. This is emphatically true in my experience of mission in a multi-cultural church context. It has led me to explore searching questions, including about how deeply converted I am willing to be, and about how true to the gospel of Jesus is the gospel I proclaim.

It is uncomfortable being a Christian. It is disturbing to follow someone who says he himself, not some safe propositional format, is 'the way, the truth and the life' (John 14.6). It follows that if truth is personal, then personal stories can sometimes help us see more clearly. It is in this hope that this chapter tells a number of different stories and makes a few connections between them. The narrative that emerges is provisional, because it is only a series of snapshots. The stories move on. The hope is that they connect with the stories of those who read them, and in turn help connect us all with the great story of God.

The story of William Seymour[1]

In discovering the story of William Seymour, I found a new hero. Born in the deep South of the United States in 1870, Seymour is in many ways the father of modern-day Pentecostalism. In 1906, Seymour's congregation in Los Angeles experienced a breakthrough of the Spirit, which led

---

1 For a brief account of William Seymour's story, see R. Foster, *Streams of Living Water: Celebrating the Great Traditions of the Christian Faith*, Bath: Eagle, 2004, pp. 102–12.

to the Azusa Street Revival. The intense spiritual searching that led up to that revival reminds me of the atmosphere in many churches during the charismatic renewal of the 1970s and 80s. Many of the manifestations of the Spirit are common to both.

What was striking about Azusa Street was that for Seymour the revival was never primarily about tongues and that category of phenomena. For him, the power of the Spirit released in revival was primarily, as in the book of Acts, to bring healing to the world by sweeping away the barriers of race, gender and nationalism. One journalist summed up the signifi-cance of the events at Azusa Street by saying that 'the "color line" was washed away in the blood'.[2] Describing this new kind of Christian com-munity that was emerging, Seymour wrote that 'the people are all melted together … made one lump, one bread, one body in Jesus Christ. There is no Jew or Gentile, bond or free.'[3]

The story of Azusa Street does not have a happy ending. Cultural norms are strong and powerfully resistant even to the challenge of the gospel. This was a deeply racist era in a profoundly segregated society. Seymour invited Charles Parham, a well-known white evangelical leader, to join him in leading the new movement. However, coming to Los Angeles, Parham was so uncomfortable in such a mixed community that he took about two hundred of Seymour's white followers and set up his own meet-ings. Slowly, all the other white leaders also followed. Ecstatic experiences of the Spirit Parham could cope with, but not the multi-cultural commu-nity that flowed from it.

The story of Chatsworth Baptist Church

Discovering Seymour's story helped make sense of another story I was part of, the story of Chatsworth Baptist Church. We joined this story in January 1990.[4] By then, the 1960's high-point of a membership of over five hundred was well past. The church was already diverse, with a num-ber of black members, including two deacons, mainly from the older West Indian community. There had been an exodus of white families from the area in search of affordable housing and better schools. The community

---

2 F. Bartleman, *Azusa Street: The Roots of Modern-Day Pentecost*, Plainfield, NJ: Logos, 1980, p. 55.

3 Foster, *Streams of Living Water*, p. 107.

4 In January 1990, my husband Peter and I moved to Chatsworth as joint pas-tors. In 1995, Peter joined the teaching staff at Spurgeon's College, and Chatsworth invited me to stay on as senior pastor, with Peter serving as an honorary associate pastor.

had changed, and the church perceived itself to be ageing and in decline. Indeed, someone calculated that if current trends continued, by 2008 we would have minus fifty members.

In September 2007, when we moved from the church, membership stood at 190, with 350 people from 28 nationalities on the pastoral list. The diaconate reflected the membership, with approximately one-third being West Indian, one-third African and one-third white British, European and Antipodean. We had also been part of establishing a Spanish-speaking, Latin American congregation, which grew alongside CBC, independent but part of the Chatsworth family. Similarly, for three years we had hosted Trinity Baptist Church, now one of the largest churches in the Baptist Union, until they moved to their own premises half a mile away.

Chatsworth was not only ethnically diverse. It was equally diverse across social and generational cultures as well as embracing a wide variety of personalities, preferences and theological viewpoints. Students coming to us on placement accurately described us as 'complex', and some of those who were initially excited at the idea of a multi-cultural church found it a disturbing and uncomfortable experience.

Chatsworth was indeed a challenging and at times uncomfortable place to be. This struck me afresh when the Baptist Union organized a conference in 2005, 'Leadership in a Mixed-up World', which a number of Chatsworth deacons attended. Organized by the Racial Justice department, the speakers and perspectives were predominantly black. Many of these people were my friends, and it was in that context I personally heard them. As the day drew to its close, it became obvious that some of our white deacons were feeling uncomfortable. One leader summed up their experience: 'I'm feeling guilty that I'm white.' Some of that is entirely appropriate: there is a lot to be ashamed of in our history. It is no bad thing to experience discomfort akin to others. However, the question is how to handle that discomfort in a way that enables us all to grow.

The fact is that when black Christians are empowered, white Christians often feel disempowered. That disempowerment is entirely appropriate, but also extremely hard to handle. The reaction of many is to flee. Reflecting on that day, my initial reaction was a desire to thank those white families who had stuck with this painful journey. Then I realized it was not only the white members who were making that journey. In a multi-cultural community, everyone is outside their cultural comfort zone: everyone could choose to be in an easier place.

What makes people hang in together through this journey? Could it be that we recognize that this is the church the Bible describes? Could it be that we sense this is the same journey Jesus took, as 'he did not consider equality with God something to be grasped, but made himself nothing' (Phil. 2.6–7, NIV)? Could it be that deep down we know the gospel is not designed to make us comfortable, that this discomfort is somehow part of our being formed into the image of Christ?

Speaking with one of our deacons who had journeyed with us, while his children, now baptized teenagers, had at times been the only white children in some of our groups, he commented, 'I wish I could say it was something we'd anticipated and embraced. The truth is more that it just happened.' But did it 'just happen'? How did it happen?

How did it happen? The story of God and his church

In many ways, it did 'just happen', in the same way a plant 'just grows'. Ministry is a form of spiritual midwifery. Ministers act as midwives to the new life God brings to birth. What we saw at Chatsworth was God's work, the *missio Dei* breaking surface. However, this plant grew in fertile soil. I find myself fascinated by the way churches have personalities. Perhaps it is something to do with the way they are planted, with the DNA that is bred into them in their early years. Looking back over Chatsworth's history, it was striking how, in spite of dramatic changes in the appearance of the membership, there is a consistency over the generations of ethos and vision.

Planted in 1878, one of a string of new causes sponsored by C. H. Spurgeon and the London Baptist Association in the developing London suburbs, Chatsworth has consistently held to a 'generous orthodoxy', an evangelicalism that couples deep commitment to Scripture with openness to the world.

I was thrilled a few years ago to discover a poster from a rally held at the Royal Albert Hall in 1909 protesting against human rights abuses in the Congo.[5] The rally was chaired by the Archbishop of Canterbury, with Dr John Clifford one of the keynote speakers. The poster lists well-known ministers who supported this protest, and there in the list of evangelical luminaries, alongside the likes of Campbell Morgan and F. B. Meyer, was the name of D. J. Hiley, Pastor of Chatsworth Baptist Church. Hiley was an unashamed evangelical preacher with a passionate social concern. Looking back a hundred years, in West Norwood we could see a church engaged with both Scripture and the world.

---

5 A. Hochschild, *King Leopold's Ghost: A Story of Greed, Terror and Heroism*, New York: Pan Macmillan, 1998.

I was equally proud of a photograph from the early 1960s of the young-est Sunday school class, with a number of smartly dressed West Indian children in it. At least some attempt had been made to welcome the grow-ing West Indian community, by this stage expanding from neighbouring Brixton.

Here is a plant growing in fertile soil, but also one that has been tended in particular ways. What were those emphases that contributed to the church growing in this particular way?

It began with the Bible. Chatsworth is a church with a love of the Bible and preaching. If people could see something was biblical, they would go with it. The church of Scripture is undoubtedly a barrier-breaking, ulti-mately multi-cultural creature.[6] We rejoiced in Scripture and allowed it to shape our worship and our ethos.

We also sought to model our diversity. My aim was that on any given Sunday any visitor would catch sight or sound of a range of people par-ticipating in some way 'from the front', or would hear or see something with which they would be able to identify. It was an impossible aim, but an important principle to work to. Such diversity in worship necessitates a willingness on the part of the congregation to give and take, and some-times liberties were taken and mistakes made, which had to be forgiven.

Diversity in worship requires something to bring coherence. For us, that was again our commitment to Scripture, read and preached, but also enriching and guiding our worship. Beneath it all, however, as with most things about the church, holding things together were relationships and trust.

Peter and I both worked hard and in different ways to relate across this vast spectrum of people. A church that is working at becoming multi-cultural undoubtedly attracts others from across the cultures, caught by the same vision, and many of those people developed in time into leaders in the church.

Then we had to learn from one another. We had to learn the import-ance of being there, when an African or West Indian grandmother had died. We had to learn that Korean young people expect you, if you are older, to speak to them first before they feel able to speak to you. We had to learn to make allowances, when we tripped over something rooted in our histories or bred into us by our cultures. This was significantly done in deacons' meetings, which could be fierce and bruising at times. We often tested the power of grace – but it held. God was at work, even among

6 For a stimulating account of multi-cultural church in Vancouver and a discus-sion of its biblical foundations, see B. Milne, *Dynamic Diversity: The New Humanity Church for Today and Tomorrow*, Nottingham: InterVarsity Press, 2006.

such a flawed and failing community of people as we undoubtedly knew ourselves to be. Church is a miracle. For us, it had to be.

Seeking to be church in a multi-cultural context is hard work for everyone. It can be glorious and joyful, but also painful, exhausting and frustrating. Why do it? Evangelism is hard enough, cross-cultural evangelism harder yet. Is all this a distraction from preaching the gospel?

Why do it? The story of God and his world

We have identified the growth of a multi-cultural church at Chatsworth as an expression of the *missio Dei*. Quite simply, it was God's idea and doing. Furthermore, we have seen that it grew from a desire to be a Bible-shaped people, and the recognition that the church in the Bible is a radically barrier-breaking community. However, as we followed along this path, we made other discoveries.

- *We began to recognize the power of cultural captivity.*
  The early Church was culturally captive, and it took a breakthrough of the Spirit for it to be set free. Many of us can identify with Peter's heartfelt cry that day in Joppa when God commanded him to do something his culture told him was profoundly wrong (Acts 10.1—11.18). With Peter, we began to recognize how deeply, for good and for ill, we are shaped by our cultures.

- *We began to understand that we live in a globalizing world.*
  'Over the last century the centre of gravity in terms of world Christianity has shifted inexorably southwards, to Africa, Asia and Latin America.'[7] If we want to see the Church of the future, with all its beauty and its flaws, we should perhaps look to Africa. The need for the Church today is to grow global Christians, disciples for a globalizing world.

  This is not only true for London. While visiting family in Northern Ireland, we meet young Poles running remote village shops, and we worship in a Church of Ireland parish, whose rector is Rwandan. We all of us live in a rapidly globalizing world.

---

7 P. Jenkins, *The Next Christendom: The Coming of Global Christianity*, Oxford: Oxford University Press, 2002, p. 2.

- *We began to recognize that we had been brought together to be part of the mission of God in this place.*
Through Jeremiah, God calls his people to 'seek the peace and well-being of the city to which God has carried us' (Jer. 29.7). It takes time for an immigrant community to find its feet in a new culture, perhaps more than a generation. However, with a second and third generation of Christians of Caribbean heritage and with an influx from sub-Saharan African Christians, who are often highly qualified as professionals, in many ways the black Christian community has grown in confidence and influence. This is the confidence out of which initiatives like Street Pastors have come. Black leaders are emerging not only as pastors to the diaspora, but want to identify with and reach out to the longer-established communities.

As the power dynamics are changing in the global Church, so they are beginning to change in the UK urban church scene. It will take much grace to negotiate the shifting contours of power, both from those used to being powerful and for those to whom being powerful is a more recent experience.

- *We discovered that mission is done by God in us and among us as well as through us.*

  > Mission in not primarily about *going*. Nor is mission primarily about *doing* anything. Mission is about *being*. It is about being a distinctive kind of people, a countercultural, multinational community among the nations. It is modelling before the world what the living God of the Bible really is like.[8]

To be brutally honest, organizing a series of mission events and activities is much less challenging than facing the things in ourselves God wants to change. It is also humbling to recognize that God reveals himself to the world through our struggles and even our failure, as we live by the grace we preach. Mission is not something we are in control of. It is the dynamic of God who, in the process of challenging, forgiving and changing us is also revealing himself to his world.

- *We discovered the gospel is far greater than we thought.*
During the 1930s, a revival began in Rwanda that brought new life, power and joy across East Africa. Fifty years later, Rwanda was

---

8 H. Peskett and V. Ramachandra, *The Message of Mission*, Leicester: Inter-Varsity Press, 2003, p. 123.

engulfed again, this time by a genocide that killed 800,000 people in the space of a hundred days. Many of the people implicated in the genocide were church people, sometimes church leaders. How can the gospel have taken such shallow root? Of course, we ask the self-same question of ourselves. Why does the gospel so rarely change us at depth?

The heart of the gospel is reconciliation. That reconciliation is, first, between people and God, then worked out in reconciliation between people. To misquote slightly yet surely stay within the spirit of John the apostle, '[God] has given us this command: whoever is reconciled to God must also be reconciled to his brothers and sisters' (1 John 4.21). Anything else surely is cheap grace, and a denial of the gospel we proclaim. How often, I wonder, do I sell short the gospel of Jesus?

The story moves on

The story of mission in a multi-cultural church context moves on. It is now three years since I moved on from Chatsworth. I have a raft of new questions. Charlton, the place we moved to, has experienced rapid growth in ethnic diversity over the last decade but is also home to a significant white working-class community. What does it mean to be English or to be working class today? How does a black-majority, multi-ethnic church reach out to such a community? Why do communities that suffer injustice seem so often to scapegoat one another? In what ways might black Christians reach across that divide? What does mission look like here?

Mission looks like Jesus. Mission is the life of the local church, because Jesus is the life of the local church. This Jesus is living truth and red-hot forgiveness. We can no more hold the gospel than we can hold a red-hot coal. It is alive and dangerous. Grace changes us or is no grace. This Jesus is the living way, always disturbing us onwards, calling us beyond our present frontiers. This Jesus is life, the life that truly is life, and ever birthing new life.

This Jesus is the mission we are called to live.

9

City-centre Mission

Methodist Central Hall Westminster

MARTIN TURNER

The Methodist Central Hall Westminster (MCHW) is a unique centre within Methodism. It is the nearest that Methodism has to a cathedral-type building, though it was funded not by a few benevolent benefactors but by one million ordinary Methodists giving a guinea each in response to the appeal of the then Wesleyan Methodist Church to raise one million guineas to mark the centenary of the death of John Wesley. Around a quarter of the amount given went towards building MCHW, which was to serve as both the headquarters building of the denomination and also as a mission centre at the hub of power within London. In many ways, it also has to be said that the building that opened in 1912 was a statement of Nonconformist strength at the close of the nineteenth century. The huge building seemed to be shouting across Victoria Street to the ancient Westminster Abbey that it now had a rival!

The missionary movement, which spawned not just MCHW but forty other city-centre missions across the country, was the Forward Movement. This movement was the answer of Wesleyan Methodism to the problem of the enormous gulf that was opening up between respectable Methodists and the poor and marginalized of society. The response to this gulf was to build city-centre missions, which did not resemble churches but had more in common with a theatre or concert hall. The intention was to create a non-intimidating but welcoming building, where ordinary non-churchgoing people could feel at home. The work varied according to the context, but the emphasis was always upon strong evangelistic preaching set alongside practical educational and social work.

For MCHW, the time of greatest strength came during the Second World War. For four years, it hosted the largest air-raid shelter in London other than the Underground. The then Superintendent Minister, the extraordinary Dr William Sangster, moved his family into this shelter and lived there for four years. An outstanding preacher, the queues to get a seat for worship extended round the building, and, when it was full up, Dr Sangster would suggest that worshippers might like to cross the way to the Abbey, where there would be plenty of room! In these years, MCHW was the largest congregation in London.

Since the War, the story was one of gradual decline in spite of huge effort on the part of a succession of very able superintendents. Ultimately the local congregation decided that they could no longer cope with the vast expense of maintaining the building, and handed it over to the national church. Within Methodism, there was then a very serious debate as to whether or not MCHW should be kept or sold. The Methodist Conference decided it should stay open, but fairly soon after that also decided to move their headquarters team away to another site. It seemed as if a perfect storm was gathering made of the combination of a declining congregation and the loss of the main source of income through the rent paid for the offices. The response to this was twofold. First, the trustees decided to set up a trading company to operate a conference centre in the building. Second, those seeking a new superintendent in 2001 decided that a more distinctive evangelical ministry was needed, and I was appointed. I had started my ministry as an assistant minister in a very similar mission in Bradford at the Eastbrook Hall – thus I had no illusion as to the scale of my task!

The worshipping congregation is key

Crucial to my thinking and focus is that the main worshipping congregation is the key focus for mission. In some contexts this would not be so, for those worshipping would be much the same group Sunday by Sunday, and the focus for evangelism lies outside of the building, but this is not so in a central mission. Week by week the congregation changes at an extraordinary rate. One of my predecessors as Superintendent, the late Revd Dr John Tudor, told me that ministering at MCHW was like ministering on an escalator! Few worshippers are there every week. Some spend their time between London and West Africa; some see MCHW as their church, when they make their annual visit to London; some have been hurt by their experience in a local church and seek anonymity; some come worn out by their local church and seeking a rest; some are seekers who come to explore faith; some are so eccentric they would not easily fit into a small local congregation; and, of course, week by week many are tourists for whom their visit is a one-off. In the face of this rich variety from across a spectrum of society and from across the world, it is clear that only excellence in worship is acceptable. When I arrived I had every intention of changing much of what was already happening. The services seemed overly traditional to me with their strong fixed liturgy, robed choir and use of the organ all the time. However, I fairly soon came to the conclusion that to try to bring change here would split the congregation, and that was totally against my aim of creating a community of love. Therefore, I changed very little of the worship envelope, but tried to make what was going on within the envelope far more relaxed and varied. Thus, I like to think that the presentation, the music, the preaching and the praying are all of a very high standard, although in the formality of the traditional form allowing space for the Spirit to work. Most important of all, however, is not what we do but the atmosphere and ambience of the church, thus the key words are love and welcome – I believe Jesus meant it when he told us that we are to love one another.

As a Methodist, this desire to build a community of love finds its expression in the welcome we offer. 'Secret shopper' exercises with friends revealed simple problems, such as how difficult it was to get into the building, how easily people could be missed by welcome stewards and how intimidating the actual worship sanctuary was. In response to this, welcome stewards are now positioned at every level of our multi-level church to greet and point onwards. Stewards also receive training and regular briefings as to how to look after people, and the fabric has itself been re-ordered.

All this is undergirded by the strong Arminian theological emphasis, expressed succinctly in the 'Four Alls' of Methodism – 'All need to be saved, all can be saved, all can know that they are saved and all can be saved to the uttermost.' Never before have I had to wrestle so much with what this really means! Within our congregation, there are people involved in same-sex relationships, irregular heterosexual relationships, difficult and aggressive people who have lurched from church to church and finally ended up with us, and some odd and eccentric people who can be problematic and demanding. But for us the love of God for 'all' overcomes any other factor; a community of love must be a community where all find a welcome and a place. From a practical point of view, this means that harsh words or inappropriate behaviour are challenged and strategies are put in place to make sure everyone is included.

Time and again, when asking new worshippers what has attracted them to us, they have mentioned the music and the preaching, but gone on to say that the most crucial factor has been the welcome and the atmosphere. In the city centre, where people often have a sense of being lost and just one among millions, entering a space where they are intentionally valued regardless of any other factor has an immense impact. If mission is to have credibility, it must be rooted in a congregation, who model the love of God, which is being shared and preached.

Buildings are important too

In a good year, our cafe and conference centre facilities will give us a footfall of around half a million people. In my previous churches, I have always organized ministry on the streets, door-to-door visitation and a variety of outreach activities off site, but at MCHW the key mission opportunity is with those who actually cross our threshold; our resource and context shapes our mission.

When the building was erected, British society was operating from a broadly Christian base, and the task was to create a worship centre that deliberately did not look Christian in order to attract in the unchurched. At the beginning of the twenty-first century, I decided that the issue now was that in a secular society we needed to flag up clearly what we were. To achieve this, large pieces of Christian art were purchased; a prayer request board was placed in the lobby, leaflets were printed explaining what the church was about and poster cases both outside and inside the building offer the opportunity to reveal who we are and why we do what we do.

For our staff, rather than asking visitors why they had come and politely turning them away if they had no good reason to be there, we have instead appointed two full-time visitor services hosts, who organize a team of volunteers to provide a warm welcome, a tour of the building and an explanation of who we are. A dedicated Visitor's Centre has also been opened as a really helpful asset for this work. Pastorally, there are requests nearly every day to speak to a minister, and we make coming down and making space to talk to people an absolute priority.

With our buildings, two new six-storey lifts have opened up disabled access, the tip-up seats in the Great Hall have been replaced with more comfortable movable chairs that allow great flexibility, and the platform has been redesigned so that those leading worship or meetings are more among and on a level with the people. Redecoration has been carefully accomplished, with a colour-coding system for each floor, a cyber cafe introduced into Wesley's Cafe and, perhaps most exciting of all, what was a bank taking up the key front corner of our building has been converted into a chapel, in which many sit quietly during the day and which has become a focus for smaller worship services midweek.

We are now clean, warm, comfortable, bright and welcoming. I am a firm believer that the physical context speaks of God; a £9 million expenditure has enabled that voice of God to be better heard.

A team of specialist ministries

When I arrived at MCHW, I entered a tradition of over ninety years, where the focus had been upon the Superintendent, but I neither felt equipped to cope with this nor did I feel it to be right as the day of personality preachers is long gone. We have therefore built a team, not at all unusual within American churches or within large British ones, but fairly unique within Methodism. Together, we now have individuals who carry responsibility for ministry through pastoral care, healing, young adults, the media and women's ministry respectively.

On a wider front, we have networked across London Methodism and host regular services for the Ghanaian, Nigerian and Philippine communities. We have a particular responsibility to link in with Parliament, and in that work have developed strong partnerships both with national denominational officers and with ecumenical friends. Through this team, the scope and reach of our work has thus been considerably widened, while our worshipping congregations have benefited in that the different personalities appeal to different people. We have learnt that as a group we can appeal to far more than any individual might do. The other very positive contribution that this team ministry is able to make is to demonstrate at the heart of the Church the love and unity that I have already said we see as the crucial spiritual dimension.

Advertising

The use of radio advertising on our local Christian radio station has also been important to our growth. We pay for basic generic advertising to run all the time, plus fairly intense campaigns for special occasions. Added to this is the additional exposure of three members of staff broadcasting on weekly programmes. This may seem an odd area of mission to people listening to Christian radio. It might be expected that they already have a faith and a church, but our experience is that a number of folk come to join us for whom the radio was the way in, or the way back, to faith in Jesus Christ. Because they have heard the advertising and also regularly heard our own voices, they feel safe to come along to church, there discovering the extra dimension of fellowship that the radio cannot offer.

This has been particularly effective in relation to our monthly ministry of healing, where numbers have doubled since we started regular broadcasts and specific advertising.

In reflecting upon our growth as a church where congregations have just about doubled and the membership risen from 220 to over 400, I have to say that I still have a measure of disappointment. Compared to the average Methodist church, we are very big indeed, but set alongside many of the large Anglican and Independent churches in London we are very small indeed! Of course, I have reflected upon why this is. What we are offering in terms of a large congregation with a traditional framework, a robed choir, evangelical preaching and room for the Holy Spirit to move is I believe unique in London, but it is not what attracts.

Church growth suggests that to be effective we should aim at a target group and work to offer what is attractive to them, particularly with music but with wider ministry too. We have deliberately not done that. I take the view that each church should not be a separate unit of the Kingdom but a slice of the whole Kingdom. By that I mean that within worship there should be contemporary and traditional, there should be folk of every ethnic group living in the area, and there should be young, middle-aged and old. To share in such worship and live in such a community takes grace in that no one is particularly catered for, but to my mind part of the Christian life is affirming other people, rejoicing in our differences and allowing the love of God to hold us together in spite of them. Each congregation should be a slice of the Kingdom, for when we stand together in heaven that will be the type of mixed group we are with!

Holy opportunists

I remember being at a conference for ministers of larger churches. As these multi-talented leaders shared their home-group and cluster-group strategy involving hundreds of people and dozens of groups, I felt despair. Eventually, I could stand it no longer and stood up and said that our church is fairly chaotic, things do not always work well, people come and go all the time and when they do turn up are often late, offices are hard to fill, and were it not for a small group of key lay people who are totally committed and reliable we would collapse. After the session, the vicar of a thriving church in the East End of London came up to me and thanked me for describing his church!

In the average city-centre mission, there are not the swathes of talented and educated middle-class people who can open their large homes for fellowship groups and run everything smoothly. No, we struggle from one thing to the next, but always with an eye to the main chance, and I do believe that the key strength of my leadership is in looking for the opportunity, linking in one person to another, making the contacts and using them to bless all concerned. The best minister in the city centre is the entrepreneur – or dare I say it, a sanctified Del Boy!

Over the years, we have seen a number of significant developments happen through chance conversations and opportune moments that needed to be embraced and explored:

- The opportunities to develop a family centre on our site alongside the Roman Catholic Vincentian order, now serving over 170 families in the locality.
- Working with Premier Radio on major events has led to the carol service, for example, growing in number from 67 worshippers in 2001 to 800 plus in 2009.
- Partnering with a whole variety of different churches and Christian agencies has meant that we host top events that bring in people from across the UK. Making space for others to operate is a special part of our mission in which we gladly share.

To sum up, there is no grand strategy in place, no master plan for growth in the future! Too often we are event- or crisis-driven, and we would do well to make more space for reflection upon what is happening and upon where we might feel God wants us to go. We do have certain principles to which we hold. I have spelt out our priority to be a loving community where all are welcome as the first principle, but we also try our best to be a praying community and a community seeking to encounter God and enable others to encounter God through our worship and ministry. As we do this, we are in many ways counter-cultural, because we value our tradition of music and biblical preaching, which does not always sit easily with contemporary society. Our Conference Centre offers both the opportunity to encounter those of other faiths or no faith but also leads us into the tension that the more successful either one of us is, the less space there is for the other to operate. Our site places us naturally at the centre of national and international life.

We could be said to be successful in that we have grown in numbers, social outreach and in Christian affirmation from both within Methodism and outside of it. And yet there is so much more that we could have done and should be doing. That is the tension of mission in the city centre, and all the time the busyness of the world and the depth of human need we encounter mean that even when we do try to plan a way forward we are either hijacked or sidetracked!

What a muddle! But we thank God that he seems to bring blessing and growth out of it, and while he does so we keep our eyes open for the next opportunity. Perhaps above all else that is what city-centre mission is all about.

10

Cathedrals and Mission

Coventry and Birmingham Cathedrals

YVONNE RICHMOND TULLOCH

It was in 1990 that my attention was first drawn to a rising interest in spirituality in people outside church. In due course this led me to conclude that cathedrals today are probably one of the best vehicles for the Church's evangelism. I was worshipping at the time in an open evangelical church and had become disillusioned by the amount of energy and financial resources that were being poured into evangelism projects with what appeared to be a diminishing return. Having been raised in evangelical circles, I was well used to evangelistic missions and events, where a guest service or special event with an evangelist preaching a sermon leading to an altar call for commitment to Christ was the common model. Still today in many churches this is the perceived best and only practice. But then, and even more so now, this approach was becoming less welcomed; the culture was changing rapidly, and simply stepping up our evangelism efforts or shouting our message louder didn't seem to be the answer. If the gospel message – that Jesus is the Son of God and Saviour of the world, who offers new life on earth and eternal life in heaven – is as true as we believe it to be, then surely this should be very appealing? Although we have the same 'good news' as conveyed in Acts, we aren't seeing the same level of response. Rather, the story has been more likely to be one of decline.

Troubled by this, in 1990 I stopped trying to do things my way for God and stepped back from my numerous church responsibilities to give space and time for God to speak. In the following weeks, ten individuals became Christians through conversations I found myself having with them about their spiritual experience. A nurture group emerged from this group, where spiritual experience was central, and, as they shared their ongoing stories, worship arose naturally from a desire for a symbolic expression of the emotions that emerged. This was a whole new style of evangelism for me, which, rather than rely on apologetic proof, conviction and persuasion of the need for Christ for conversion, instead gently nurtured spiritual interest in the direction of the one, true, living God and sought opportunities for experience of the Holy Spirit in advance of a rational explanation or understanding of the gospel. It expected God to be at work by his Spirit in people's lives, it discovered that he *was*, even though the person couldn't necessarily articulate it that way. Then it gently directed the individual to more experience of God's life-transforming power and led them to an awareness of Jesus as Saviour – the one who had made such transformation possible.

The bearing of all this upon evangelism for today, and not least of all for cathedrals in their mission, should not be underestimated, because since then spiritual interest has notably increased. In the spiritual vacuum of post-Christendom and with the pick-and-mix, individualistic, 'truth is established by experience' nature of postmodernism, there has been a burgeoning interest in – or at least acceptance of – spiritual experience over recent years, seen most clearly in the growth areas of alternative therapies, alternative spiritualities, psychics, paganism and 'Body, Mind and Spirit' fairs. Furthermore, symbolic expression has returned, noticed clearly at the death of Diana, Princess of Wales, and since then at other national and local tragedies and in the emergence of roadside shrines. In addition, the ancient spiritual expressions of the Celts, of monasticism and pilgrimage have increased in popularity.

In the year 2000, research by David Hay into the spirituality of people outside of the Church showed that up to 76 per cent of people acknowledged having had a spiritual experience. It showed that people are open to exploring those experiences, when given the right context in which to do so, and that although they can't necessarily articulate the source as being God, a large majority of people refer to there being 'something there'. My own research, 'Beyond the Fringe' (2005), supported this. It showed that people outside formal religious affiliation are indeed having spiritual experiences and often referring to a sense of awe. It showed that they are asking big, spiritual questions born out of – often hidden – spiritual longings, most notably whether there is a divine being or 'god' and if so whether they can connect with such a being. Accordingly, some had tried church, but found that either it didn't provide them with the experience they longed for, or it sought to draw them in and convert them to a particular way of thinking. Commonly, these people didn't go to church because of its being alien, 'club-like' or unspiritual and because, most alarmingly, they saw no relationship between their spiritual longings and Christianity or church.

Hence cathedrals! Cathedrals are regarded by many as public property, as belonging to everyone. They can be easily stepped into and sampled. They represent spirituality. They are a place of pilgrimage, of prayer, where one might connect with the divine, where a spiritual search might begin, where God – if he, she or it exists – might be sought and found. They are a place where such a discovery might be made on one's own terms, in one's own space and in one's own time. They are a place of anonymity and are generally open – a place where a person might decide to come at a time of personal need. They are where a candle might be lit, where emotions can be expressed, where quiet reflection can take place and where one could hope not to be disturbed. They are a place where one might connect with the ancient spiritual expressions of mystery, of wonder, of awe. And, I suggest, they are the place where those with spiritual longings today are most likely to go if they are to try out church at all – not necessarily because they intend to try out *church*, but because cathedrals provide a doorway to spiritual experience. They also provide the best of worship, where occasional visitors are accepted, and since they are the church of the land – where that is understood – they are the accepted standard or norm.

As a consequence, cathedrals regularly have many visitors to their services. It is not surprising, then, that there has been widespread increase in attendance at cathedral services over recent years. At a time when much of the rest of the Church has been in steady decline, cathedral attendances since the year 2000 have been rising, with total Sunday and weekday adult attendance from 2000 to 2008 increasing by more than 20 per cent and total under-16 attendance by as much as 57 per cent. Christmas attendance shows another promising picture with Christmas Eve/Day attendance rising in the same period by some 27 per cent.[1]

Of course, such people will not necessarily be actively seeking spiritual awakening or expression, but it has to be acknowledged that something amazing is happening. I turn now to the various areas of cathedral mission that might engage the majority agnostic public – those who are neither committed to any faith nor confessed atheist, but who, nevertheless, are likely in today's spiritual vacuum to be open, at least, to spiritual things.

---

1 Church of England Research and Statistics (www.cofe.anglican.org/info/statistics).

Pastoral mission

With cathedrals being in city centres, the pastoral needs within which they are immersed are great and varied. There is a stressed working community in need of the cathedral's peace, the homeless in need of her shelter, the mentally ill, who are increasingly left to fend for themselves in the day-time, in need of her love, and refugees/asylum seekers in need of her assistance and support. Invariably, the daily acts of worship at Birmingham Cathedral have the added challenge of people coming and going, causing a disturbance, drunk, not speaking English, snoring in the corner! In addition, Birmingham Cathedral's Green provides a welcome oasis for a lunchtime or shopping break. During the summer of 2008, Acting Dean Peter Howell-Jones did most of his work from a gazebo on the Green, and found that faith conversations naturally arose. Our volunteers in the cathedral shop have seen this too over the past two years as several conversations over free coffee for the homeless and refugees have resulted in baptism and/or confirmation. Here is an enormous opportunity to express the love of Jesus, but no longer can the diminishing armies of cathedral chaplains and volunteers, nor the overstretched cathedral clergy, cope with such demand.

Tourist evangelism

Related to this is the area of tourism. A visit to the cathedral is a must for any tourist to a city. The history, art and architecture of most are a great draw, and for many people, cathedrals will be one of their few experiences of church. A comprehensive survey by ORB in 2009 showed that the vast majority of cathedral visitors are from Britain, that more than half of them come from outside the immediate area, that about half are first-time visitors. Naturally, many never return. Any evangelistic endeavour with tourists will necessarily serve the Church at large rather than seek to build the cathedral community or congregation.

Several cathedrals are well developed in their educational leaflets and tours, but much more could be done to engage tourists spiritually on their visit. Evangelistic exhibitions are obvious, as are leaflets with prayers and reflections to take away. In our changing cultural landscape, these require great care in their presentation and language, aiming primarily to spark or nurture interest in Christian faith and encourage personal journeying and expression of faith. They should avoid jargon, any focus on the institution and any tendency to preach. The ORB survey showed that although for 41 per cent of visitors the main reason for going to the cathedral was for its history, architecture and art, and for only 10 per cent was it for a moment of reflection or to think about a loved one, 59 per cent of visitors said a prayer or lit a candle when there and 27 per cent stated the ambience of peacefulness and calm was the thing they liked most. It also showed high satisfaction levels from visitors, particularly where there was participation. Most cathedrals could, therefore, make much more of their buildings to encourage, through prayer stations, reflection and symbolic action, a personal spiritual pilgrimage once inside.

In 2005, I was privileged to help initiate a project of evangelistic exhibitions with accompanying response cards in partnership with the Deo Gloria Trust and the Christian Enquiry Agency. Via a national freepost address the cards were used to request follow-up literature, a Bible or a contact with a Christian or local church. A number of cathedrals have since taken up the opportunity of the exhibitions and hundreds of cards have been received. SGM Lifewords has also produced useful resources to engage visitors to historic churches. 'Look Around You' is designed to lead visitors around any traditional church, using the layout and the common features of the building as a basis for prayer and reflection. 'Inspiring Prayer' features a series of written prayers and prayer exercises, and I have found Lifewords' prayer cards with tear-off slips for prayer requests to be very popular, with hundreds being picked up each month. At Birmingham Cathedral, we currently provide regular art/prayer stations on a seasonal theme. These again are popular, but as with any exhibition, they are costly for cathedrals to fund, as are leaflets on the scale that they are taken.

Religious education

Related to tourist evangelism is the area of educational visits. With very few children having any knowledge of Christianity and schools hard pressed to deliver National Curriculum requirements, cathedrals have a unique opportunity to provide educational tours and programmes on church and Christianity that enable children to have a positive experience of church and know where to go should they ever want to know more.

The majority of cathedrals now employ at least one qualified teacher as an education officer, and together with volunteers they welcome many thousands of school children each year. Education centres have been set up in several cathedrals, where children can be welcomed, taught and offered hospitality. School carol services remain popular, and Christingle services are increasingly welcomed. Out of these can come special invitations to Christmas family or crib services or other family and children's events.

Many cathedrals offer 'schools days' or leavers' services. At Wells Cathedral, all leavers from church primary schools are invited – and nearly all attend – which means three thousand children from the area visit the Cathedral over a two-day period. Chichester holds days for sixth-form students, which have increased with demand, and Ely attracts four thousand children to the cathedral on four days in October.

The schools department at Coventry Cathedral now sees every primary school child in the county at some stage in his or her education, to teach about the dangers of conflict and war and the Christian message of peace. Thousands attend a succession of Christingle services before Christmas with their teachers, and many hundreds return with younger siblings, parents and grandparents for the increasingly popular 'Journey to Bethlehem' service on Christmas Eve.

Ely Cathedral organized the 'Pilgrim Train' with the local railway operating company. Four hundred school children from Harlow in Essex were dropped off at Ely Station and walked the half-mile up the hill to the cathedral. They were met by fully robed vergers and clergy halfway up and walked in procession to the south door. The intention was for them to turn east on entering the cathedral and proceed to St Etheldreda's shrine, on which they would place bunches of flowers. It had all been rehearsed, but when the children entered the cathedral and looked up at the beauty of the octagon, with the sound of the great organ playing, they were completely overcome. The pilgrim train came to a grinding halt. The cathedral stewards couldn't move them on, because the children seemed so overwhelmed – in awe. It took half an hour to get to the shrine!

In an interview with the then Canon Missioner Mark Ryland in 2005, David Risden of Exeter Cathedral said he had detected a different attitude from the schools' perspective over recent years. Where teachers had previously been wary and 'scared stiff of indoctrination' by the cathedral in the mid-1990s, there was more intrigue and curiosity as to 'where God related to this vast building and to people's lives'. This was affirmed by Laura Arends, the Education Officer at St Paul's, who felt that the understanding of the Christian faith among teachers had decreased over the previous five years. This she attributed to the fact that most teachers she saw were 25–35 years old and therefore were unlikely to have benefited from Christian nurture in school, home or church. However, she noted that many of these teachers seemed 'curious' about the Christian faith, not just the artefacts. In this sense, the lack of knowledge seemed to spur interest and a positive attitude.

I myself have seen teenagers, intrigued by what they have noticed when passing the door, walk into Coventry Cathedral part way into its worship, presumably unaware that church or Christianity is supposed not to be 'cool', and sit down at the front!

Events evangelism

A fourth area is that of events. The capacity, location and nature of cathedrals as 'Mother Church' mean that cathedrals lend themselves to large gatherings. Community and civic events are as much needed today as they have ever been, and, once inside a cathedral, many thousands naturally come under its spiritual charm. There is opportunity for clergy to welcome and introduce events and while doing so to draw attention to the cathedral's being a 'house of prayer' and point guests to its spiritual ambience. In an age when those outside church have little or no understanding of denominations, cathedrals are also a natural focus for Christian unity. Large church events held at cathedrals can positively raise the profile of the Church, especially where they are ecumenical or involve young people, and can be a much needed source of encouragement to increasingly hard-pressed local clergy. Wedding fairs, exhibitions and life courses, such as those for parenting, bereavement or debt management, can also resource not only the diocese but churches across the region, as well as serve the local community.

When I was at Coventry Cathedral, we held regional marriage preparation courses each year as well as marriage enrichment courses. These were attended by many who had little or no church connection. At Birmingham Cathedral, the Canon Liturgist Janet Chapman's Valentine's Day renewal of marriage vows service has attracted couples from near and far, who wish to recommit to each other, either because of a special anniversary or because their marriages have been challenged by illness, redundancy or bereavement.

Cathedrals are also ideally placed to hold specific, large-scale evangelistic events. Emerging from the research 'Beyond the Fringe' and its ensuing practical reflections with mission leaders was the question, 'What does a spiritually open society, preferring to "try out" faith for itself rather than be preached at, with little understanding of church and a belief that Christianity is unspiritual, mean for the evangelistic event?'[2] The answer was 'Spirit of Life', a Christian Body, Mind and Spirit fair held at Coventry Cathedral on May Day Bank Holiday in both 2006 and 2007. Deliberately

---

2 See S. Croft et al., *Evangelism in a Spiritual Age*, London: Church House Publishing, 2005, and S. Hollinghurst, Y. Richmond and R. Whitehead, *Equipping Your Church in a Spiritual Age*, London: Group for Evangelization, 2005.

advertised direct to the public in non-religious terminology, it offered '[a]n opportunity to engage with the Spirit of Life through meditation and mysticism, prophecy and dream interpretation, massage and therapies, street entertainment and seminars, poetry, art and the senses, angels and blessings, anointing and healing prayer, plus so much more'. Christian contributors from across the country and representing the breadth of Christian tradition and spirituality provided seventy stalls and activities for participators to sample and experience. Over sixteen hundred people came to the first event and over four thousand to the second; the response more than exceeded our expectations. Many said, 'If we'd known it was going to be this good we would have brought our friends.' Unexpectedly, some became Christians on the day and more afterwards. Several commented on how helpful the day had been in their spiritual exploration. One Iranian man, having had a dream poignantly interpreted, spent several hours trying to find me, as the organizer of the event, to ask 'What is all this? What should I do?', just as they did in the days of the early Church. We were privileged to lead him into a living relationship with Christ.

'Spirit of Life' was expensive and involved a lot of work. It is therefore unsustainable .in the long run. But it was a valuable experiment in attractional evangelism, proving that the public will readily explore Christian spirituality given the right context – an opportunity for spiritual experience in an environment where they can choose – and it provided important lessons to Christians about the Spirit's work in all Christian traditions as well as in several activities, which some would have deemed out of bounds! Similar 'Spirit of Life' events have since taken place in other cathedrals and in simpler forms in churches across the land.

One such initiative was a series of Blessing Days, which Canon Missioner Nigel Hand and I recently held at Birmingham Cathedral on the cathedral's Green. Massage, anointing and healing prayer, life coaching and baby blessing days provided a welcomed opportunity for many to be blessed as they relaxed over lunch or simply passed by. They led to many meaningful conversations, and for the baby blessings, in particular, people travelled a very long way. Sadly though, the programme for 2010 had to be abandoned due to lack of available volunteers.

Exeter Cathedral's 'Life on the Beach' and Manchester Cathedral's 'Angels' and 'The Lion, the Witch and the Wardrobe' initiatives are further examples of the creative use of cathedrals for evangelistic events, the first adopting a 'go to them' strategy for evangelism and the second a 'come to us'. With the large number of people with whom they have contact, cathedrals can easily develop a 'mixed economy' approach to evangelism, encouraging the return of the prodigals as much as reaching out to the unchurched.

Cathedrals as mission fields

This brings me to how cathedrals are a mission field in their own right. The numerous acts of worship and activities attract a variety of people for a large number of reasons. In this consumer model of church, there is a sizeable church fringe, presenting great opportunity for enquirer courses. But by the same token, few are committed to building the life and witness of the congregation, so volunteers, when it comes to sharing faith, are hard to find. People also gather in different communities; the choirs, archivists, bell ringers, shop personnel and so forth lending themselves naturally to fresh expressions of church if appropriate acts of worship are introduced. Coventry Cathedral has an ever-growing network of bereaved parents called 'Remember Our Child', who meet monthly to do just that, and who find strength in simple acts of remembrance. Gloucester Cathedral has a valuable ministry to the Goths who gather on the Green. Every existing congregation or emerging fresh expression has the potential of developing as a church in its own right to provide a variety of worshipping opportunities, but this requires energy, initiative and vision.

Coventry Cathedral's 'Cathedral Praise' on a Sunday evening provides an informal service of praise to complement its more formal choral tradition. This attracts young people and those who are seeking or who are new to faith, as well as church leaders and Christians from across the region, who come for spiritual refreshment.

Lighting the beacons

Cathedrals today offer an unprecedented opportunity for people of all walks of life to develop their spirituality. In an age of decreasing Christian knowledge, they will not necessarily bring those individuals to a point of committed faith but are uniquely placed to enable thousands with whom they have regular contact, or through an occasional visit, to encounter God and take steps on their journey of faith. Rather than being outdated or defunct, cathedrals are growing in popularity, when large swathes of the Church are in decline, and are well placed not only to point individuals to faith and Church but also to serve the needs of the wider Church in mission. To do that effectively two important challenges will need to be faced.

The first is finance. Apart from limited support from the wider Church, each cathedral has to 'fend for itself' irrespective of historic reserves or potential for income generation. The cost of maintaining buildings and choral traditions means that most struggle to maintain the status quo let alone resource evangelism. The thousands of people who come into nominal contact with cathedrals are not committed enough to provide substantial support, and often assume that cathedrals are public property and do not need a donation. Thus, cathedrals have to rely heavily on grants and appeals. Sadly, many have had to begin to charge for entry, making them less accessible for spiritual needs and necessarily focused on fundraising rather than mission-orientated events. The Church at large desperately needs to channel more resources into cathedrals to enable them to continue to give of their best and become the centres for mission they could be. Second, deans and cathedral clergy will need to be selected for their heart for mission and their entrepreneurial and management ability. Ideally, at least one residentiary canonry should be allocated specifically to mission. Unfortunately, since cathedral appointments are senior posts and regarded within the church as a career step, mission is seldom a priority, politics often come into play and relationships of competition and conflict can exist.

Nevertheless, things are happening. In October 2006, I hosted a 'Mission-Shaped Cathedrals' conference at Coventry Cathedral to which, astonishingly, representatives from thirty-six of the country's forty-two cathedrals came. Following a similar conference in Peterborough eighteen months earlier, they came because they had observed a changing climate and growing opportunity and wanted to discover what could be done. There was an excitement in the gathering as stories were shared and issues discussed. It appeared as though the Holy Spirit was gathering momentum and we were about to ride a wave. Sadly, since then little has happened to progress cathedral mission. If anything, the burdens identified weigh heavier now than they did before. If the challenge for mission today is to 'see what God is doing and get on board', I finish by appealing to the Church to recognize the potential of cathedrals and address their needs, because it is clear that with not much imagination and greater allocation of funds, cathedrals could become beacons for the gospel across our land.

Mission and Eucharist

The Greenbelt Worship Co-operative

MICHAEL VOLLAND

... On the Greenbelt front.

... How about a Beat Eucharist? I'm thinking Allen Ginsberg, *Howl*-esque liturgy, with adapted monologue readings in a Kerouac-like stream-of-consciousness *On the Road* manner. I'm thinking music-ally, the high tempo, ska-lite jazz that induces trance-like euphoria, as described in Kerouac. I'm thinking smoky jazz club visuals with sharp contrasts of mountain, wilderness beauty à la *Dharma Bums*. I'm think-ing intercessions that are called out like a voice in the wilderness, some wild-eyed prophets, Old Testament or 50s California ...[1]

So read part of an email I opened in the early hours of a Wednesday morn-ing, as the train on which I was sitting sped from the snow-laden streets of Durham towards London. I closed my laptop and sat back in my seat. I was inspired. We had to make this happen.

I was responsible for programming the Worship Co-operative venue at the 2010 Greenbelt Festival. The Saturday evening slot was as yet unfilled. I'd been thinking about the possibility of a Punk Eucharist, but it hadn't taken long to decide against this, since I didn't know either a Punk band or a priest who I thought could resolve the tension between the essentially nihilistic philosophy of Punk and the radical affirmation of life that is at the heart of the Eucharist. A Punk Eucharist might have been an interest-ing headline-grabber, but that was about it. A Beat Eucharist, however – that seemed both possible and brilliantly unique. As I considered the email, it was clear to me that since thousands of Christians who attend Greenbelt pick up ideas for innovative worship that goes on to form an integral aspect of the life of their local church-in-mission, a suggestion

---

1 Tim Watson, Durham, 2010.

that appeared to have such obvious potential for invigorating the worship – and therefore the mission – of local churches would be a great addition to what Greenbelt could offer.

The emailed suggestion came from one of my tutees at Cranmer Hall – a young ordinand called Tim Watson. A few weeks prior to Tim firing his idea at me, I made an announcement at college explaining that since I was involved in programming the worship at Greenbelt, if anyone felt inclined to put ideas together for a particular offering, there was a chance that it would make the Festival. A small group emerged under Tim's direction and began to bash ideas around. Various possibilities bubbled up from initial discussions, though none of them seemed right. Frustration began to set in. The conversation stagnated. I began to wonder if anything innovative would result. It was then that Tim found himself inspired and threw out the suggestion of creating a Beat Eucharist.

Initially, the use of the term Beat caused a little confusion – both at college and further afield at meetings of the Greenbelt Worship Planning Committee. Not everyone had read or even heard of Kerouac's *On the Road* or Ginsberg's *Howl*, and the term seemed to be easily confused with Merseybeat or some form of Hip-Hop. In the context of this chapter, it is worth explaining that Beat, as Tim suggested we use the term, was essentially a form of writing and a cultural phenomenon that emerged in North America in the 1950s. Beat as writing and lifestyle was characterized by a number of elements, including the articulation of a hunger for experience and meaning; be that through live jazz, recreational drug use, sexual experience or the attempt at achieving Zen Buddhist enlightenment. The Beat writers used language to craft vivid literary images. They stretched the meaning of words to express a desperate generational search for something more.

In Durham, the little collective starting to work on the Beat Eucharist began by taking the Beat use of language and hunger for experience and meaning and marrying them with a desire to communicate something of the intensity and wonder of living out of Christian faith in general and what is proclaimed and experienced at the Eucharist in particular. The collective were not attempting to parody or in some way recreate the original verbal delivery style of Beat poetry and writing. To do so in the UK in 2010 would have verged on the ridiculous. Instead, they took the emphases of Beat and laid them down in a new context. There would be a stylistic change, but the desire and urgency to use spoken words in ways that attempted to transcend the usual boundaries of experience would remain. For the Durham collective, Beat began to be defined by a chasing of intensity in writing and a striving to articulate the emotions experienced in a desperate longing for encounter with God. The Beat that would find its way into the Worship Co-operative at the Greenbelt Festival in 2010 was not Beat as form or genre but Beat as essence and intent.[2]

The Durham-based collective were, and continue to be, involved in local churches in and around the city. Each member is actively committed to the reality of the local church-in-mission. The collective aimed to create the Beat Eucharist out of this lived reality. The desire was to feed the lessons and energy generated by this project back into local contexts. In this sense, the Beat Eucharist would be both a product of and resource for the local church-in-mission. In the preparation stage, ideas were bashed around with local Christians. We spent time considering how a Beat Eucharist might best serve the work in which local churches were involved – if at all.[3] From the outset, a central focus was our longing to develop and inhabit an expression of Christian spirituality that celebrated the best of the times in which we live and that challenged the worst. As a collective, we had been exposed to and blessed by a huge diversity of worship styles, but we were searching for fresh ways to express our desire for God; for forms that had the potential to draw in those who had not been touched by what was already on offer – those for whom the emotional intensity of Beat and its stretching of language resonated. The collective began to develop a sense that if it were constructed and delivered well, a Beat Eucharist might have the potential for opening previously unnoticed doors for the local church-in-mission.

We began to get excited. The energy levels rose. Ideas were thrown around. Then came the inevitable pause and reflection, as we asked ourselves why we were opting for a Eucharist rather than a Beat sermon, or a Beat-rant about injustice or a Beat praise service. Why had we chosen to focus on celebrating a sacrament? Was there a chance that this would be alienating for some – not drawing them in but pushing them away? The very term Eucharist was arguably non-comprehensible for those outside the Church, and loaded with unhelpful baggage for a good number of those inside it. There was the possibility that this could backfire straight away. Instead of being a resource for the local church-in-mission, we needed to consider the possibility that the Beat Eucharist was of extremely limited use and would only appeal to a goatie-stroking, philosophy-reading, minority. We discussed the matter at some length and eventually decided that of all the things we could potentially develop in the Beat style, the creation of a Eucharist had the most to offer the church-in-mission.

---

2 This paragraph is adapted from a definition of Beat written by Tim Watson, Durham, 2010.

3 I joined the collective early on, although it remained under Tim's direction.

The Eucharist is understood by Christians in a host of different ways – ranging at the extremes from being an almost irrelevant sideshow to being virtually the only thing that really matters. As an Anglican priest, I am pretty well convinced that the celebration of the Eucharist by the local church should occupy central ground alongside a range of other habits and practices. I haven't always thought like this. Although I am a life-long Christian, I was not raised in the Anglican Church and until my mid-twenties sat rather light to the importance of anything that the local church-in-mission did other than a good forty-five-minute expository sermon. In spite of there being lots to commend a decent sermon, I eventually learnt that it is not the beginning and end of the matter for the local church-in-mission. I think I'd like to argue, however, that the Eucharist is – or certainly has the potential to be – a crucial focus and potent driver for the local church-in-mission. By this, I don't mean that if only more priests celebrated more Eucharists with more style there would be a widespread renewal of the Church, a surge in Kingdom-related activity or a plethora of converts to the way of Jesus Christ. What I mean is that, for the local church-in-mission, regularly gathering around a table and engaging with the story of the life, death and resurrection of Jesus, sharing broken bread, drinking wine from a common cup and praying that they be sent out in the power of the Spirit to live and work to the praise and glory of God is both a starting place for mission and a major source of sustenance along the way. The celebration of the presence of the living God at the Eucharist is a defining act for the local church-in-mission. Our little collective in Durham – all longing for local churches around the UK, and indeed the globe, to be renewed in worship and equipped for mission – felt that if the act of worship we were to host at Greenbelt was to create a space for fellow Christians to be inspired and energized for engaging in worship-driven mission in their own contexts, then this would be best served if we focused our creative efforts on constructing a form of the Eucharist.

Having resolved to construct a Beat Eucharist, we were left with questions about content. Because of the pressure on time that we would experience on the night, we decided to drop the sermon but to include every other component of the *Common Worship* Eucharist: the gathering, a time of confession, an absolution, a psalm, a Gospel reading, a creed, intercessions, sharing the peace, a valid Eucharistic Prayer, the distribution of bread and wine, and a sending out. We felt that, in many ways, the service had the potential to act as a sermon in its own right. It was possible to argue that teaching and learning would be taking place, along with the issuing of prophetic challenges and a call to a vigorous and faithful following of Jesus Christ. All of this would be rooted in Scripture and in prayer and, like a sermon, its fruit-bearing potential would be entirely dependent on the animating presence of the living God. These were high hopes indeed! But lofty expectations were par for the course. We were caught up in the creative process – dreaming dreams and seeing visions. Our prayer was the prayer that every preacher must have on their heart as they prepare to address the people of God: that every concept, every line, every word, would be from and of God and would go out into the world and effect change in hearts and lives.

In the midst of all this grand thinking, we did some rough calculations and estimated that the Eucharist – including distributing bread and wine in a full venue – would take approximately half an hour. The problem was that we had a three-hour slot to fill. The obvious solution also seemed the most radical, and, ironically, the most Beat. We would finish the first service and roll straight into a second. Since we had three hours, we would have to celebrate *six* Beat Eucharists back-to-back! Far from being excessive or odd, somehow this seemed just right. We felt that the repetition of the same words had potential to coax open the hearts of those who would gather and propel us towards euphoria in our worship. Hosting six Eucharists didn't mean that those who came had to stay for the whole thing – or even arrive at the beginning. We would begin and then just keep on going. Worshippers would be free to come and go as they pleased.

The currency of the Beat Eucharist was words. This fact presented us with the question of how worshippers would take part – especially those who came after we'd kicked off. Did we use PowerPoint? Somehow PowerPoint didn't seem very Beat. We decided that generating an authentic Beat vibe demanded a book. A slightly tattered paperback if possible – something that everyone would be given as they came in and could take away if they wanted to. But if people were going to come and go throughout the three hours, we'd need quite a few books. We estimated 500. We knew that 500 books, even at discount, were likely to cost hundreds of pounds. However, a book was Beat, so we set our hearts on raising enough money to make a book happen[4] – entirely disregarding the 'but-people-today-don't-read!' mantra being bandied around by various writers on mission in the emerging culture. The book wasn't the essence of the Beat Eucharist. The essence, or life, of the Beat Eucharist would exist in the heartfelt delivery of line after line of expressive text yelled at freight-train speed in a darkened venue among a crowd of worshippers eager to meet with God. The book wasn't the essence, but the book was a physical thing existing in time and space, and copies of it would out-last a one-off

---

4 St John's College Durham generously provided £700 to cover the cost of printing books and fliers.

experience at Greenbelt in 2010 and would travel back to 500 local contexts. Here, it was hoped, they would remind their owners of something experienced: something alive and raw and transformative; something that might prompt new ideas and expressions, which would have the potential for lighting local fires.

Tim wrote the creed early on, and we gathered in a room at Cranmer Hall to take a look. He explained that it would work best if we just read it through together and out loud. As soon as we began, it was obvious that this was something inspired and powerful. The atmosphere in the room changed. Our pulses raced. Excitement built. The words were pounded out passionately:

> As one we affirm belief in God, Father, all wonderful, Creator of skies above, earth below, then, now and ever after, of all things, seen and unimaginable. As one we affirm belief in the Divine, in Jesus, who lived and walked and loved and died Singular son of the one God of all ...[5]

At the end, a resounding Amen was pronounced. There were smiles all round. We were buzzing. But more, and deeper, than this: we felt changed. If the rest of the liturgy was going to be like this, it was clear that it was a gift from God and had genuine potential as a worthwhile missional resource for the wider Church.

I slotted the Beat Eucharist into the programme for the Worship Cooperative. That was it. It would definitely be happening. The creed was in existence, but we were now fully committed to producing a whole service based on the *Common Worship* Eucharist. We had a few months to write the full text, get it printed, produce a soundtrack and visuals to accompany the service, and prepare our hearts and heads for delivering it. This was a demanding to-do list in the midst of already busy lives, but space would have to be created. We were excited and energized. We prayed and knuckled down to work.

As the writing evolved and the text of the Eucharist came to life, we made decisions on a host of practical questions. These ranged from which members of the collective would do what during the evening, to how we would set up the venue, to whether we needed to demonstrate that I – as the presiding minister – was ordained, to exactly what we would use for eucharistic elements and why, to how we would welcome people, and how we'd communicate page numbers and distribution instructions. There were a hundred practical considerations – the things that accompany any public act of worship and that can seem to stifle the life of the thing you

5 Beat Eucharist Creed ©Tim Watson, 2010.

are trying to create but without which it cannot live. Our job would be to enable people to encounter God – to facilitate worship and to do this with minimum fuss and intrusion. Good planning and preparation now would mean avoiding confusion and clumsiness on the night. We were not aiming for something slick – or for an environment in which worshippers were passive consumers. But we were aiming to honour God by preparing adequately and by hosting an act of worship in which people were able to concentrate on him rather than being distracted by avoidable glitches or glaring omissions.

After months of preparation, the Festival weekend finally arrived. The members of the collective piled 500 books into a car alongside tents and sleeping bags and made the long journey from Durham to Cheltenham. On Saturday night, we set up the venue as we'd agreed – fairly minimally. We had just over an hour to prepare. Only just enough time. We worked calmly but urgently. We were eager to leave time to pray and to settle ourselves. We were leading worship, and this meant that as well as seeing to all the practical issues, we needed to focus on the main thing: God.

Seven-thirty approached. With three minutes to go, we started the soundtrack. White noise hissed out of the speakers. The visuals flickered on screens around the venue. People began to file in. The space filled up very quickly. The members of the collective were dotted around, books in hand, ready to go. Tim was standing on a small, raised platform. To his right, also on the platform, was a table, simply set with bread and wine. The venue was packed. People looked at each other, at their books, at the screens, at the ceiling, at the sound-desk. Perhaps some were wondering when Tim would give a welcome – or a notice. He opened his book. The white noise stopped. A deep bass line punched out. Tim stepped to the mic and impassioned words began flying in every direction.

The atmosphere was electric. There was a palpable sense of the presence of God, both as we thundered through the text and during the silence at the distribution. With the first Eucharist complete, people filed out of the venue, the doors were re-opened and those waiting in the queue outside poured in for the second. The same happened with the third. By the fourth, there were fewer people. By number five, we were down to a dozen or so. Our bodies and voices were tired. Spiritually, emotionally and physically, the members of the collective were on the verge of exhaustion. We discussed stopping. We'd run well over on time, and apart from us and the technical crew, the venue was empty. At that moment, a middle-aged American woman poked her head around the door. She explained that she was with four friends and asked if they could come in. For a moment, I was tempted to send them away, but then thought better of it. And so we celebrated our last Eucharist of the evening with all the energy of the previous five in the presence of a handful of people; an excellent contrast to the first one, and just as powerful.

When we had finished, the woman who had poked her head around the door came to speak to us. Her comment was brief but hugely encouraging: 'That was the most profound Eucharist I have experienced in my life.'

In fact, during the evening, in the brief moments between Eucharists, a good many people had approached us to say how helpful they had found it and to ask whether we would mind if they used it in the churches, schools and universities in which they were involved. This was what we had hoped for: that the service would be a resource for worship and mission in local contexts. Beyond this, it is our hope that the sharing of the Beat Eucharist story in the context of a missiological text will bear further fruit. For the members of the Rough Edge Collective, working on this project has highlighted the fact that worship and mission are two sides of the same coin. The people of God are entirely defined and characterized by both of these things. We *are* worship and mission. This is how we live. This is our essence. We encounter the missionary God – who lives in community and who is everywhere and always engaged in his reconciling and redeeming work – we encounter *this* God as we gather in worship. And it is in the corporate worship of this God that we are genuinely and deeply transformed, and also – simultaneously – caught up in his activity and propelled out into the world as his co-workers in mission. A Eucharist proclaims and celebrates the reign of God in Jesus Christ and it calls those who are gathered to participate in a radical new reality. The Beat Eucharist was an attempt to articulate God's new reality in a form that was surprising enough to jolt our minds, bodies and souls into fresh response to the gospel. For us, that response has been a new inhabiting of the radical life – a viral inhabiting. An inhabiting capable of fanning fires into flame in the local church-in-mission.[6]

---

6 The members of the Rough Edge Collective are Tim Watson, David Austin, Matt Allen, Andy Stinson, Rich Wyld, Dan Pierce and Michael Volland.

12

Mission in a Mainstream Church Context

MARTYN PERCY

Thomas Tweed has recently done something very unfashionable. He has tried to define religion. Few would attempt such a thing these days, but this is what he says:

> [Religions] ... are confluences of organic-cultural flows that intensify joy and confront suffering by drawing on human and supra-human (i.e., divine) forces to make homes and cross boundaries.[1]

I am rather drawn to this definition of religion. At its best – and one presumes a passionate real faith in a real God as a basis – good religion performs four important tasks, which churches will know much about.

First, it intensifies joy. It takes the ordinary and makes it extraordinary. It knows how to celebrate lives, love and transitions. It blesses what is good and raises hope, thanks and expectation in prayer and praise. It lifts an institution and individuals to a new plane of existence – one of blessing and thankfulness for what is and can be. And it not only moves, but also intensifies. Just as a birth becomes even more in a baptism, so in mission and ministry does a ceremony become more with prayer and celebration. Second, suffering is confronted. Working with pain, bereavement, counselling and consolation will be familiar to all ministers and churches – providing the safe space and expertise that holds and slowly resolves the suffering that individuals and institutions carry inside them. Third, the making of homes is a profoundly analogical and literal reference to the function of faith. Making safe spaces of nourishment, well-being, maturity, diversity and individuation; our 'faith homes' are places both of open hospitality and security. Fourth, faith helps us to cross boundaries – to move forward and over the challenges of life to new places. It can be

---

1 Thomas Tweed, *Crossing and Dwelling*, Cambridge, MA: Harvard University Press, 2006, p. 12.

crossing deserts to find promised lands; or passing from darkness to light. Religion never keeps us in one place; even with our homes, it moves us.

When ministry causes the Church to transcend itself

This might all sound like a lot of effort for those engaged in mission and ministry. And to some extent it is. However, I also want to suggest that the *manner* in which we engage with our institutions is just as important as the actual programmes and events that might be offered. Sometimes, it is the way of being and the character of individual ministry that carries more weight and resonance than those things that seem concrete and planned. This is not surprising, since faith communities often make contributions to social capital that are not easily calculated or calibrated. Because they foster and focus distinctive values, which provide leaven in complex contexts, faith communities often find themselves promoting forms of goodness that secular and utilitarian organizations might miss. In this respect, Bruce Reed explains how religion partly functions by drawing on an analogy from nature:

> If bees could talk, and we came across them busy in a flower garden and enquired what they were doing, their reply might be: 'Gathering nectar to make honey.' But if we asked the gardener, he would most certainly answer: 'They are cross-pollinating my flowers.' In carrying out their manifest function to make food, the bees were performing a latent function of fertilising flowers. The mutual dependence of bees and flowers is an analogue of churches and society.[2]

Here, Reed offers us a vivid picture of mission and ministry that we might recognize. Through a simple ministry of 'deep hanging out' with the people we serve,[3] attentiveness, hospitality, care and celebration, ministers often do more good for the parishes, communities and institutions they serve than they can ever know. This may simply be through the offering of regular lunches or open house for tea and coffee at any time – and these are manifest intentions, of course. But the potency of the gesture and practice lies more in their latency, and is significant. These practices say something about the possibilities for different kinds of spaces in communities – social, pastoral, intellectual, spiritual, to name but a few. They open up a

---

2 Bruce Reed, *The Dynamics of Religion*, London, Darton, Longman & Todd, 1978, p. 139.

3 A phrase misappropriated from Clifford Geertz.

AS A FIRE BY BURNING

different side of the humanity of the institution to those individuals within it. In being there with programmes and events, as well as in being purposefully hospitable, churches enable the institution to begin transcending itself. Put simply, the ministry says 'there is more to life than what you are currently absorbed by'; 'look deeper'; 'think with your heart'; 'let your mind wander and wonder'; 'we are all beginners in prayer'.

This should not surprise us. Karl Barth, no less, suggests that churches need to focus first and foremost on their *intensive* relationship with God, and only after that the *extensive* concerns – especially in relation to growth. Put another way, Christians are first to love the Lord with all heart, soul, mind and strength and to love their neighbours as themselves. And concerns for mission and growth can come only after that. Put another way, faithfulness to Christ comes before any absorption with success:

> The true growth which is the secret of the upbuilding of the community is not extensive but intensive; its vertical growth in height and depth ... It is not the case that its intensive increase necessarily involves an extensive. We cannot, therefore, strive for vertical renewal merely to produce greater horizontal extension and a wider audience ... If it [the Church and its mission] is used only as a means of extensive renewal, the internal will at once lose its meaning and power. It can be fulfilled only for its own sake, and then – unplanned and unarranged – it will bear its own fruits.[4]

Missiological steroids

Yet churches are easily seduced into formulae and blueprints that purport to deliver growth – especially the quick, almost instant variety. The body of Christ finds it difficult to resist missiological steroids. And like all miracle diets or fitness programmes that promise so much for the body, the beguiling seduction of the packages on offer appear to be simple. That is why there is more than a fair degree of certainty and simplicity in Dean Kelley's thesis, *Why Conservative Churches are Growing* (1972).[5] Kelley asserts that in order for a church to grow numerically, there has to be some kind of clarity about its purpose. Religion, claims Kelley, is about providing ultimate meaning for people: making sense out of existence and also

---

4 Karl Barth, *Church Dogmatics IV.2, The Doctrine of Reconciliation*, Edinburgh: T & T Clark, 1958, p. 648.

5 Dean M. Kelley, *Why Conservative Churches are Growing: A Study in Sociology of Religion*, San Francisco: Harper & Row, 1972.

answering the question, 'Why do bad things happen?' So Kelley argues that in order for a strong sustainable community to develop, there needs to be a sense that the community itself is so important that it *demands* commitment, and that this same commitment needs to be at some cost to the members. Correspondingly, for a church to grow numerically, there needs to be a sense that it has something to offer in making sense of life and that it demands a commitment by return. If it costs nothing to belong to such a community, it can hardly be worth joining.

Kelley discusses the importance of strictness in upholding the values and boundaries of such a community, and reflects on Kierkegaard's call for 'serious religion'. Here, Kelley asserts that liberal and mainstream churches have lost the sense of 'defined boundaries', with the principle of religious tolerance and individual freedom being embraced to such an extent that the churches no longer espouse a faith that people deeply and sacrificially commit to. Such churches are 'lukewarm', and though they may be engaged in much good work, they do not have clarity in their religious expression.

Correspondingly, energy is expended into espousing a good cause or practical service, which, though implicitly connected to the understanding of faith, is not about the churches' main purpose of drawing people in to a community of salvation. Kelley therefore argues that the more conservative churches have a better record in turning round the lives of the socially excluded, by converting them to a new meaning in life, which demands a changed lifestyle.

To be sure, Kelley's ideas constitute a simple, compacted and logically coherent thesis. But the question contemporary ecclesiologists, missiologists, practical theologians and sociologists of religion might ask is also simple: 'Does it make sense, and does it ring true?' The answer here must at least be in some doubt, for we know that even in measuring numerical strength, there are multiple ambiguities. How does one account for the large rise in numbers attending cathedral services in the Church of England, where there is patently no relationship between strictness and strength? Equally, how would one explain the burgeoning number of metropolitan churches that attract niche neo-liberal groups? Even a preliminary survey of churchgoing habits in the twenty-first century suggests that there are more exceptions to Kelley's 'rules' for growth, which therefore renders the thesis somewhat unsafe.

That said, there can be no denying the importance of meaning in churches. But defining the purpose of the Church need not be strict or exclusive; it can also be inclusive and open (and no less attractive for this). The complex struggle for mainstream and liberal churches remains, stubbornly, centred on how to continue to encourage commitment, and how to communicate the seriousness of the gospel and teach people about the cost of discipleship. Or put another way, the task might be to discover ways of being unapologetic about faith that do not inhibit those same churches from being tolerant. Is it possible to be religiously tolerant and yet truly communicate a faith that is life-changing?

It might be said (and perhaps this is something of a caricature) that mainstream churches do not expect too much from their members. They tend not to worry about members who miss three of four Sundays. Anxious to avoid inducing guilt and equally concerned to under-communicate a sense of urgency, mainstream churches typically adopt a mellow attitude to belonging and tend to tolerate a variety of inchoate expressions of belief. In one sense, mainstream churches are reconciled to understanding their congregational composition: a mixture of loyalists and consumers.

Yet this attitude should be contrasted with more evangelical churches, where the 'non attendance' of a member is interpreted rather than tolerated. Perhaps the person is 'backsliding'? Maybe they are struggling with their faith and need support? Where Kelley is correct is in understanding that evangelical and conservative churches grow first and foremost by engaging their members in deep bonds of commitment and then again through evangelism. Such churches readily accept that people want to make seriously informed choices about church attendance.

But church growth has never been such a simple matter. There is a multiplicity of institutional and contextual factors that can account for the numerical growth of a church. In England, a popular junior Church of England school can lead to extensive community involvement in the church. Other demographic factors may also have a bearing, such as class, ethnicity and wealth. If action flows from identity, then a community with a close-knit sense of itself may find its religious expression more 'productive' than a more disparate community. In general, effective evangelism flows out of a sense of purpose, excitement and mission. Correspondingly, strictness and strength may not be, as Kelley suggests, such decisive factors.

That said, the most fundamental problem for the ebbing mainstream churches is often the lack of compelling reasons for people to participate. Mainstream churches can be embarrassed about talking about God, and their fear of intolerance can then lead to a chronic lack of religious conversations and overt religious output in the local community. All too frequently, mainstream and liberal churches can lose their core public identity in asserting their breadth and diversity – that is, tolerance – rather than communicating that they do, in fact, believe in God.

Formulae versus doing what comes naturally

In her recent *What Mothers Do*, Naomi Stadlen intriguingly subtitles her thesis, *Especially When It Looks Like Nothing*.[6] She argues for a focus on 'being' rather than 'task-orientation' in motherhood, and we think that her observations translate well into the field of contemporary missiology and ecclesiology, by setting a fresh agenda for growth and development.

What Mothers Do: Especially When It Looks Like Nothing offers a beautifully simple argument. Stadlen says that contemporary culture is gripped, almost mesmerizingly, by formulae and recipes that seldom correspond to reality. So-called 'Mother and Baby' books are a good example: they offer step-by-step advice, which appears to be simple and effective. But, argues Stadlen, most of these kinds of books tend to infantalize the mother. What happens if I have a baby who doesn't do what the book says? Guilt, frustration and anger can quickly set in. Or try another book: but then what happens if that also fails to mould the child in the image of the author? The 'how to' books, says Stadlen, reduce motherhood to a series of tasks, instead of concentrating on the relationship between mother and child. She argues that mothers rarely need to be told how to care; it is learnt and developed in relationships, not through advice lines and programmatic books.

The heart of the book suggests that mothers are always doing something with their offspring, and most especially when it looks like *nothing*. They are *engaged* with their child. They are relating. They are being with and being for the child. So the question, 'What have you done today?' – often asked of a young mother – needs no obvious reply, even though it often prompts guilt and embarrassment. Simply to have been with the child is enough; to have discovered a song or a sound that comforts him; or something visual that simply amuses and stimulates her. This is enough.

I have opened up the argument in this way because it seems that one of the most pressing problems that besets the Church today is that it too is gripped by a culture of formulae. Many ecclesial recipe books have appeared in recent times: *How to Grow Your Church*; *How to Manage Your Congregation* (surely a work of satire?); *Ten Steps to Growth*; *Mission-Shaped Church*; *The Purpose-Driven Church*; or Alpha Courses; and who can forget 'the decade of evangelism' (RIP)? Each of these initiatives is well meaning, but also deeply formulaic; a kind of panacea for panickers. And clergy – and sometimes congregations – are easily seduced

---

6 Naomi Stadlen, *What Mothers Do: Especially When It Looks Like Nothing*, London: Piatkus Books, 2004. See also Emma Percy, 'What Clergy Do: Especially When It Looks Like Nothing', PhD, University of Nottingham, 2012.

by such things. Many wince at Christmas when someone sidles up to them at a drinks party and says: 'So, Vicar, your busy time then.' Because the flip-side of the question often asked of clergy is also implied by this remark: 'What exactly do you do all day, Vicar?'

Clergy are often stumped for an answer. Communion in a residential or nursing home for five senior citizens, a couple of visits, some paperwork, morning and evening prayer, one meeting and some thinking doesn't sound like a very productive day. But here clergy are at one with mothers. They have been doing a lot; it just seems like nothing. They have formed, deepened and kindled relationships. They have related to lots of people for whom dependency is a fact of life and concentrated deeply on being, not just doing. They have made somebody's day, simply by dropping by or by smiling.

Formulae, like recipes, anticipate success: and churches are usually too tempted to worship both the rubric and the outcome. But unlike recipe books, those courses and books that address the apparent malaise of the Church forget that just as every child is different, so is every congregation: a uniquely constituted set of ingredients. What works in one place probably won't in another. So the moral of this analogy is simple. Don't impose formulae for growth on children or churches; and don't try and cook up congregations in the same way that you might try and cook up some food. Respect what has come naturally, and work with that, even if that simply means just being and apparently doing nothing.

Organic growth

One is also struck by how many of the metaphors that Jesus uses to describe the numerical increase of the Kingdom are organic and require a slow patience in husbanding growth. The parable of the sower, for one, hardly anticipates a packed schedule for the sower. After her work is finished for the day, what does she do? She will need to wait, water and wait. Similarly, the parable of the mustard seed reminds us that although there is an extensive outcome to be enjoyed, the process of moving from seed to tree is 'natural' rather than 'driven'. Of course, the organic parables on Kingdom growth that Jesus tells do not give permission to the clergy to sit back and do nothing. But they suggest that the true growth worth striving for is more likely to be crafted through patient tending, working empathetically with natural ingredients, rather than with 'instant' formulae that produce growth for its own sake. Thus,

He told them still another parable: 'The kingdom of heaven is like yeast that a woman took and mixed into a large amount of flour until it worked all through the dough.' (Matt. 13.33, NIV)

Here, Jesus tells us most of what we probably need to know about mission and ministry. He suggests that the Kingdom of heaven is like yeast that is mixed in with dough. Yeast? That microbe fungi? That discardable and forgettable material that is, oddly, the key to so much of our lives? It would seem so. For yeast is what ferments the wine and beer; and it makes the dough rise to make the bread. It is the tiny, insignificant catalyst for our basic commodities and the formation of our communities. The leaven in the lump; the difference between bread and dough; juice and wine; refreshment and celebration.

Yeast is, of course, small. Moreover, it is lost and dispersed into the higher purposes to which it is given. And when Jesus talks about the Kingdom of God as yeast – and our ministries too – he is not advocating the concentrate of Marmite in the jar: yeast for the sake of yeast. Rather, in Jesus' imagination, we as ministers are invited to disperse purposely. To lose ourselves in something much bigger – the institution or body in which we minister. But not pointlessly. Rather, in 'dying' to our context, we activate it. We become the catalyst that brings flavour, strength, depth, potency and growth. Without yeast, there is no loaf; just dough. Literally, we die to ourselves for growth. We are the ingredient that makes bread for the world.

But this is not a call to us to be dying or dissolving. God wants us alive, not dead: actually, the more alive the better. So the notion of our ministry is not that we are the yeast, per se, but rather that we offer a yeast-like type of ministry. It is about being the agent of transformation that is often small, or even unseen. It is about being immersed so deeply in the world and the parish that the depth of growth is often unquantifiable. As Einstein once said, that which truly counts in life can seldom be counted. The work of yeast is one of deep fission.

Baking bread, if you have ever done it, is rewarding work and very therapeutic. But it also offers us a rich analogy for what we are about. John Paul Lederach offers a rich meditation on our calling to be yeast. Consider this: the most common ingredients for making bread are water, flour, salt, sugar and yeast. Of these, yeast is the smallest in quantity, but the only one that makes a substantial change to all the other ingredients. Lederach says you only need a few people to change a lot of things.[7] So

---

7 J. Paul Lederach, *The Moral Imagination: The Art and Soul of Peacemaking*, Oxford: Oxford University Press, 2006.

yeast, to be useful, needs to move from its incubation and mix into the process – out of the seminary and into the parish. Clergy – like the prover-bial manure – do most good when they are spread around.

But yeast also needs to grow – it requires the right mix of moisture, warmth and sugar. And it initially needs covering and cultivating before it is ready to do its work. (The analogy for clergy training and formation could hardly be more fruitful here.) Only then should the yeast mix with the greater mass. In bread, it is kneaded into the dough; it requires a bit of muscle. And it also requires someone else to light the fire to make the oven. Bread, in other words, is not just about the yeast, but about a con-text – one of feeding, desire, need and the skills of others. So in talking about small fungi that produce change and growth, Jesus is asking us to imagine his Kingdom – one in which tiny spores mixed into the social mass can make a massive difference. One of my predecessors at Cuddes-don had this to say about ministry:

> Confronted by the wistful, the half-believing and the seeking, we know what it is to minister to those who relate to the faith of Christ in un-expected ways. We do not write off hesitant and inadequate responses to the gospel. Ours is a church of the smoking flax, of the mixture of wheat and tares. Critics may say that we blunt the edge of the gospel and become Laodicean ... [but] we do not despise the hesitant and half-believing, because the deeper we look into human lives the more often we discern the glowing embers of faith.[8]

The consistently levelled criticism at Donald McGravran's work on church growth in this respect is worth noting: namely that his relentless push for growth was not unlike introducing steroids into the body of Christ. The results were fast and looked spectacular (judged from one perspective); but the long-term health implications were less than convincing. Build-ing up the mass of the body can be a form of idolatry. There is no real substitute for healthy, natural and sustained growth. One must beware of etiolation.

Four hallmarks of priesthood and a priestly church for natural organic growth

The question naturally arises, 'What would ministry to a developing con-gregation look like?' There are several ways of being in a congregation

---

8 Robert Runcie, Retirement Address to General Synod, 1990.

that shape the task of ministry, but are fundamentally centred on role rather than any particular outcomes. One would recognize, to begin with, that the Church as the body of Christ – as a metaphor – is imperfect, since the Church is never complete and cannot complete or delimit itself. In one sense, the Church has an open definition, because its boundaries and identity are, at a fundamental level, contested and open. Who belongs, who attends occasionally but not frequently, who believes this or that, will be a feature of even the most conservative congregation. Tight definitions of a church will seldom correspond to its grounded context; there is always a gap between ideology and reality.

What, then, is the minister or priest to be or do in such an ambiguous situation? Clearly, it is tempting to be seduced by recipes and formulae that deliver clarity. But I would suggest that a focus on the role and identity of the minister is a more fruitful path towards encouraging super, natural, organic church growth. Four hallmarks of priesthood and a priestly church are offered here, in terms of organic growth, by way of a brief conclusion.

Ministry is sacramental–transformative

To be a priest or a priestly church is to have an understanding that ordinary material – such as bread, wine and water – can be transformed by prayer and worship into something through which God speaks to us and spiritually nourishes us. But one cannot confine this axis to the standard tokens of the sacramental life of the church. Congregations and ministers find that casual conversations, pastoral encounters, acts of service and other activities are also sacramental and transformative; they become 'places', where the life of God meets the life of the world. The more alert a congregation is to how God feeds and sustains his people, the more likely it is that this food will be shared, and more people transformed.

Ministry is reciprocal–representative

That is to say, that while the minister or priest may undoubtedly represent Christ to the people, the congregation continually looks for the ways in which Christ is present within them and the outsider. This is an important dimension in mission, for it affirms the activity of the Holy Spirit beyond the borders of the Church, and reminds congregations that Christ can be encountered in new and alien ways, for which the congregation needs to be receptive. At a contextual level, congregations that grow organically will tend to have deep partnerships with a variety of secular agencies that complement its work and mission, so that the 'common good' and the blessing of social capital becomes an enlarged and shared task.

Ministry has a sacrificial–receptive dynamic

Obviously, priesthood, as with other forms of ministry, is costly. But the cost is often found not in the output but in the receptivity to the input. Individuals will confess and confide in priests and pastors all kinds of things that can go no further. Here, the priest has a role as absorber of pain; of receiving knowledge that cannot be shared; of taking upon themselves burdens that are being finally deposited, once and for all. There is something salvific and cathartic here, to be sure. But it can also be noted that when an individual finally feels 'they can tell you anything' (and not be judged, but simply loved), they finally feel free to belong to the body of Christ. The costly ministry of sacrificially receiving people's lives and stories allows individuals to be grafted into the Church.

Ministry is also a delicate combination of the pastoral–prophetic

The old English adage expresses it well – clergy are there to comfort the afflicted and afflict the comfortable. The imperative to offer love, nurture and tenderness has to be balanced with the responsibility to speak out, which can be costly. Sometimes, growth and popularity must be sacrificed to truth and justice. Natural, organic church growth sometimes requires heavy pruning and an interventionist cultivation. In all of this, it must be remembered that it is God alone who gives the growth. It can be engineered, and such engineering can be effective in terms of numerical growth. However, I remain convinced that the only true growth is the natural and deep kind that God invariably bestows upon a faithful, hopeful and joyful people. So may the Spirit blow on those embers. May we glow; may we grow.

13

Mission in Youth Ministry

Wokingham

CLARE HOOPER

I have a confession to make: there's nothing special about my story. There's never been any great plan, amazing curriculum I followed or programmes I've delivered. I've just been a disciple, who wants to change the world and who finds loving people so much more appealing than judging them.

I've been working with young people in a local Baptist church in Wokingham for fourteen years. It also happens to be the place where I've lived since I was eight. My favourite English teacher lives just down my road, and I've seen the baker's become a tanning salon, the children's bookshop become a nail bar and the butcher's become yet another empty shop.

When I first started, I was the only church-employed youth worker in the town, and I worked closely with the ecumenical schools worker for the area. Our area now has around half a dozen church employees working with young people, the schools worker has morphed into two roles and we have another Christian youth work charity all delivering competing – or should that be complementary – youth work! My context has evolved, and so have the expectations placed on me. I have to remind myself why I got into this 'business'. I'm not here to fill the young people's diaries with yet another event in their already overloaded weeks. I'm not here to cajole, bribe and plead with young people to come on a Sunday, just so I can get their parents off my back. I'm involved in the church and with the young people, because I love God and because I love people, and I want to change the world; I think it's called being a disciple and helping others be disciples too. But in a context that desires value for money and tangible outcomes – on being told about some of the amazing conversations that have happened on the streets with the detached work a church member asks, 'But when will we be seeing them in church?' – I'm finding my longing to make disciples in danger of being drowned out by the voices and demands of others.

Like the majority of youth workers who studied with me at the Centre for Youth Ministry in Oxford for three years in the late 1990s, I see myself as an informal educator, influenced by the educational philosophy outlined in Paulo Freire's book *Pedagogy of the Oppressed*.[1] My approach to youth work has always been relational, informed theologically by the incarnation and biblically by Paul, who was happy to share with the church in Thessalonica not only the gospel but his whole life (1 Thess. 2.8). As a reflective practitioner, I have embraced praxis, understanding that my faith shapes the youth ministry and equally my experiences in youth ministry inform my faith. And like many, I breathed a sigh of relief when I read Mike Yaconelli's book, *Contemplative Youth Ministry*.[2] I found a book that encouraged me and gave me space to be, rather than made me feel intimidated or guilty about what I wasn't doing and providing.

My heart is for all young people, and so I find the distinction between churched and unchurched uncomfortable and unhelpful. All young people need to get connected with God, and I've found that many of the challenges facing young people who've been brought up in faith households are the same as for those who haven't. All young people need to know and be reminded of the hope and the freedom that is found in God and God's Kingdom; as do I. I have found that one size doesn't fit all, and therefore a more fluid approach to working with young people has been useful. It's unwise to hold things too tightly. What connected with the young people from my area five years ago might not be what's needed now; what one person might need to encourage them on their faith journey might not be what another person requires. How I challenge one person might be different from how I challenge another. I'm really comfortable with this approach, recognizing that Jesus dialogued with people differently, requiring different things of them. I also recognize the dangers too: a potential for inconsistency and reliance on my judgement can be about being sensitive to the Holy Spirit or it can just default to my own opinion.

There is only one way to get connected to God and that is through Jesus. In our heads, we understand that there must be many ways to Jesus, different ways of engaging with Jesus that enable people to flourish and thrive. In John 3.3, we have Jesus telling Nicodemus that he needs to be born again. But in Matthew 4.19, we have Jesus simply calling out to Peter and Andrew, 'Come follow me'. In John 8.11, the woman who is

---

1 P. Freire, *Pedagogy of the Oppressed*, second edition, London: Penguin, 1996.
2 M. Yaconelli, *Contemplative Youth Ministry*, London: SPCK, 2006.

caught in adultery is told to leave her life of sin, while in John 4.1–30 we have another woman who was also very friendly with the men, and yet Jesus doesn't seem to place any demands on her. She just responds to who he is. In Matthew 19.21, the rich young man is told that he needs to give up all his possession, while in Luke 19.8 Zacchaeus gets off lightly with only giving away half his possessions plus paying back four times what he cheated people out of. It seems that God's expectations, challenges and entry points to the good news are not standardized, and yet so often we've reduced it to a simple prayer of commitment.

Drawing on the work of Paul Hiebert in his book *Anthropological Reflections on Missiological Issues*,[3] I'm aware that in my work with young people I am seeking to help them face towards and journey towards Jesus, the cross and the good news of the gospel. I am more concerned with the direction that the young people are facing then a line or boundary that they have crossed. I recognize that many are uncomfortable with this because faith in this instance isn't always articulated in a bounded way, where 'we usually begin with a test of orthodoxy, with verbal affirmation of belief in a specific set of doctrines, such as the deity of Christ and the virgin birth. We often add tests of orthopraxy or right behaviour. We look for evidences of faith in the changed lives of the people.'[4] But I feel that a journey towards the light from darkness isn't a one-off line that is crossed but a constant process of becoming more Christ-like. One way of looking at salvation, conversion or coming to faith is – this was my old life, and this is my new life; my new way of being, behaving and my new beliefs. However, my experiences in working with young people have rarely matched up with this. People with depression still continued with that struggle. People with eating disorders still wrestled with their self-image. People with addictions weren't set free. People who have constantly been put down still struggled to trust others. People who loved possessions still bought more than they needed. The way I now understand salvation, conversion and coming to faith acknowledges that people are unique and that their contexts and situations are unique. It allows for the fact that people do not have the same start in life and therefore what Jesus asks of them in response to him may well be different for different people. It communicates that our life and faith are being constantly aligned with the will and purposes of God.

After working in a local authority junior youth club for several years, it felt right to quit and for the church to provide a drop-in on a Friday

---

3 P. Hiebert, *Anthropological Reflections on Missiological Issues*, Grand Rapids: Baker, 1994.

4 Hiebert, *Anthropological Reflections*, p. 115.

night for the older young people, who would normally be hanging around on the streets or in the parks. At the same time, a member of the church, who had previously been involved with the local authority doing detached work, wanted the church to be engaged in working with the young people on the streets, who didn't want a drop-in provision. Although the two contexts were different, we were one team with the same approach and values.

Both these ventures taught us so much as we allowed the stories of the young people to change how we communicated our faith, our understanding of discipleship, and, for me personally, it redefined aspects of my faith regarding salvation, mission and evangelism. The following are a couple of stories that reflect something of that journey.

A tragic event

In September 2005, two young lads got stabbed to death by a friend. It was the longest week of my life. Not only were we working with young people obviously devastated by the loss, but we were working alongside the girlfriend and the brother of the young man who committed the murder. We knew the young people through the drop-in we were running at the time and through the detached work that we were doing. There was definitely an element of this for which no training could have prepared me. The rawness of the grief, the pain and incomprehension of the event were huge. I felt so small, unprepared and insignificant; who was I to try and support these young people? We spent hours hanging out with the young people, walking with them in their grief, providing food for them when they forgot to eat, providing a space for them to put on their own memorial, listening to them as they shared their memories and questions. There was no agenda behind our compassion. We did what we did because we loved the young people. These 16-year-olds have all celebrated their twenty-first birthdays now, and it's so amazing to be still in touch with several of them. A couple of them found faith during the dark time, and they now occasionally help with some of the youth work. A few more of the young people didn't find faith, but did find a place of belonging with us, and they too help with some of the youth work. I'll get phone calls or Facebook messages from others updating me on their news or asking for a chat when they need a listening ear. Six years later, the church got a letter and a cheque from one of the parents thanking us for being there and supporting her daughter and her friends during that tragic time. I love the way that God's love continues to unfold in the stories of these young people whom I've had the privilege of knowing. God's love isn't bound by our timings and plans. It's gentle, forever patient and forever present; something we try modelling in our youth work but obviously often falling short.

Seaford Court

For two years, a committed team from church have been visiting Seaford Court, a hostel for homeless young people in Wokingham. They go in every Tuesday night. Beforehand, they meet together to pray and reflect; this provides them with the space to grow spiritually together through their mutual experience. This work seeks to do three things:

- to build trust and rapport with the young people through regular visits and small group activities;
- to explore issues that are important to the young people through the use of creative resources and discussion;
- to provide opportunities for the young people to take part in experiences outside of Seaford Court that help them look outside themselves, build them as a team and give them a greater appreciation of the wider community.

Here are some reflections from one member of the team:

As we all know, youth work often has a one step forward two steps back feel about it, and this characterizes the last two years at Seaford. We have known tremendous highs – the achievement of completing the raft races, a young woman's involvement in the pantomime and evenings when the residents are full of questions about life, God and the Bible and sharing their small but significant achievements – getting onto college courses, completing NVQ modules, getting a job.

However, invariably these triumphs will be followed by disappointments and feelings of failure. These young people very much live in the moment and the biggest challenge we have found is trying to support them to see something through. The poverty we see at Seaford is typical of the poverty that exists all over this country. It is poverty that says 'I am not loved, I am not loveable – this life is as good as it gets for me so I may as well escape from it' – and so we see all their money going on drugs and alcohol and other forms of escape. It is heartbreaking to see achievements being followed by such things as evictions through nonpayment of rent, being kicked out of college courses through inability to control a temper, failure to turn up at interviews, drunkenness leading to violence. Our role is to keep being there, when they let themselves down and when they let us down. Our role is to keep the faith and to try slowly but surely to help them grasp that they have the potential for a good future, that they are precious to God just as they are, but that he longs for them to be so much more fulfilled.

Our prayer for the young people past and present at Seaford is that they will learn to love themselves and start to make the right choices and become the people that God created them to be.

I have been, and sometimes still can be, guilty of having strategies, plans and forward thinking, and forgetting the call to love people and not play a game of chess. The young people I work with are so special, unique, gifted, funny, vulnerable, wise, imperfect, flawed, troubled; how dare I treat them as a chess piece helping my game look good or the church look like it's thriving. I feel so much more at peace providing space and opportunities to show and tell the young people that they are loved and that they too have amazing potential to love God, themselves and others.

14

A Fresh Expression of Mission

Cafechurch Network

CID LATTY

A defining moment

There are moments in history that take your breath away. Like the glare of the midnight sun in Norway, they are amazing yet bewildering experiences that can take you by surprise. For me, the emergence of the Cafechurch Network is one of those experiences. When we started our first cafechurch in 2006, little did we know that we were beginning a movement that would see scores of other churches follow suit. I did not know that it would lead to so many questions being raised about the nature of church and that well-established organizations would seek our help and advice.

As I began to write articles for denominational newspapers and magazines, speak on radio and appear on TV, I too was learning and growing in my understanding of what all this could mean for the Church. This is what I called 'theology on the run', because I did not have all the answers – I was learning in motion as I went. For me, the recurring question was, 'Is cafechurch a good way for the Church to reconfigure itself to appeal to a cafe culture?' I have grappled with this question, sometimes encountering criticism but always challenged to move forward, because the fruit of what we have done has been so good. Before we look at some of the issues, I will look at what I mean by the term cafechurch.

Connecting with the community

How do we connect with our community? This was the question posed when we began a cafechurch in Welwyn Garden City in 2006. What would it take to keep our church tradition, while sensitively seeking to 'incarnate the gospel'? We could see how a thriving cafe culture was rapidly developing in our town. Coffee shops were opening up everywhere, and this was replicated all over the UK. In fact, by 2008, a staggering 50 per cent of the UK adult population was visiting coffee shops. Our own church congregation were a part of this cafe culture, many of them using coffee shops as 'third places' between home and work. With this in mind, we asked our local coffee shop if we could develop a community in there and were amazed when they said yes.

What we planned was a themed event with quizzes, a short talk, discussion and live music – all with the added benefit of being served by friendly coffee shop staff. Our purpose was to help people engage with issues like debt, parenting or the environment from a faith perspective. We called it 'coffee with a conscience'. People would not only be invited to enjoy a lively evening of music, chat, hope and humour, but we would offer them resources and prayer to help them take action after the event was over. All this would form the basis of our emerging community.

There are challenges that come with developing communities in this context. The word 'church' is loaded for some people – they may have misconceptions and issues with their experience of church, and for many it can be off-putting. While running a cafechurch, we often found ourselves having to reassure people that what we were doing was inclusive and not abrasive. We also found that we ourselves had to learn what it meant to communicate in a cafe context. For instance, while it may be acceptable in churches to expect people to sit politely through services containing wordy sermons with little present-day application in them, in a high street cafe context this is not the case. People come ready to talk with each other and are familiar with the more relaxed environment. If the subject is not engaging, and the talk is too long or monotonous, people will begin to talk among themselves, and the whole evening may be lost.

What we began to say to cafechurch leaders is, 'Whatever you do, don't be boring, and keep the talk short'. We saw it more beneficial to keep the meeting lively and make a mistake – correcting yourself later – than to be dull and risk jeopardizing the whole meeting. We emphasized the significance of allowing people to engage in conversation like 'iron sharpening iron' and to see the talk as a prelude to this. On reflection, I think food and drink helped to create the right environment for this to happen too. The precedence of eating food together as a context for sharing life is certainly a biblical one. The thrill and challenge of serving in this context kept us keenly 'charismissional', as we sought to re-dream what church could do in this context.

Our cafechurch proved to be so popular that I began discussions with Costa Coffee Management, and a few cafechurches were piloted in other stores. Due to the success of these, Cafechurch Network[1] was formed. This registered charity was later given the 'OK' to put a cafechurch in every suitable Costa Coffee store in the UK, and Costa Coffee have asked that all churches wanting to use their stores come through the Cafechurch Network. Stores from other coffee shop chains have also opened their doors to the Cafechurch Network. It was at this point that we set out the values that would link the cafechurches together. Our strap-line was 'Welcome, warmth and words'. We sought to welcome people into a warm community of friendship and to convey the biblical message in ways and words that relate to real life 'discipleship' issues.

We held our first conference in 2008, and over a hundred people came with great excitement from a wide range of denominations to hear about how they could run a cafechurch. Monthly training days followed soon after this, as the demand grew. I remember being wary of creating a large organization, which would mass produce a concept. Allowing people to explore what this could mean in their own context without creating a big institution appealed to my postmodern sensibilities.[2] So I gave away lots of information, which meant that people could run a cafechurch without joining our network. Even so, our network grew to sixty cafechurches, with scores more churches developing their own ideas in many high street venues.

As I have encouraged others, I recognize that three main forms of cafechurch have emerged. Some cafechurches are 'cafe style' worship – a 'normal' worship service with people gathered around tables for a combination of songs, sermon, conversations, communion, collection, readings, prayers and coffee. This type may use various multi-media or other interactive elements to engage those who attend but is usually hosted in a church building. If the location varies, the content remains a comprehensive covering of all the elements of a customary church service.

Some cafechurches are run in privately owned coffee shops, in which a church serves meals or light refreshments with optional prayer, conversation or counselling. The emphasis here is generally on unobtrusively serving people while being ready to respond to their needs if requested.

The third form of cafechurch is one where a local church takes over a commercially run coffee shop, usually 'out of hours', to run an event. This type looks at issues such as parenting, politics or poverty with the use of quizzes, talks, live music, interviews and chat, all hosted in a branded

---

1 See, www.cafechurch.net for further information.

2 B. Walsh and S. Keesmaat, *Colossians Remixed*, Downers Grove: InterVarsity Press, 2004, p. 22.

store. Stores benefit, as cafechurch helps them as a business to grow as part of the local community, and there are great benefits for the Church too, as people who might not enter a more traditional church setting interact with people who do. This may be one of the first steps for some towards going to church. For others, they may decide that cafechurch in a high street location is the kind of community they want to belong to. The challenge then is to add other elements on to the cafechurch experience like a discipleship course, which can help people move forward in their faith journey.

Misconceptions of the Church

Let us return now to the question I posed earlier: 'Is cafechurch a good way for the Church to reconfigure itself to appeal to a cafe culture?'

I was sitting in my office as Senior Pastor of a church that was hosting a blood donor session. A steady flow of people were coming in, and I over-heard one conversation between two women. After greeting each other, they began to talk about giving blood in a church. One said quizzically to the other, 'Do you go to church?' The reply came almost without hesita-tion and humorously: 'Do I look like I go to church?'

What misconceptions do people have about the church? Do they say it is out of touch? It is a cold building? A boring service? A place for old people? Sometimes we add fuel to these misconceptions by the way we behave. I once visited a church with my family, and when we got there, all the doors were locked. We could hear the singing, but could not work out how to get in! It seems quite humorous now, but at the time I thought, 'They do not want us in there'. I'm sure that the church did not intend to be unwelcoming, but that's all I can remember about it. For many, this 'first impression' is crucial to get right, if the church is to be anything more than one of those places you visit when you have to.[3]

Reflecting on cafechurch and my experience of being locked out of a church building, I was reminded of this Scripture: 'Each builder must choose with care *how* to build on it. For no one can lay any foundation other than the one that has been laid: that foundation is Jesus Christ' (1 Cor. 3.10–11, NRSV, emphasis mine).

Very often we try and 'fix' the Church instead of starting again in the right place. The place to start is with God and to work from there. It is

---

3 The story of the Jesuit, Robert De Nobili, who arrived in South India in 1605 and set about 'removing unnecessary offence' from the Church might be a helpful case study here. See G. Cheesman, *Hyperchoice*, Leicester: InterVarsity Press, 1997, p. 115.

all too possible to build a church that is without good foundations. In our focus on God in Jesus, we must allow the church to be shaped by him. The tension is to consider Jesus' statement; 'I will build my church' (Matt. 16.18) is not a call to sit back and let things happen around us but an invitation to enter into the cosmic 'struggle' as we diligently work with God in building his Church.[4] How can we do this? Stephen Croft describes how the Church is called to be shaped by the character of Jesus and that this is best seen in the message given in the Sermon on the Mount.[5] The fruitfulness of the Church comes out of its ability to be grounded in the nature of Jesus. In short, Christology shapes our ecclesiology. Our view and understanding of the Church should be shaped by our connectedness to Christ. To develop church in the right way we need to ask then, 'What is God like?' This may seem simple or complex depending on your bias, and that debate is amply covered elsewhere.[6] The Old Testament prophet Joel exclaims of God, 'for he is gracious and compassionate, slow to anger and abounding in love' (Joel 2.13, NIV). God has attributes that are conducive to forming a relationship with us that delivers unconditional acceptance. God himself takes outcasts, 'converting'[7] and transforming them into friends as they walk together through life's experiences.[8] The Church underestimates this at its own peril. Therefore cafechurch seeks to makes transformational relationships a priority. I suggest that this alone makes it a vital endeavour.

If God is like this then what kind of church should we be?

Paul prays for the Church that it might engage in a vibrant relationship with God and 'know this love that surpasses knowledge' (Eph. 3.18, NIV). Intellectual agreement and academic understanding are important, but something more than these is at work here. In a very real sense, Christians get to know God as they follow Jesus. Knowing God through the humanity of Jesus is essential. The Church must somehow incarnate that truth, so that others may look into the 'shop window' of the Church and discover God for themselves. How is this applicable to running a cafechurch? I will illustrate this with what I call the 'least preached on verses in the Bible':

---

4 G. Ladd, *A Theology of the New Testament*, London: Darton, Longman & Todd, 1994, p. 114.

5 S. Croft, *'Jesus' People: What the Church Needs to Do Next*, London: Church House Publishing, 2009.

6 See R. Harries, *The Real God*, London: Mowbray, 1994.

7 Ladd, *Theology*, p. 34.

8 Harries, *Real God*, p. 37; Ladd, *Theology*, p. 34.

The next day John was again with two of his disciples. He saw Jesus walking by. John said, 'Look! The Lamb of God!' The two disciples heard him say this. So they followed Jesus. Then Jesus turned around and saw them following. He asked, 'What do you want?' They said, 'Rabbi, *where are you staying?*' (John 1.35–38, NIrV, emphasis mine)

Here we have the leading prophetic character of the day declaring that the one who looks like any normal man is actually the long awaited propitiation for the sins of the world. This groundbreaking statement is so captivating that John's disciples immediately begin to follow Jesus. The strange thing is, the first question they ask Jesus is not about how he was going to take away sin, how this man came to this role or something theological. No, instead they ask, 'Where do you live?' It seems to me they are saying something like 'Let us connect with you as a person, see how you live, what you value and this will help us to relate to you.' This approach was the one Jesus encouraged and it must have worked because John records that 'The Word became human and *lived here* on earth *among us* ... and we have *seen* his glory.' (John 1.14, NLT, emphasis mine). Literally, as Jesus co-habited with his people, immersing himself in the culture of the day, people connected with God.

In some way, cafechurch seeks to do exactly the same thing: inhabit the cafe culture without allowing the culture to dictate the DNA of the Church.[9] We draw alongside it, diverting its selfish consumerist focus to the needs of others by engaging in issue-based conversations. We deliberately befriend people, because we love them, and hope that they may become friends with God. I think this follows more closely what Jesus did rather than adopting a condemnatory stance over an 'idolatrous' consumerist society.[10]

Admittedly, cafechurch has its shortcomings and weaknesses, but this is hardly unique. If cafechurch is said to be a soft option, this is only because our ability to put people at ease is seen as superficial compared to more traditional patterns of church. However, traditional church can have all the right content in the service, but an inability to grow. It is in that context that newcomers can be told, 'You can't sit there, that's my seat'. Or are left feeling embarrassed if their children make too much noise in the service. Services may also be filled with Christian jargon and in-house protocol, all of which can be a hurdle for a newcomer. After the service, there may be tea and coffee served, but people may brush past visitors to connect with their friends or concentrate on their church-based respon-

9 Harries, *Real God*, p. 34.
10 G. Cray, *Disciples and Citizens*, Nottingham: InterVarsity Press, 2007, p. 70.

sibilities. This can all lead visitors to conclude that we know what God is meant to be like – loving, compassionate, gracious – but the experience of the church does not match up. Not all churches fail in this way, but a surprising number do. As John Drane observes, there seems to be a 'credibility gap' between what is offered and our experience of it, and so we can lose the very people we are seeking to reach.[11]

As I have reflected on the way we do cafechurch, I have become convinced that focusing on welcome as a first step to friendship and conversations that form disciples is not a soft option at all, but rather the key to the life of a faith community. Someone once asked me, 'When is cafechurch going to get onto "spiritual issues"?' My reply was that issues such as parenting, debt and the environment are all spiritual issues. Talking about issues from a faith perspective is a vital part of the lifelong learning that friends of God enjoy. Therefore cafechurch has an important contribution to make.

Jesus our example

The difficulty with cafechurch is that it requires us to have friends to invite, and this for Christians is often the problem. We may discover how few friends we have outside church and how hard it is to form a community of friends in a transient society. I cannot claim to have discovered the solution here except to seek to rediscover God's own passion to be where people are.

We have said that Jesus is our example of befriending people. He left where he was and came to us. But he did not come seeking that we first know how to pray or read the Scriptures – as good and as essential as these things are. For the devil himself knows how to pray and has a grasp of Scripture; we only need to appreciate the story of Job or read about the temptations of Jesus to discover that. What he did ask his followers to do was to make disciples and to teach everything they had learnt from him (Matt. 28.18–20). Every day and everything is a teachable moment for the apprentice.

Let me illustrate this. A few people who went to cafechurch decided to join our Alpha course. They had little or no experience of church so this made it a challenge for them and us at times, because they did not know the Christian protocols. Right in the middle of my talks they would shout out if they felt they had an illustration that emphasized one of my points.

11 John Drane, *After McDonaldization*, London: Darton, Longman & Todd, 2008, p. 43.

On a weekend away, they were deeply touched by the teaching and the ministry of the Holy Spirit. But on the Saturday night, the bar was open, so it was as if they said 'now we know what to do'. In the comfortable bar area, they proceeded to drink, until they were totally drunk. The next day they slept off a hangover, as the rest of the group attended the closing service for the weekend. It was after this incident that I had the opportunity to speak about the radical call of Jesus to become true disciples; how Jesus had something far more fundamental to say to us than learning the mechanics of prayer, reading the Bible, listening to sermons and attending services. To be a disciple of Jesus will affect how we spend our time, energy and money. It will be about the choices we make in life. It will cause us to rediscover Christian disciplines like prayer and fasting, sacrificial giving and cross-cultural mission. It will compel Christians to live what they sing, love what God loves and be in accountable relationships. To live in the harness of God's love makes all of life the arena to form relationships with people. As a result, greater stories are yet to be told.

Where do we go from here?

I believe it is time for the Church to dream again about what might be possible. Because cafechurch offers a way to follow the example of Jesus, I believe it is a key element in reaching people in our present-day cafe culture.

I would suggest, however, that:

- Cafechurch is one of many missional ventures that can widen the spectrum of the Church's reach and create a good 'first impression' for those outside of the Church.
- The unction, permission and example has been given for us to 'go'. We, however, may need to recover confidence in these words of Jesus.
- Christian leaders who have pioneered before will need to encourage others to pioneer today.
- Engaging with the culture is messy. In doing cafechurch, we have seen people come to faith, churches raise their profile in the community and scores of initiatives inspired by this story. Even so we have been accused of being little more than a money-making scheme for coffee shops. To be missional is a bit like planting wheat knowing that tares are present and that they both look the same as they grow. The challenge is to work towards the harvest even so.
- Having times to review, evaluate and plan as a team will enable your cafechurch to develop in a healthy way.

- We may need to reset our priorities so that we can spend time being in situations where we can make friends with people who do not go to church. We may find it easier to invite people to a coffee shop as a result, rather than to a traditional church building. We may also need to take the pressure off ourselves to see instant results.

Theology to go

Dietrich Bonhoeffer is reputed to have said that it is an act of faith to 'seize fervently' the moment to build friendships. The precedent has been set by God, the opportunities are all around us to connect wholeheartedly with a cafe culture and form friendships. Let us learn theology as we go. Cafechurch is a good way for us to do just that.

15

Pioneering Mission

The Net Church, Huddersfield

DAVE MALE

I was shocked to read an article in a local newspaper that suggested that 53 per cent of people in Huddersfield had no contact with any religious institution. This meant the majority of people in the town were outside the orbit of church. I also assumed that for people like me in their thirties the percentage was much higher. This revelation coincided with a process working within me over the previous ten years that had left me with lots of questions about the Church and its mission. I had previously been involved in leading two churches in very different social settings. One was a small church on a tough council estate in the Midlands, and the other was a larger eclectic church in a middle-class area. But in both places I discovered the same issue. There was a very limited sense of mission to those outside the church. There were great people in the church, but the vast majority of their energies were being put into 'running the church', most activities were church-centred, and even our vocabulary was an internal church language that was mostly impenetrable to anyone else. There was evangelism taking place, and people were very welcome to join the church, but the underlying message was that you have to fit in with us, because we are not going to change anything for your benefit.

I am very aware of how this 'slow cook' in me was a long process, but it was not a solitary journey. Some people had short-term input into my thinking, while others travelled with me for much of the time, as I discovered that I was not alone in feeling and thinking this way. So when the opportunity came through a conversation with my bishop to have a space to try something new and different in Huddersfield, some of the foundational thinking had already taken place and some key fellow travellers had already been found.

In one of our first ever meetings of the newly emerging team, I asked them what most excited them and frightened them about our new venture together. As we went around the room answering the question, nearly everyone had the same answer to both questions, 'starting with a blank sheet of paper'. We agreed it was wonderful to start from nothing with no pattern we had to work to, but it was also incredibly nerve-wracking to begin from scratch. We were unusual in not developing something that was already in existence. But I felt that it was also a great privilege to begin from the very beginning. In our beginnings, there were three key factors in operation that worked together to produce something exciting.

Team

There was a small group with me in this from day one, and over the first few months we added more to the group, so that by the time we began the church we had twenty-eight adults committed to 'The Net'. It was a great help that my wife and myself had already been in Huddersfield for five years and so had developed many links and were rooted in the town. This was particularly helped by having young children at school. Many of our initial contacts were made at the school gate, which then took us into myriad networks.

We spent nine months meeting together talking, praying, dreaming and eating, as we shared together our hopes for this new beginning. For the first four months, we met on a Tuesday evening in our lounge to talk and plan together. It was during these times that we came up with the name 'The Net', our values and vision and how this fledgling community might grow and develop. As the pioneer leader, I knew how easily this could become my thing, and I was totally convinced that it needed to be God's thing, in which we all were partners and shared together.

Our two great theological driving forces were mission/evangelism and community. We wanted to create something that genuinely was for those outside the Church and that transformed us, them and our town. We had a genuine passion to see these people become disciples of Jesus with us and a growing vision that this could happen in Huddersfield within our networks. But we did not want to be simply a mission station or an exhausting institution that wanted to suck all the energy and life out of us. We became more and more convinced of the importance of community in God's economy. The more we looked at Scripture the more we saw the central role of community within God's mission and purposes. God used the community of Israel, the disciples and the emerging Jewish and Gentile churches as vehicles of his mission. Much of Scripture was not written to individuals but to these communities. The problem was that so often we viewed church as a collection of individuals rather than a reflection of the community at the heart of the Trinity. We worked really hard at not only learning about mission and community but also being involved in God's mission and being community together. We wanted not simply to be church-focused, and we aimed not only to share ideas, thoughts and dreams but also our lives together. We spent time being with each other. The danger is that this can so easily be lost in the rush to 'do' the work. One of our annual highlights was the church weekend away, when we had some input, but most of the time we enjoyed being in each other's company and seeing this happen across the generations.

Listening

I think there is a real danger, fuelled by our vision and excitement of rushing in too quickly to make concrete plans. We spent nine months together before we had our launch event. Looking back, I sometimes wonder if we could have taken even longer. We spent time listening to God through Scripture, prayer and each other. We kept coming back to Jesus' words about being 'fishers of people', and we had long discussions about what that might mean for today. We also listened to each other and learnt much from others. There was such a wealth of experience. This from people who had often felt marginalized by the church in the past, because their focus was not on church activities, and they were therefore not in attendance at every meeting. We learnt from other people and churches that had gone before us.

On one particular occasion, I learnt much from going to talk to a church leader who was doing something similar to what we hoped to achieve but who was about a year ahead of us. This meeting produced many positive things we could copy but also some things that made me come away thinking, 'I would never do it like that.' Lastly, it is really important to listen to those outside the church. I often talk to church leaders who tell me what people outside the church want. I then ask them how they know that. Usually, they don't really know it but have simply assumed what people want from the church. One of the best listening exercises we did was to invite some of our friends to a local pub for a meal, a meal that we paid for, and then we asked them to tell us about their experiences or impressions of church and what they might imagine church could be like. We were helped by having a skilled facilitator in our community, who was able to lead the discussions and draw out the participants. We made sure there were only a few Christians present and that they kept quiet as we wanted this to be a time for us to listen only and not try to defend the church. This proved to be a very simple exercise to produce but a profound experience of listening for us.

Focus

I was fed up being part of churches that either had no focus or so many foci that they achieved very little. I felt we had a very clear focus from God to connect with people in Huddersfield who had no contact with any other church, through being God's community. I discovered over the years of The Net that my main function as the leader was to keep us focused on the focus. It was very easy for us to get diverted into lots of excellent tasks, but ones that were not part of our particular calling as a church.

We worked over many weeks to clarify this vision into a meaningful statement for ourselves. Eventually, we produced, 'By loving God and each other we seek to enable non-churched people to develop a real and relevant relationship with Jesus.' This really did become very much the focus of our church life as it enshrined our key values of mission and community. We used the language of vision and focus, but this can be expressed as an overarching and guiding story if people are nervous of using more management-style language. Our focus was very much the key story at the heart of our life together.

We felt we needed to think about how our mission might work out in a detailed way so that we could clearly answer the question, 'Who is this mission for?' When I have subsequently met those involved in pioneering situations who are struggling, it is almost always because they have not answered this question clearly enough and have not closely defined who their mission is for. Our past and present experiences and our reading and thinking led us towards a more network style of church. We were very aware that many people in our age group (twenties and thirties) were not restricted by geography but lived their lives through networks. They might live or sleep in one place but work elsewhere and enjoy their social life in another location. Our primary networks were through our friendships and relationship links, but we also identified a number of networks such as sport, the internet and work, through which we worked over the years. We felt also that God was calling us to reach people similar to our age. This didn't mean we restricted The Net purely to unchurched young people living in a network manner, but we were clear that these people were our focus.

This focus also impacted the way we organized church. We did not have to meet in a particular geographical area, but what was important for

such people was accessibility and parking. When we met was also important. For our worship events we still used Sunday, but for other mission
events we found Friday or Saturday night much better. We tried to look
at everything we did through the eyes of these people and changed what
we did accordingly. We continually asked, 'What is the gospel for such
mobile people and how can we communicate it to them?'

We found quickly that they did want to be part of a community and
were often searching for good relationships with others. They wanted to
hear what we believed, but they also needed the space and freedom to
question and challenge what they were hearing. Although we found film
a great media to use with them, we quickly discovered that they were fascinated by the gospel stories, most of which they did not know. Often we
found ourselves getting out of the way to help them meet Jesus through
the Gospels. We discovered they loved stories generally, and we searched
out Christians within and outside The Net with great stories to tell of
their lives and God's work in it. Finally, we worked hard at creating a
community where it was safe and acceptable to belong and to be finding
out about Jesus.

One of the dangers of church is that it can give the message out that
if you don't believe fully within the first few months you are not really
welcome. We realized some people felt strongly they belonged to us and
were part of us, while also being clear that they were on a long journey of
discovering faith in Jesus. To help with this, we even created a membership of The Net that was not dependent on their Christian belief, so there
was an authorized sense of their belonging with us.

The only restriction we had once the initial team was formed was that
we strongly dissuaded Christians from other churches in Huddersfield
joining us at The Net. People have been surprised and shocked by this,
and I concede we could have grown much more dramatically without this
rule. But we imposed it to maintain our focus. Often the problem with
Christians joining later is that they want to impose other foci or they are
more interested in recreating church in the image of what they already
know and feel comfortable with. I think this was the main reason why we
so successfully maintained our focus and saw many of our unchurched
friends become disciples of Jesus. We were very united around our focus
and our founding story. Often I would meet Christians who had come
along to one of our events, and they would tell me that three people from
The Net had already told them over coffee they couldn't join the church
as they belonged to another church!

Initially, I assumed that I didn't need to remind people about our focus,
as we had worked this out together and owned it so strongly. I soon real-

ized this was a very naive view. I was amazed how quickly the focus could slip. Business people have claimed that focus can be lost within thirty days for any organization, and even with all our history of starting from scratch I soon discovered this to be true. So I tried to find as many places in our church's life and calendar simply to remind them why we were here, why we started The Net and who it was for. Most months, there was a time in an event or when leaders gathered, where I could simply say, 'Remember why we did this and remember that's why we are doing it now'. I found loads of ways to do this, but at the heart of it all was the simple message to remember our focus. If you do that, you will not go far wrong. It needs to be a clear focus, but it also needs to be communicated regularly.

It is now four years since I left The Net. It is still going strong despite a few hiccups and setbacks along the journey, with a totally lay leadership team now. As I reflect back on my experiences and use them in my present posts of resourcing, training and supporting pioneers, I am sure that the leaders of such ventures need to be robust spiritually, mentally and physically. Leading The Net was, at times, like being on a roller coaster on which you experienced the highs and lows at the same time. It concerns me that some leaders end up being burnt out by their experiences. I think at the heart of the leader's life must be assurance of his or her own standing in Christ, in order not to be rocked by the vicissitudes of starting something from scratch. It is easy for the leader to end up carrying so many hopes of the new fledging community that are not possible for one person to fulfil. There certainly needs to be great faith, but also a healthy dose of realism. Often under the pressures frailties and weaknesses can be easily exposed.

Linked to the need for robustness is the importance of support. I found the advice of an advisory group that we set up for The Net very important in helping me to gain perspective and counsel on many tricky issues. Their wisdom, love and support got me through a number of difficult situations. But also close friends outside the church, to whom I could turn, were equally important. It was wonderful to have a place where I could let off steam. It was a very necessary outlet. I worry for leaders whom I find have become isolated from support and friendship. I love God's words to Adam in the garden, 'It is not good to be alone.' I think this has much wider resonances than simply marriage. We must not allow leaders to become alone, and the responsibility for that lies with the leaders themselves in finding places of support and recreation.

Starting a church from scratch is a great privilege, but it is not always easy. I think working through these three factors of team, listening and focus were vital in our development of a church that was really able to connect with those outside. We saw many such people join our community and become disciples of Christ. I am not sure we were necessarily pioneering in our style of worship or the methods of our evangelism, although we were very open to experiment, but in starting from scratch we concentrated on our focus through our combination of mission and community that had emerged from our lengthy listening process. We would not allow ourselves to be diverted from this. This was not always easy to do, and it was costly for the leadership team at times. But we were convinced of our calling from God and the need to fulfil this for the sake of our town, the people in it and the glory of God.[1]

---

1 For more information on the story of The Net Church, Huddersfield, see Dave Male, *Church Unplugged*, Milton Keynes: Authentic, 2008.

16

Mission and the Local Economy

TERRY DRUMMOND

Definitions

In seeking to describe the contribution of the church and ministry within the local economy, it is important first to define what is meant by both terms and from this identify how local Christian communities work with the business community and with public authorities, which are the key players in economic development in most areas.

The church in this context is the local worshiping community, from which those with responsibility seek out ways of offering pastoral support to people who work within the area for which pastoral responsibility is taken. In the case of the Church of England, this will be the parish. For other denominations or gathered congregations, it will be self-defining by the church's leadership/pastoral team.

The local economy for the purpose of what follows is the combination of both large and small businesses that employ individuals and are responsible for their working conditions. It may be a small manufacturing company, an office or the myriad small and large shops that are found in all communities. All of them employ full- and part-time workers who have pastoral needs, and while it may be unusual for a minister of religion to take an active interest in their pastoral care, there is an opportunity for sharing the gospel that should not be underestimated.

In addition, it includes all the statutory bodies, which by definition may not be businesses but are large-scale employers whose staff contribute financially to the local community through their purchasing power with local shops, food outlets and leisure facilities. In their contact with these businesses, they are helping to sustain the financial underpinning of the community.

Work-based pastoral ministry

The employee base of most companies and workplaces will probably live outside of the economic catchment area, and therefore be the subject of pastoral care from their local church, but it is important to recognize that there can be an identifiable pastoral role and ministry for people in their workplace, where it must be said they spend more time than in their home.

It is also important to note that for many younger people who are in the category of being reasonably high earners, making use of restaurants and other leisure facilities, their residence is a place that offers a base to go out from rather than the traditional understanding of the home.

In reaching out to these often well-educated individuals, a pastoral model based in the workplace may bring opportunities that are not available in any other place. The problem is one of breaking through barriers that are those of both the workers and the managers. A sensitive approach is necessary, but if access can be negotiated, relationships can be made, which can be of immense value to both the pastor and the recipient of the pastoral care.

Another area for consideration is what is described as the new economy, the not-for-profit sector that organizes and manages projects and businesses that are seeking to create social capital. The growth of the not-for-profit sector includes voluntary organizations, charities and local faith communities, which make their buildings available often on a subsidised basis for work that serves the local community. The workers will often be offering a service for the least well off in a community, through work with pre-school children or the elderly.

The projects that are developed in this way will employ individuals who contribute both directly and indirectly to the local economy. Their financial contribution can be identified not only through their spending power, but also via the less obvious contribution of social capital, which is not usually defined in financial terms.

The contribution of the local churches' mission is all-encompassing, and yet it is the case that some areas of the life of a local community as described above will be seen to be less important than others. The particular example is that of linking into local economic development and the business community. The day-to-day work of regular worshippers takes up the majority of their time, but it is often the case that the local minister will have no idea what this means for the people who are regular worshippers in his or her church.

It is important that opportunities are found to assist ministers who have no knowledge of the working life of the members of their congregations. The Industrial Christian Fellowship 'Take Your Minister to Work' initiative[1] is an interesting example of bringing together local church ministers with their church members in the latters' workplaces. In addition, the exploration of an individual's faith during Sunday worship offers an opportunity for bringing together the experience of Monday to Friday and placing it within the context of worship. In both cases, greater understanding can be gained by the whole worshipping community.

It is also probable that the economic life of the community that is being served is taken for granted but not understood. Even though economic change can be a key to understanding how a geographical area may be changing, either in the context of decline or improvement, in both cases the changes will have an effect on local residents and therefore on how strategies for mission and pastoral outreach are developed.

This is of particular importance at the present time, when the national government is seeking to cut budgets, which additionally leads to reduction in investment by local authorities, which have a specific responsibility for economic and social regeneration.

In the period between the mid-1980s and the election of the coalition government in 2010, investment in local communities has been a key to community improvement, and in many cases local churches have entered into partnerships to develop projects that contribute to both economic and social improvements.

With the investment from public authorities normally being financial, occasionally augmented with contributions from local businesses, the churches' support matches this in kind through the use of buildings or other plant, sometimes with the time of both clergy and local Christian volunteers. It is important to note that the social capital that underpins much regeneration, while not strictly defined in financial terms, is a valuable contribution that can be evaluated and given a monetary value, which itself can be set against the total budget and be seen to be a contribution to the overall investment programme.

Industrial mission and chaplaincy

In considering the role of the local church in the context of the local economy, it is important that consideration be given to the historical antecedents of this particular example of mission and outreach.

The contribution of the churches to understanding mission in what is described as the local economy has a varied history. It is best represented

---

1 See http://www.icf-online.org/tymtw.php for further details.

in the work of industrial mission and chaplaincy, which was at its height in the late 1940s, when heavy industries of steel and coal and small workshops were the norm. A key element of their work was to be a link between the trade unions and management, and in most cases their focus was politically left wing and theologically liberal. Their decline came in the 1980s with the shift from an industrial-based economy to one where the focus of employment was located in the service sector.

The pastoral model of chaplaincy did continue in some areas, and there was an additional shift to retail chaplaincies in the new shopping malls like the Metro Centre in Newcastle and Bluewater in Essex. The placing of chapels in these shopping malls was an attempt to make the connection between faith and commerce by offering support to shop workers and a place for shoppers to stop and say their prayers. The model used was and is pastoral and based on the Anglican parish system of a priest for every community.

The development of faith and work groups that have a link to organizations that offer support and guidance is a reasonably new development; for example, Transform Work UK offers support to Christians who organize their own meetings in their workplace.[2] Unlike traditional industrial chaplaincy, the groups are more evangelical in focus and are volunteer-led and organized. The model builds on the traditional faith and work groups that are found in some businesses and public authorities, which bring people together for Bible study and prayer with little or no contact with local churches.

A new working model is Market Place Chaplains Europe, which offers chaplaincies to companies for a fee and is an extension of their human resource departments.[3] The model is contrary to that of industrial mission, where independence was considered to be of the foremost importance, the argument against payment being that the chaplain was able to maintain a critical and prophetic voice to the companies they visited. The key issue here is that of not 'biting the hand that feeds'.

The shift in understanding of the contribution of the local church in thinking about the economy is in part a response to financial cutbacks by the major denominations for chaplaincy outside of an institution, a model that takes clergy and ministers away from a local parochial or chapel ministry and does not contribute to the ongoing costs of stipends or their equivalent. The interesting exception is the development and growth of the local clergy who volunteer to be chaplains to their local Asda store. The volunteer chaplain gains access to the shop floor and can offer a min-

2 See http://www.transformworkuk.org for further details.
3 See http://www.mchap.co.uk for further details.

istry to both the staff and the shoppers. The model is one that needs a sympathetic management and, perhaps most important of all, agreement by the senior directors.

The church and local economy development

In considering the issue of local economic development, it is important that the economy is seen to be more than finance-led. The church and wider community sector has much to offer in what is called social capital, or, in the words of the Church of England report *Faithful Cities*, 'faithful capital'. The underlying idea is that Christians are responding to their call to mission and discipleship by serving their local neighbourhood. In this model, the contributions of volunteers' time and the offer of space in churches for community activities at no financial cost to the user is seen as contributing to the growth of a capital that is the antithesis of a finance-led model, while it also contributes to the building up of stable communities. However, such a model demands a change of approach with regard to how a local economy is defined, and is a challenge to both the theological and philosophical ideas of what constitutes it.

This changing focus offers an opportunity for new ways of thinking with particular reference to how best to relate to local economic development in the context of a local business community and its workforce. In addition, it is important that consideration be given to the impact of changes on communities that are the result of the government's cuts in expenditure and the downturn of both the national and local economies. A particular concern are the problems associated with budget cuts in planned regeneration programmes that would have improved communities and neighbourhoods both socially and economically.

In most local authorities, economic development is, or was, the responsibility of a department carrying a very clear role in working to improve economic viability across its area. In some cases, the work would be undertaken by an arm's-length company wholly owned by the local authority, while retaining independence to encourage local initiatives.

The election of the coalition government in May 2010 with its commitment to austerity measures in the light of economic decline means that many of these departments and companies are being reduced, and their work is being maintained by a much reduced number of staff, if at all. The disadvantage for the church is that relationships that have been built up are lost, and the few staff who remain in post can no longer give time to ensuring that the specific needs of an area can be addressed by a sharing of local knowledge.

The problem for a local church that is seeking to identify a role in local economic development is that it has lost a key partner and potential ally. Working with the officers of these bodies could lead to creative partnerships, which ensured that information was shared and projects developed that brought together representatives of the statutory bodies, the local community and the Christian community. While there may be residual bodies with smaller budgets, the possibility of new partnerships seems to be far less likely.

The loss of these partnerships and the government's rhetoric and policy proposals regarding the 'Big Society' can mean that local Christians may reach the conclusion that they might be able to fill a gap and in some ways contribute to the local economy by seeking to replicate the statutory services that have been reduced due to budget cuts.

The local church might for instance identify professional services for both the young and the elderly to be areas of work that they might, with funding, offer to the community they serve. In this way, they build on existing good practice that, while small, is successful, because of their understanding of the locality, their ability to recognize and respond to local circumstances alongside mobilizing volunteers.

In taking this direction, it is possible that the local church can contribute to the economy by offering employment and bringing limited financial investment to areas where economic decline is endemic. The creative element of this model of working ensures that local income is spent within the community in which it was generated. Though the assumption must be that in replacing statutory services the new projects will be funded in such a way that meets all the costs incurred, in a period of economic retrenchment this may not always be the case.

In a situation where financial investment in communities is being constrained, it is important that the finances of any local project are seen to be sustainable. The cuts and reduction in grant aid that would traditionally be used for underwriting such projects point to the importance of careful financial planning for all projects, and especially for new ones.

To move in this direction the local church or voluntary organization needs to be clear that its business plan is robust and that recognition is built in to the proposals from the beginning that funding can be finite and at any time financial cuts can lead to situations where work may be terminated at short notice. The effect is the loss of jobs, reduction in services and emotional traumas for all involved, especially those who rely on the services that are being offered.

On the positive and creative side, in serving the local economy in this way, the church is contributing to the creation and the building up of a society where the weakest are supported and local jobs can go to local residents. In this way, the local economy is being well served and the church is making an important contribution to both the social and economic well-being of the communities it serves.

In looking forward to the contribution of the local church in developing links that contribute to economic development, it is important that consideration be given to what is possible and deliverable.

Three areas for consideration

In the light of the above and considering how to move forward, there are three areas that deserve consideration:

- *A commitment by the local church to consider seriously what ministry might be possible to the business sector and other workplaces in a parish or community that is being served.*
  Identifying sympathetic managers, who understand the need for pastoral care of their employees, can lead to a ministry that meets the needs of people in the space where they spend most of their time. It will be important to ensure that a contract is agreed as to what is being offered and in particular a recognition that overt evangelism may not be appropriate. Rather, by offering implicit religious support, people may be assisted in understanding what a positive contribution faith can make to the wholeness of life.

- *The local church needs to take seriously the working life of worshipping members of their congregation.*
  Opportunities to share their experience from working life can liberate theologically and spiritually both the community of faith and the individuals who make up that community. It also brings into focus the day-to-day realities of what constitutes the Monday to Friday experience of many people.

- *In the light of the discussion of what constitutes the 'Big Society' the local church can and should be involved in asking questions about services for local communities.*
  The key element is not to become a service-delivery agency that seeks to emulate and replace services that are normally associated with local authorities. The creative response of the church will be to contribute by offering its traditional pastoral care, which also ensures that whole communities are being served. It will also lead to an important contribution

to the wider conversation about what the post-2010 debate about the national economy means for local communities, where the services are offered that are to contribute to a healthy and creative local economy.

In seeking to find ways for the local church to be involved in the local economy, it is important that local churches work together and find ways of offering pastoral outreach that meets the needs of individuals and families. It is also necessary to challenge statutory agencies, the business world and the third sector to recognize the personal and spiritual needs of the people they employ.

This demands a church that is able to look outside of itself and is able to reflect theologically on the contribution it can make to create a healthy and holistic community where faith and work are seen not to be two parts of life but the whole that makes people what they are.

17

Mission and Ecclesiastical Collaboration

TOM STUCKEY

The Anglican priest did not like Methodists. An apocryphal story went around the village that whenever a Methodist died, he would drink a glass of sherry. Unfortunately, the Methodist minister's manse faced the parish church. Being a friendly soul, the new minister on his arrival visited the vicar. It was not a warm reception, but the vicar announced, 'I say prayers in the church every morning from 7.00 to 7.20; you can join me.' The minister thought he had better go. The next day, he crossed the road, entered the church, was given a book and told by the vicar to sit in the choir stall opposite him. It was a cold start to a practice that continued for the next seven years, until the minister left. Both subsequently testified to the discovery of an enduring bond of friendship and deepened spirituality, which neither had known before. Beautiful ecumenical events can grow from the most unpromising beginnings.

The chemistry of ministerial relationships

One hears stories of new ecumenical initiatives that arise when two ordained persons, generally Anglican, Methodist, URC or Baptist, get on so well that they want to work together at some specific project. Such personal relationships can result in joint services, the sharing of buildings, neighbourhood-watch schemes, drop-in centres, hospitality arrangements and a growing together of congregations. New creativity occurs, because the ordained, through mutual trust and friendship, step out in faith beyond their own denominational walls. These initiatives, however, can hit ecclesiastical barriers. Members of the local congregation, excited by the progress made, ask 'Why can't we now do this?' or 'What is stopping our local preacher from celebrating in your church?' They become puzzled when told that it is not allowed. Creative ecumenical initiatives at local level sooner or later come up against structural, theological and legal difficulties, many of which have still to be resolved at a diocesan or national level.

While this is frustrating for those who want to forge ahead, what leaves local congregations bewildered, angry and demoralized is a denominational staff change, which brings a new minister or priest who has little understanding or sympathy with what has gone on before. The new incumbent then proceeds to rein in the initiatives, pulling the congregation back within his or her own control. While a good chemistry in ministerial relationship can open things up, the opposite can be devastating. Having been involved in training Anglican, Methodist, Baptist and URC ministers in an ecumenical college and in other contexts, I sadly recognize that there are some ordained and lay persons in leadership positions whose theological and ecclesiastical agenda is conditioned by power, control and hubris. If mutual respect, acceptance and trust are absent, then local collaboration is doomed no matter what happens at the macro-ecumenical level. Unfortunately, things have stalled at the macro-level, which is something we must now examine.

The twentieth-century ecumenical drivers of organic union

For the last forty years as a Methodist minister, I have witnessed failed attempts between my church and the Anglicans to remove the macro-level blockages that prevent our achieving organic union. John and Charles Wesley were staunch Anglicans, so union should have been possible. However, the Methodist children in the nineteenth century, instead of remaining in the family home grew away from it, fell out with each other and became totally estranged from their ecclesiastical parent. Nevertheless, a hundred years on, in the 1960s, the possibility of a restoration and renewal of the relationship between Methodists and Anglicans seemed achievable.

The chief stumbling block lay in our different interpretations of the role and authority of the ordained minister/priest and of the nature of episcopacy. To many bemused lay people it seemed like a disagreement over status and power and the desire to preserve a 'closed shop'. The question of episcopacy cannot and should not be so easily dismissed. All churches have episcopacy (oversight) in some form or another. It exists even in the most independent or democratic churches. It is the particular form of episcopacy that is the problem. In its association with bishops, episcopacy goes back to the very early days of the Church, as the Orthodox and Roman Catholics rightly affirm. Apostolic succession through a line of bishops, although a fiction, serves to remind us that the Church of the present must always be in communion with the Church of the past if it is to be the Holy, Catholic and Apostolic Church of the future. To assume otherwise is to fall into of the postmodern spirit of our age that increasingly chops away at history, labelling its legacy as malign and oppressive.

The pursuit of organic union between Methodists and Anglicans was not the only story of ecumenical pilgrimage in the twentieth century. Conversations had also opened up right across the ecclesiastical divide, some of which, like the union in England between the Presbyterians and Congregationalists to form the URC, produced tangible results. It should, however, be noted that the more independent evangelical churches viewed the process with suspicion. Beyond Britain, in the former 'mission fields' of Africa and India, the ecumenical dream was being realized far more quickly. One much quoted example was the formation of the united Church of North and South India, where the acceptance of bishops appeared not to pose such a threat as it did for some Methodists in Britain.

The main drivers of twentieth-century ecumenism were the wish to realize the prayer of Jesus 'that they may be one as we are one', so that the world would believe, and the Lund principle that 'we should not do anything apart which we could do together'. Mission was the aim; ecumenism and co-operation the means.

During my year as President of the Methodist Conference, not only did I visit Methodist churches overseas, which had their own bishops, but I also participated in conferences of church leaders in England as well as addressing some county ecumenical bodies. I noted the theological arguments and rationale for ecumenism to see if they had any relevance for the Church of the twentieth century. My discoveries were not encouraging.

The failure of a dream

Although much had been achieved and significant dialogue taken place between Protestants, Roman Catholics and Orthodox Christians, the last century is littered with glitches and false starts. Attempting to achieve organic union has proved to be costly in time and energy. Problems with buildings, local loyalties, theological cussedness and psychological perceptions keep getting in the way. Issues of identity and power also haunt ecumenical discussions. Ecclesiastical mergers, it has been suggested, instead of enabling growth precipitate decline. A number of Local Ecumenical Partnerships, once thought to be the vanguard of the 'future great Church', also failed to fulfil the hopes of those who pioneered them; some trying to act independent of their parent communions; others suffocating under a blanket of ecclesiastical red tape.

Callum Brown,[1] charting the decline of Christian Britain, pours scorn on the responses of church leaders who think they can reverse the process through ecumenism, changing the ecclesiastical structure or updating the liturgy. He says the cultural changes that have taken place are of such magnitude that the Church in its present shape will only continue 'to exist in some skeletal form'. Before 1800, Christian piety had been located in 'evangelical masculinity'; after 1800, in femininity. The 1960s signalled the 'ungendering' of British Christianity, which has resulted in a religious vacuum. The search for faith is now conducted outside traditional Christian institutions, fostered by ideas of personal development and consumer choice. Consumer choice is an important ingredient when examining some of the so-called 'growing' churches in Britain. What often happens is that dissatisfied Christians from the 'dead' churches 'shop around' for a more lively church. Membership growth in one church precipitates a further fall of membership in another within an overall saga of decline.

The ecumenical dream is fading fast. It is a fantasy of faith to believe that renewal will come when the traditional mainline churches accept each other and pool their resources. The present disenchantment with institutional religion has deeper causes. In any case, we live in a multifaith society where diversity and multiplicity are the order of the day. The old ecumenical dream, according to Alister McGrath, has 'become the last refuge of the theological bore'.[2] The twentieth-century ecumenical agenda can no longer work, because its liberal assumptions are irrelevant in today's world of growing conservative evangelical churches.

I now believe that 'organic union' is something given by God at the end of history. This, however, does not mean we should abandon the hope of some limited form of 'visible unity' that manifests itself in a common profession of apostolic faith; a complete sharing of baptism and Eucharist; and a common acceptance of the diversity and interchangeability of ministry and oversight. Nevertheless, where does this leave us?

A new ecumenical vision?

The central ecumenical question of the last century seems to have been, 'How can we demonstrate visible unity between diverse and divided churches?' This question is now compounded by a new problem. While 'division' between denominations remains an obstacle, we are now wit-

---

1 C. Brown, *The Death of Christian Britain*, London: Routledge, 2001, p. 198.
2 A. McGrath, *The Future of Christianity*, Oxford: Blackwell, 2002, p. 85.

nessing the possibility of fragmentation occurring within single-parent communions as the different denominations attempt to come to terms with issues of sexuality, justice and diversity. I therefore proposed to the leaders of Churches Together in England that the key ecumenical question for the opening decades of this century should be, 'How can we together as churches celebrate unity and diversity for the common good of the planet and for all people everywhere?'

I suggested this question for two reasons. First, ecumenism, like ecclesiastical restructuring, is in danger of becoming an end in itself and a way of rationalizing the problem of surplus buildings and fewer ministers. Although done for the sake of mission, it becomes a displacement activity for mission. Bevans and Schroeder in their huge book on mission begin with the sentence, 'One of the most important things Christians need to know about the church is that the church is not of ultimate importance.'[3] This is a stunning sentence for two Roman Catholic theologians. In my inaugural address to the 2005 Methodist Conference, I said that mission is seeing what God is doing in the world and joining in, and that we in the West, having substituted 'Church' for 'Spirit' as the third person of the Trinity, have reversed God's understanding of mission. God has a mission; we are invited through the Holy Spirit to participate in it.

> When the Church does not join with what God is doing in the world, then church ceases to be church and becomes a club. What some view as the decline of the Church institution is simply God passing judgment on nostalgic religious clubs.[4]

Second, our theological understanding of the relationship between unity and diversity has undergone a radical shift. Jonathan Sacks in *The Dignity of Difference* wrote:

> God, the creator of humanity, having made a covenant with all humanity, then turns to one people and commands it to be different in order to teach humanity the dignity of difference ... Biblical monotheism is not the idea that there is one God and therefore one truth, one faith, one way of life, it is the idea that unity creates diversity.[5]

---

3 S. Bevans and R. Schroeder, *Constants in Context: A Theology of Mission for Today*, Maryknoll: Orbis Books, 2004, p. 7.

4 T. Stuckey, *On the Edge of Pentecost: A Theological Journey of Transformation*, Peterborough: Inspire, 2007, p. 7.

5 J. Sacks, *The Dignity of Difference: How to Avoid the Clash of Civilizations*, New York: Continuum, 2002, p. 53.

The Christian Church in the West is starting to embrace a more dynamic model of the Trinity that emphasizes the distinctness of the persons. The celebration of diversity should become an important ecumenical ingredient for the Church as she engages in mission. This is a good foundation for further reflection.

Four fresh responses

First, on 22 September 2005, at Lambeth Palace, the Archbishop and I commissioned the first Fresh Expressions team of Anglican and Methodist missioners. This was an innovative evangelistic expression of the Covenant relationship ratified between our two churches a few years before.

Fresh expressions, which are now multiplying at an encouraging rate, provide a hopeful counterpoint to the declining traditional church as we evolve a diverse 'mixed economy' church. The name 'fresh expressions' has become a blanket term covering a wide range of imaginative attempts to engage with those who hover on the edges of church or who have no contact whatsoever.

Second, not all fresh ecumenical responses to mission have to be evangelistic or worship-centred. Some focus on 'presence'; namely, being with those who need us most. The 'street pastors' initiative is proving to be a creative ecumenical experiment as Christians from both the traditional churches and the new churches take to the streets with the defined task of listening and offering practical care.

Third, when the 2010 January floods devastated the Cumbrian town of Cockermouth, the first people on the spot were Christians. The Local Churches Together emergency procedures had snapped into place. Christians in florescent jackets directed traffic, offered comfort, rescued people and were giving advice before the emergency rescue teams took over. Churches remained open as refuge centres; food, drinks and support were given to the relief teams. This type of ecumenism is practical and down to earth. It was an action event arising from a long ecclesiastical process.

Fourth, on 2 July 2005, as G8 leaders met in Scotland, a tidal wave of 225,000 marchers swept through the streets of Edinburgh in a never-ending flow. Whistling, drumming, singing and chanting, this was a good-natured advocacy of Make Poverty History. I was there as President of the Methodist Church and was later able to meet with Gordon Brown and Alistair Darling. The whole event, which had a carnival atmosphere, was multi-faith and multi-cultural. On the march and in the meadows, I was able to share with people of different religions, ideologies, faith and no faith. What brought us together was a concern for global justice. This too was an ecumenical event; global, post-denominational and post-Christian.

Global ecumenism

In 1893, 80 per cent of the Christians in the world lived in Europe and North America. Now almost 60 per cent of Christians throughout the world live in Africa, Asia, Latin America and the Pacific. Pentecostalism has globally transformed the Christian landscape. It has been estimated that by 2050 only about one-fifth of the world's three billion Christians will be non-Hispanic whites.[6] The era of Western liberal Christianity is passing and the day of Southern conservative Christianity has dawned. But there is also another growing conservative faith – Islam. The political, sociological and economic conditions that make people in parts of the two-thirds world open to Christianity also make them receptive to Islam. In many situations, Islam is even more attractive, because it offers a counter-cultural alternative to the globalizing and exploitive tendencies of the rich West, which in the imagination of many is still identified with Christianity.

The mission of the Church is to plant itself in every place and culture as a sign of hope, but any global or national ecumenism must beware lest it try to realize some former dream of Christendom. Instead, as a response to the challenge of globalization, Robert Schreiter has suggested that the Christian faith should seek to renegotiate its understanding of catholicity. He mentions three aspects of a new catholicity: the acceptance of the idea of 'commensurability of culture', that is, Christianity will not be homogeneous; second, an awareness of the fragmented and partial experience of cultures; third, churches will focus on 'the boundaries between those who profit from and enjoy the fruits of the globalization process and those who are excluded and oppressed by it'.[7]

The search for unity remains an imperative for the Church. In a confusing, fragmented world, ecumenism witnesses to the integrity, the identity and the historic continuity of the Church as a sign of the Kingdom of God.

---

6 P. Jenkins, *The Next Christendom*, Oxford: Oxford University Press, 2007, p. 3.

7 T. Stuckey, *Into the Far Country: A Theology of Mission for an Age of Violence*, Peterborough: Epworth, 2003, p. 129.

A new Pentecost

In my book *On the Edge of Pentecost*, I argue that the elective winds of the Spirit are blowing across the planet, and that for Britain a '*kairos* moment' of the Spirit is at hand, as God calls us to step out in faith.

The events of 9/11 have jolted the Western nations out of their 'comfort zone'. Credit crunch and debt now gnaw at our existence. Consumerism is not satisfying the deeper longings of people. Although the prophets of the 1960s predicted the demise of religion as the God of the gaps was pushed to the edge, this has not happened, much to the dismay of Richard Dawkins and others. Instead religion has become deregulated and is enjoying a remarkable renaissance.

It would seem that if mission is to be local, national and global, then ecumenism will have to wrestle with the new spiritualities, the growing conservative nature of Christianity, sexuality and the status of women, as well as attempt an open dialogue with Islam.

So what of the future? The diverse tapestry of Christian communities will increasingly reflect the rich colours and patterns of the Trinity in whom the many are one and the one many. The Church will assume diverse forms representing some aspect of the multiplicity of languages, peoples and cultures. Unity will not be the product of ecclesiastical joinery but of the Spirit who baptizes with fire and generates diversity. The ecumenical agenda will include items about partnership links between churches, through prayer, project, shared learning and mutual exchange of clergy. Above all it will focus on justice issues. If ecumenism does not seriously address the gap between rich and poor, it will cease to serve the Kingdom of God. Justice for the planet and its peoples will also provide the locus for partnerships with those of other faiths and of no faith. God is not creating a new set of ecclesiastical institutions but rather a 'fluid', inclusive, emerging church reflecting the dancing life of the Trinity. I shall let Rowan Williams have the last word:

> The Church is first of all a kind of space cleared by God through Jesus in which people may become what God made them to be (God's sons and daughters), and that what we have to do about the Church is not first to organize it as a society but to inhabit it as a climate or a landscape. It is a place where we can see properly – God, God's creation, ourselves. It is a place or dimension in the universe that is in some way growing towards being the universe itself in restored relation to God. It is a place we are invited to enter, the place occupied by Christ, who is himself the climate and atmosphere of a renewed universe.[8]

8 *The Christian Priest Today*, on www.archbishopofcanterbury.org/1185.

18

Mission in a Global Context

BMS World Mission

DAVID KERRIGAN

Turning the tables – what on earth has world mission to teach the local church?

As a mission agency head, you'd expect my passion to be for strong local churches that are committed to world mission. Correct, but not complete. I am also passionate about bringing back home the insights gained in world mission to strengthen the local church in its outreach.

A story. A few years ago I was invited with a colleague to spend a week-end with a church that is now entirely surrounded by a large South Asian Muslim community. Their concern is how to reach their neighbours. I tell them that they will probably never see a day when their neighbours would walk into their church on a Sunday morning! What's more, they shouldn't even be praying for that to happen. Their puzzlement is mixed with a strange sense of relief – they had never actually believed this would happen anyway! But I go on to share with them a way of reaching out to their Muslim neighbours that is bearing fruit in mission work in the Indian subcontinent, South East Asia and in parts of Africa and the Middle East. I suggest this is something they could pray for and implement, and on hearing the details, they are excited. And they're convinced this is something they can work towards.

C1 to C6 Spectrum[1]

What was it that I shared as I spoke with this church? To answer that question, we need to go back to the early 1980s and the commitment of

---

[1] Although this spectrum is described as it is experienced in the Islamic context, where it began, there are similar so-called insider movements within Buddhism and Hinduism.

a group of missionaries in a Muslim-majority country in Asia to encourage Muslim enquirers or converts, few as they were, not to join the local church. Instead, they were encouraged to gather together with others, who were also from a Muslim background. Today, these groups are commonly called Isa-believer groups,[2] Isa being the name for Jesus in the Qur'an.

John Travis (a pseudonym), himself a part of this movement, first documented this approach in what he called the C1 to C6 Spectrum, where 'C' refers to a Christ-centred community.[3] Through the range of models on the spectrum, he was attempting to show the degree to which each type of Christ-centred community connects, or fails to connect, with the prevailing culture. In other words, the degree to which a Christ-centred community is 'contextualized'. The church in the story above was a Christ-centred community that was concerned that it was not connecting with its Muslim-majority community. Its life and witness was not contextualized.

So imagine any one of a number of Muslim-majority countries in which a variety of forms of Christian communities might be found.

C1 would be a traditional Western[4] church using a foreign language throughout: this may be an international church, which worships in English, mainly for expats, and probably has a foreigner as a pastor. This church really doesn't connect with the local Muslim community, though one or two more educated, wealthier, English-speaking Muslim converts may attend. Music will be non-indigenous – guitars and keyboards are not uncommon. Hymns and songs familiar to Western Christians will be the norm, as will pulpit and pews. A visiting Westerner would feel at home. C1 believers call themselves 'Christians'.

C2 is a traditional national church and would probably trace its roots back to missionary work from the West. But this church uses the local language for worship and is probably led by a local, national pastor. Many local believers have been Christians for generations. They dress either as Westerners or as local people dress, but observe fewer local customs. For example, men and women may sit together. Some local instruments are used for worship, as well as keyboards and guitar. People will still tend to sit on pews or chairs. There will be more Muslim background believers

---

2 Isa rhymes with Lisa.

3 J. Travis, 'The C1 to C6 Spectrum: A Practical Tool for Defining Six Types of "Christ-Centred Communities" ("C") Found in the Muslim Context', *Evangelical Missions Quarterly* 34.4 (1998).

4 In this chapter, 'Western' and 'the West' are used as generic terms to refer to people or expressions of mission that have roots primarily in Europe, North America or Australasia. As such it is more a cultural reference than a geographical one.

Muslims and Jesus: The C1–C6 spectrum						
	C1	C2	C3	C4	C5	C6
Description	A foreign church transplant (e.g. an international church). Mostly Westerners attend. Foreign in culture and language. Pew and pulpit the norm.	Like C1 but using local language. Mostly national believers. Pews and pulpit still the norm. No separation of the sexes. Many men dress in shirts and trousers, but not all.	Like C2 but using local cultural elements, e.g. national dress the norm, traditional musical instruments, separation of sexes etc.	Like C3 with some biblically acceptable Islamic practices, e.g. hand-washing, prostrate prayer, dress-code. Much more likely cell group than congregation.	Muslims who have accepted Isa as Lord and Saviour but who worship in the mosque as well as sometimes in a cell group of other C5 Muslims, similar to C4 cells.	Secret believer – may or may not be active in religious life of Muslim community. Can become C4 or C5 if they meet other secret believers.
Self-perception of the believer	Christian	Christian	Christian	Followers of Isa	Muslims for Jesus	Muslims for Isa
Muslim perception of the believer	Christian	Christian	Christian	A kind of Christian	A strange kind of Muslim	Muslim

(MBBs) in a C2 church, though the gap with the local culture is still large. C2 believers call themselves 'Christians'.

C3 fellowships are much more contextual than C2. They will always use the local language, including the use of Muslim-sensitive language (such as Allah for God), if a number of MBBs are present. They will use local instruments for worship (such as the *tabla* – a small drum – or a squeeze-box harmonium), sit on the floor and separate men and women. Few, if any, will wear Western clothes (for example, men won't wear shirt and trousers but a calf-length *kurtah* or *punjabi*). Depending on the context, they may meet in a simple local church but more often in someone's home. C3 believers call themselves 'Christians'.

C4 is where the fun starts! Usually meeting in homes or a shop owned by one of the believers, the religious vocabulary of the Islamic community will be used to refer to God, Jesus, prayer, worship, offerings and so forth. These 'followers of Isa' will ritually wash their hands and faces before they handle the *Injil* (the Muslim word for the New Testament), as they would the Qur'an, and when they pray they will bow prostrate as they would in the mosque. They may keep the fast at Ramadan and will avoid pork and alcohol, as Muslims do. C4 is best described as a *Christ-centred community* and not a church, and its adherents as *followers of Isa*, not Christians. The desire for distance from the name 'Christian' is linked to a widespread perception that all Westerners are Christians; Westerners on our TVs and those we see as tourists are immoral, therefore Christians are immoral. C4 is now almost universally accepted as the norm for encouraging a gathering of believers within Islamic communities.

C5 is controversial in the way C4 once was. C5 can be best understood as a kind of messianic Muslim, not unlike messianic Jews, who stay within Judaism. Many C5 believers stay within the mosque and worship Isa within the context of daily or Friday prayers in the mosque. In fact, it's not unknown for so many C5 believers to gather together that in effect the mosque becomes a messianic mosque. C5 believers may still read the Qur'an, and see Muhammad as a prophet. While most will see Isa as the only Saviour, many struggle with the notion that Isa is the Son of God.[5] C5 believers are viewed as *Muslims of a sort* by the Muslim community and refer to themselves as Muslims, who follow Isa the Messiah. There are those, like Timothy Tennent, who argue that C5 is syncretistic and that accepting Isa as Lord and Saviour is incompatible with continuing adherence to Islamic worship.[6]

C6 seems at first glance to be something of an anomaly. So far, the move from C1 to C5 can be seen as an expression of Christ-centred communities that are increasingly contextualized with reference to the host culture. Following that logic, C6, essentially a community of secret believers, is in effect completely identifiable with the culture, because C6 believers cannot speak, or do not choose to speak, openly about their faith for fear of intense persecution and death. They will meet only occasionally, almost never with foreigners, will hide carefully any copies of the *Injil* they possess and will not share their faith openly unless with people they can absolutely trust. This usually means family members only. C6 Isa believers conform outwardly to the identity of a Muslim and are seen as such by the Islamic community.

---

5 P. Parshall, research quoted in 'Danger! New Directions in Contextualization', *Evangelical Missions Quarterly* 34.4 (1998).

6 T. Tennent, *Theology in the Context of Global Christianity*, Grand Rapids: Zondervan, 2007, pp. 193–220.

Gospel and culture

So how does this spectrum help us understand the relationship between a local church and its local culture? To frame the question differently, does culture affect our faith in Jesus Christ, and the life of worship and witness that flows from that faith?

When I read the Bible, I have to conclude that there is no such thing a disembodied-from-culture Christianity. The gospel reaches us through elements of our culture and is expressed using elements of culture. Language, song, architecture, music and dance come easily to mind. But world-view and patterns of thought also shape our faith and help us to express it.

Jesus was born into the culture of first-century Israel, and fulfilled his ministry in that same culture. His teaching was rich in cultural notation, from Samaritans to sowers, from Israel's Old Testament heritage to Israel's eschatological hope. In the Epistles, Paul constantly uses cultural references from the family, the courtroom and the marketplace to help explain doctrines. In Athens, he refers to their poets and temples. In the early centuries, the Church wrestled with issues of theology generally, and Christology especially, and expressed its answers in ways that reflected Greco-Roman world-view, vocabulary and concepts.

In later centuries, translating the Scriptures into vernacular languages enabled tribes and nations to appropriate the gospel for themselves. In many countries today, indigenous music, liturgy and architecture are emerging, and also a confident non-Western theology that reflects the world-view of myriad peoples and cultures. So to me, Christ is Lord and Saviour, brother and friend. But to many Ghanaians, he is the one they pray to as *Nana Yesu* (Ancestor Jesus).[7] And while, in the West, we have marginalized the immanence or closeness of Jesus in our daily lives, to millions in the global South he is the healer of the sick child, the protector of the pregnant mother and the guardian of the weary traveller. The same Christ, the same gospel, but experienced and expressed through different cultures.

All of this reflects the incarnational imperative of the Christian faith. Christianity is not only *capable* of finding expression in and through various cultures; it is of its *essence* that it finds expression in and through cultures. 'The Word became flesh and made his dwelling among us' (John 1.14, NIV) is not an incidental detail in the Christmas story. It is a paradigmatic demonstration of God's entry into our experience of humanity and the cultural realities, whereby we experience the world around us.

---

7 Tennent, *Theology in the Context of Global Christianity*, p. 127.

But here is the crux. While the gospel is capable of taking root and being expressed in all and every culture, those same cultures are human constructs and as such they are inevitably flawed. The gospel is truly a double-edged sword in this regard, capable of finding expression within human cultures, but simultaneously challenging and hopefully transforming those cultures to become more resonant of the character of Christ. So, for example, in a very self-centred Western culture, the gospel challenges us to think of our neighbour. In many Eastern cultures, where shame and honour are key facets, the gospel can remind us that Jesus bore our shame on the cross (Heb. 12.2). In cultures where feuds last generations, the gospel calls us to turn the other cheek and love our enemies. Indeed, any culture or subculture that is visibly patterned after the one who forgave his enemies, washed his disciples feet, ate with sinners and included those who were excluded is arguably a culture that bears the hallmark of 'redemption in progress'.

For this reason, it is vital that when someone comes to faith in Christ, how they are discipled can and should be in ways that reflect their culture. To do so is to affirm the truth that Christ is for you and your people. He speaks your language, knows your world and understands your fears.[8] Christ's disciples are called to be salt and light and yeast within any particular cultural environment. Burning bridges with one's culture is the last thing a local church should encourage a new believer to do.

Extraction evangelism

One of the greatest inhibitors for the effective mission of the Church, locally and globally, is the phenomenon of extraction evangelism, whereby new converts become immediately detached from their own culture. This is often seen in the context of witness to Muslims, where there are many stories of men and women whose conversion to Christ has resulted in their abandoning their culture or being abandoned by their culture. Such abandonment is sometimes unavoidable, but too often their rejection is

---

8 The early BMS missionaries to Mizoram, the Revd J. H. Lorrain and the Revd F. W. Savidge, despaired after six years of ministry. Lorrain wrote in his journal that these people had 'no sense of sin and felt no need of a Saviour'. But as their cultural understanding grew, they knew how much the Mizos feared the spirits in the forest. As a result, they changed their approach and presented Jesus as the vanquisher of the devil and all his powers. Once the salvation Jesus offered was invoked in the name of *Pathian*, the Mizo High-God, and new life in Christ was described using the Mizo concept of paradise, *Pialra*, conversions flowed! See B. Stanley, *The History of the Baptist Missionary Society*, Edinburgh: T & T Clark, 1992, p. 272.

the result of the gospel being presented or accepted in ways that are alien to the culture of the enquirer or convert.

For instance, the encouragement to make an individual decision for Christ seems normative to our Western minds, where individual responsibility is prized. In the West, the rights of the individual seem to trump all other rights. The right of a 16-year-old girl, or even younger, to obtain contraceptives would be considered paramount over any imagined right of her parents to know she is sexually active. The rights of a child not to be slapped supersede the rights of the parent to discipline their child as they see fit. The rights of a murderer to be freed after serving a sentence of a few years takes precedence over the rights of the victim's family who feel the sentence is lenient.

But in many cultures, the rights of the individual are considered secondary, or even inconsequential, compared to the rights of the family or the community. Indeed, such cultures are often much closer to the culture of biblical times. As a result, this clash between the individual and the community is the most common cause of tension when a Muslim man or woman comes to faith in Christ. In most Islamic cultures, the encouragement to make any major decision without involving the elders is considered deeply offensive to the family or community, and especially the head of that family. The new convert may be welcomed by the local church as a triumph of God's grace, but the cost is the severing of all relationships with that person's host community. Furthermore, the regard of the host community for Christianity is deeply damaged as they see it destroying the very values they have held dear for generations. As a result, the resistance of the community to the gospel is strengthened because of what is seen as a frontal attack on the community by Christians.[9] This is as relevant for Muslim communities in the UK as it is elsewhere in the world.

Learning the lessons

These insights, gained from years of mission work in cultures around the world, offer huge potential to enrich the mission of the local church in the West today.

The church in the north of England cited at the beginning of this chapter now finds itself in a Muslim-majority area, similar in fact to the experience of many missionaries in Muslim-majority countries. A missionary encounter with local people began with respect for that culture, and a

---

9 P. Parshall, *Beyond the Mosque: Christians within Muslim Community*, Grand Rapids: Baker, 1991, pp. 178f.

deep desire to learn. That is where mission work begins. A Muslim community on the doorstep of the church is not something to be feared, but an opportunity to serve in the name and Spirit of Jesus.

Our overseas mission workers are taught they can do nothing until they start learning the culture and language of those they seek to work with. Wouldn't it be an enlightened step if a local church in the UK sent its pastor, or outreach worker, to another country to learn the language of those now living on its doorstep? In fact, if the local Muslim community were asked to arrange it, they would probably do so with great pride! But even if that's not possible, a church should set aside serious time and resources for study and research, otherwise it will be ill-equipped for its mission. If a pastor of ten years' experience comes to us to serve in Europe, let alone Asia or Africa, we will ask them to do a year of cross-cultural studies. The principle is no different in the UK.[10]

But along with learning the culture of the Islamic community, the local church needs to find ways to allow its own culture to reflect the person of Christ to the Muslim community. Although that community may be strong in numbers, the likelihood is they feel isolated and maybe even oppressed. Since 9/11, they will be conscious of being viewed suspiciously by their indigenous British neighbours. Wouldn't it be wonderful if the church could find ways of including those whom others seek to exclude? Maybe the church premises could be used for social events for the community – the teaching of English might be a place to start. Maybe there could be an intentional programme of mutual learning put in place by the leaders of the two communities. These things must never be viewed or undertaken as a prelude for mission. Loving your neighbour is an end in itself and reflective of Christ's love for all of humanity.

Our hope will be that men and women will find faith in Christ, but the challenge is to envisage how this might happen, and how to respond if it did happen. If one or two did show themselves to be enquirers or even come to faith in Christ, joining the local church would be a case of extraction evangelism, lifting them out of their host culture and bringing them into what is in effect a C1 church when compared to the dominant Muslim community that surrounds it.

A better approach would be to encourage an enquirer to speak with his or her elders about their interest in Isa and in finding out more about him. It would be appropriate to offer the Scriptures in whatever language

---

10 Culture doesn't just mean other religions. The Black Country in the West Midlands is a completely different world from Solihull, just thirty miles down the road.Move from London to Leeds or Glasgow to Gloucester at your peril if you fail to appreciate the differences in culture.

would be most helpful. To a second- or third-generation youngster who may be English, but assuming they speak the heart language of their community, it would be good to have the Scriptures in that language too. And it should be a version that refers to God as Allah, and Jesus as Isa, not Jesu. If it is a younger person who is the enquirer, then at some early stage this matter should be raised with the youngster's father or the local imam. This should only be done with the permission of the enquirer, but showing such respect is likely to be helpful. If this is handled sensitively, the hostility of the community might be avoided. If that hostility exists, then wise counselling will be needed. It may be right to be patient and certainly it is right to avoid any premature baptism. This is seen by many Muslims as the decisive moment of breaking away from the community, and great distress would result if such a step were taken inadvisably. Get the timing wrong and much can be lost.

Even if serious tensions can be avoided, how is the enquirer best helped? Depending on the circumstances of the individual, I would suggest it is not by incorporating them into a local church, even though they may be most welcome. Rather, encourage the establishment of what, in effect, would be a C4 group. Maybe the enquirer has friends who might also be interested in exploring the Scriptures. If such a group could come together, no matter how small, it's advisable that they be allowed to read and discuss the Bible themselves and not be overtly 'taught' in a directive manner by someone from the church. Unknowingly, many cultural and theological presuppositions will be handed over in the process of interpretation. Trust the Holy Spirit to guide the group. And even if unconventional interpretations begin to emerge, be slow and sensitive in offering correction. After all, they may have discerned things we have missed because of our own cultural blinkers.

The goal here is not a stronger local church but a thriving community of Isa believers embedded in their own culture and, we trust, growing in faith and influence. By God's grace, these groups might just be seen here in the UK too.

PART 2

Mission and the Local Congregation

19

Mission and Context

'There can never be a culture-free gospel',[1] declared Lesslie Newbigin, having spent nearly thirty years as a missionary in India. Returning home to the UK, he began to apply the principles he had learnt on the mission field to Western culture. Indeed, he was shocked to discover that the application of missiological insights, such as *indigenization* and *contextualization*, had been largely ignored by the British church, even with the increasingly difficult situation that confronted it. Wider society was undergoing immense shifts and changes in the mid-1970s, as traditional social mores seemed to be dissolving away and Christian belief and observance appeared to be on the wane. In his analysis, the task facing the Church was to retrieve the integrity of its identity as a missionary presence in society: 'This will entail learning to understand this culture from a missionary perspective – its controlling myths and plausibility structure – and discerning the relevance of the fullness of the gospel in this culture.'[2]

Because of the close links between Christianity and culture in the West, he saw that the collapse of confidence in Western culture was accompanied by a corresponding faltering of confidence in the gospel. His solution was to be found in the international, multi-cultural family of the Church. Those who read the Bible with minds shaped by a different culture could bring insights and resources that enable such a missionary encounter with contemporary Western culture. In this way, the gospel would be released to address and challenge culturally conditioned interpretations of it.[3] The Church in Britain needed to understand more adequately the impact of its cultural context on its faith and practice, alongside needing to learn how to relate more appropriately to the new cultural reality that was developing around it.

---

1 Lesslie Newbigin, *Foolishness to the Greeks*, Grand Rapids: Eerdmans, 1986, p. 4.

2 Wilbert R. Shenk, 'Lesslie Newbigin's Contribution to the Theology of Mission', *Transmission*, Special Edition Tribute to Lesslie Newbigin, 1998, p. 6.

3 Lesslie Newbigin, *The Gospel in a Pluralist Society*, Grand Rapids: Eerdmans, 1990, pp. 191–7.

The emergence of the idea of 'contextualization'

While the ideas that come together to form what has become known as contextualization can be found throughout the history of the Church and all the way back to New Testament times, it is only relatively recently that they have experienced a renaissance in Christian thinking and practice. Indeed, the term 'contextualization' itself only emerged on to the theological scene in a report of the World Council of Churches' Theological Education Fund in 1972. Entitled *Ministry in Context*, it was largely the work of Shoki Coe, a Taiwanese Presbyterian. Writing out of his experience of post-war South East Asia, Coe found that the traditional missionary thinking of the 'three-self movement' – self-governing, self-propagating and self-supporting – was insufficient to enable him to engage properly with his experience and context. He had a family background in Taoism and had also studied in Japan and England, meeting and marrying Winifred while giving instruction in Japanese at London University's then School of Oriental Studies.[4] The melee of social change that engulfed the world in which he lived led him to see clearly the dynamic nature of the dialogue between Scripture and the cultural context in which it was interpreted. If incarnational ministry was to be truly transformational, then that transformation had to take place in the middle of this shifting culture.

The focus of the report was on theological education and reflection in the third world, and it contained some important insights. From the outset it acknowledged that contextualization had implications for mission and structures as well as theological education and reflection. It was also clear that the point of origin of any contextualization would be in the third world and that, as a consequence, it may develop priorities of its own independent of missionaries from the West. Indeed, it was adamant that the possibilities for renewal that contextualization addresses have to be sensed 'locally and situationally'. However, in doing so, the report was also quick to stress that an interdependence is maintained chronologically with the history and future of the specific context, and translocally, through the power of the gospel, in 'solidarity with all people in subordination to a common Lord'. It was also keen to identify uncritical accommodation as a form of *false contextualization* while affirming that an *authentic contextualization* is always prophetic.

---

4 Ray Wheeler, 'The Legacy of Shoki Coe', *The International Bulletin of Missionary Research* 26.2 (April 2002), pp. 77–80.

Contextuality, it is claimed, is the capacity to respond meaningfully to the gospel within the framework of one's own situation. Contextualization is not simply a fad or a catchword but a theological necessity demanded by the incarnational nature of the Word.[5]

While the fact that the term 'contextualization' had emerged out of the World Council of Churches gave many evangelicals cause to fear that it was inherently liberal in its theology, such fears were not to last for long. The 1974 Lausanne Congress on World Evangelization began seriously to question the relationship of the gospel to culture. Recognizing the need to invest further work in this subject, a consultation was arranged for January 1978 to consider the issue of 'Gospel and Culture' at Willowbank, Bermuda. Leading evangelical theologians, anthropologists, linguists and missionaries were present, and contextualization took centre stage. The agenda was clear, it was

[t]o develop our understanding of the interrelation of the gospel and culture with special reference to God's revelation, to our interpretation and communication of it.

To reflect critically on the implications of the communication of the gospel cross-culturally.[6]

At the end of their time together, the participants stated their overwhelming conviction that God's self-disclosure in the Bible was always given in terms of the hearers' own culture and that there was no hope of communicating the gospel if the culture factor was ignored.[7]

Evangelicals increasingly began to use the term, albeit with a variety of definitions. Even hardened opponents of the concept like Bruce Fleming were so influenced by the shift in thinking that they had to come up with their own terms to describe their changing views. Fleming's preference was for the adoption of 'context indigenization'.[8]

The widespread adoption of the term and a growing body of serious theological work on its biblical, ecclesiological and political implications

---

5 *Ministry in Context: The Third Mandate Programme of the Theological Education Fund (1970–77)*, Bromley: Theological Education Fund, 1972, pp. 20–1.

6 'The Willowbank Report', in John Stott and Robert Coote (eds), *Down to Earth: Studies in Christianity and Culture*, London: Hodder & Stoughton, 1980, p. 311.

7 'Willowbank Report', pp. 313, 319.

8 Bruce C. E. Fleming, *Contextualization of Theology*, Pasadena: William Carey, 1980, p. 78.

led the Lausanne Committee to call another consultation in Haslev, Denmark, during June 1997 entitled, 'Gospel Contextualisation Revisited'. Seeking a deeper common understanding of contextualization, the consultation was to conclude with a strong challenge to the evangelical community worldwide for this to be not just an issue for cross-cultural mission, but also a necessary practice for all churches in mission within their own culture. To this end, they called for 'an attitude of risk-taking' in engaging the good news of the gospel with the cultures in which they lived and worked.[9]

It is fascinating to note that, while the progress of an understanding of contextualization in world Christianity and within the academy was inexorable, on the ground little changed. With the publication of the landmark report, *Mission-Shaped Church*, for the Church of England in 2004, the writers still found it necessary to echo the words of Newbigin from a generation earlier:

> The theology and practice of inculturation or contextualization is well established in the world Church, but has received little attention for mission in the West. We have drawn on this tradition as a major resource for the Church of England.[10]

Contextualization as language, concern and transformation

John Corrie helpfully summarizes the developments of contextualization as engaging the issues of the relationship between the gospel and culture on three distinguishable levels.[11] The first is that of language. At this most basic level, there is the need for the message of the gospel and the words of Scripture to be translated into the forms of speech and understanding of those who read and listen. How else can the gospel be communicated effectively? The second relates to the concerns of the culture and involves identifying those things that are important within a given culture. These may be foundational traditions, shared values, perceived needs or owned priorities. They need to be understood to discern how the gospel might be a relevant or prophetic voice. Are these elements of culture in harmony with the gospel, and so might be embraced? Are they at odds with the

---

9 Editorial, *World Evangelization* 80 (September–October 1997), p. 3.

10 Graham Cray et al., *Mission-Shaped Church*, London: Church House Publishing, 2004, p. xii.

11 John Corrie, 'Contextualisation Revisited', *Missiologic* 3 (September 2002), p. 3.

gospel and need to be rejected? Or are they indifferent to the gospel and may be accepted purely on the basis of their cultural significance? The third level is transformational and results from an interactive dialogue between the gospel and a new cultural context. This operates at the level of meaning, and in the process new dimensions of gospel significance are revealed on one side of the conversation, while individuals and communities are transformed by Kingdom values and meaning on the other.

The Roman Catholic missiologist Louis Luzbetak summed up the methodology of contextualization very simply as being contained in the question and answer:

> What would *Jesus* teach and how would *he* behave if he were born today, say in Japan, Brazil, Kenya, or, in my home parish in London, Paris, Rome, Bonn or Washington – not two thousand years ago but here and now? Contextualization is the process by which a local Christian community integrates the gospel message (the 'text') with the real-life context, blending text and context into that single, God-intended reality called 'Christian living'.[12]

Contextualization is, then, the way a Christian congregation makes the connection between the Bible and daily life, between faith and action, between sacramental acts of devotion that are a means of grace and lives that are lived as people of grace. How would Jesus behave? What would he teach here? What would his values and emotions be? What would his underlying premises, attitudes and drives be, if he belonged to the community of which we are a part? David Bosch observed:

> This incarnational dimension, of the gospel being 'en-fleshed', 'embodied' in a people and its culture, of a 'kind of *ongoing* incarnation' ... is very different from any model that had been in vogue for over a thousand years. In this paradigm, it is not so much a case of the church being *expanded*, but of the church being *born anew* in each new context and culture.[13]

---

12 Louis J. Luzbetak, *The Church and Cultures: New Perspectives on Missiological Anthropology*, Maryknoll: Orbis Books, 1988, p. 133.

13 David Bosch, *Transforming Mission*, Maryknoll: Orbis Books, 1991, pp. 199, 454.

Incarnation and kenosis

Building on an understanding of the pattern of God's self-disclosure, the Willowbank Report looks to establish a theological underpinning of contextualization by making explicit use of incarnational theology, along with its christological twin, kenosis. Incarnation is the act of *assuming flesh* and, theologically, is the gracious, voluntary act of the Son of God assuming a human body and nature. Kenosis is the Greek word for *emptying* and, theologically, relates to the self-denial implied in the process of the Son of God's incarnation. Two biblical references are foundational here. Seeking to express the profound truth of the incarnation, the apostle John writes of the pre-existent Word of God: 'The Word became flesh and made his dwelling among us. We have seen his glory, the glory of the One and Only, who came from the Father, full of grace and truth' (John 1.14, NIV). Reflecting on Christ's coming and all this implied for the second person of the Trinity, the apostle Paul teaches that Christ Jesus,

> Who, being in very nature God, did not consider equality with God something to be grasped, but made himself nothing, taking the very nature of a servant, being made in human likeness. And being found in appearance as a man, he humbled himself and became obedient to death – even death on a cross! (Phil. 2.6–8, NIV)

Dean Gilliland further maintains that incarnation and kenosis demonstrate how 'receptor oriented' God is and how they are at the very heart of what God did in Christ.[14]

Meditating on Philippians 2, the Willowbank participants saw a double action of kenosis in the mind of Christ: he 'emptied himself ... he humbled himself'. The first speaks of sacrifice (what he renounced) and the second of service (how he identified himself with humanity and put himself at its disposal). Exploring renunciation, they identified in Christ's incarnation a surrender of the status he enjoyed as the Son of God in glory; the independence of his omnipotence and his immunity from temptation, limitation, need and pain. Regarding his humble service of identification with humanity, participants marvelled at the completeness of that identification in his 'flesh and blood' experiences of life, ministry and crucifixion.[15]

---

14 Dean S. Gilliland, *The Word Among Us: Contextualizing Theology for Mission Today*, Dallas: Word, 1989, pp. 23–4.

15 'Willowbank Report', pp. 323–34.

Newbigin also concludes that this is an important model for cross-cultural mission. For him, all mission is radical and begins with kenosis. The Church in mission must refuse to see itself as the cultural form that is to be adopted by any newly converted Christian community. Rather, the gospel must be given away to the other culture in the faith that the Holy Spirit will be responsible for shaping what it will become. This was the case in the early Church, as the Christian communities at Antioch and Corinth and Rome were not mere replications of the mother church in Judea.[16]

An encounter of three cultures

Newbigin suggests that 'the missionary encounter' requires a triangular model for the gospel–culture relationship. This is because he discerns three cultures at work in any encounter: the culture of Christ and the Bible; the missionaries' culture; and the target or receptor culture.[17] As missionaries prepare to communicate the gospel, it is vital they realize that their experience of Christianity has already, either consciously or unconsciously, been recontextualized from the biblical world to their own. Their task is to strip away those cultural accretions from their experience and understanding and look to recontextualize the gospel message once more. This time, however, it is formulated in terms of the experience and understanding of those they want to share the gospel with. In Charles Kraft's term, the objective is to produce a 'dynamic equivalence' of effect in the language and conceptual framework for those receiving the gospel that was experienced in the original biblical context.[18]

The place of language in contextualization is foundational, and the Gambian missiologist Lamin Sanneh believes that the place of Bible translation in the history of Christian missions cannot be underestimated, because 'language is the intimate, articulate expression of culture, and so close are the two that language can be said to be synonymous with culture, which it suffuses and embodies'.[19] This results in a radical indigenization. Such translation requires significant effort to come as close as possible to the speech of ordinary people and, when confronted with an unfamiliar audience, an acceptance that a breakthrough in communication comes

16 George R. Hunsberger, *Bearing the Witness of the Spirit: Lesslie Newbigin's Theology of Cultural Plurality*, Grand Rapids: Eerdmans, 1998, pp. 169–71.

17 Hunsberger, *Witness*, pp. 237–8.

18 Charles Kraft, *Christianity in Culture*, Maryknoll: Orbis Books, 2005, p. 297.

19 Lamin Sanneh, *Translating the Message: The Missionary Impact on Culture*, Maryknoll: Orbis Books, 1989, p. 3.

only in terms of the audience itself with the adoption of indigenous cultural criteria for the content of the missionary message. It implies that effort is expended in coming to an understanding of the culture, history, religion, economy, anthropology and physical environment of the people concerned.[20]

Such a methodology stands in stark contrast to that adopted by Islam, for example. The Qur'an cannot be translated, because God's word can only be heard in the language of Arabic, in which it was originally communicated to the Prophet. As such, Islam makes a cultural assumption about the indispensability of its Arabic heritage in matters relating to Scripture, law and religion. Christianity, on the other hand, by constantly translating its message, gives to culture a relativized status as 'message bearer'. Sanneh views the disentanglement of the gospel from any exclusive cultural definition as the achievement of the apostle Paul. He was able to translate the gospel message into both Jewish and Greek cultures.[21] In their classic text on contextualization, Hesselgrave and Rommen point out that this translation is both verbal and non-verbal in that it embraces all those activities involved in faithful discipleship, from Bible translation, interpretation and application through to worship, church organization and incarnational lifestyle.[22]

Biblical roots for an understanding of contextualization are found in a number of places. Luzbetak is captivated by the sweep of New Testament history. Christianity begins as a tiny Jewish sect, conforming to the laws and customs of their culture and enjoying popular community support, only to be transformed into a cross-cultural movement that sweeps through the Roman Empire. He points out how the message takes different forms in different communities. Among Jews, Jesus is the Jewish 'Son of David', the Messiah with accompanying genealogy. Among Gentiles, a different approach develops that is sensitive to their cultural background. Quoting their poets and philosophers, there is increased incorporation of the images of light and life, as in John's Gospel, and echoes of the mystery religions as Christ is seen as the one 'in whom are hidden all the treasures of wisdom and knowledge' (Col. 2.3, NIV).[23] Indeed, to the Corinthian church, Paul expresses his passionate commitment to adapt and contextualize to accomplish his missionary objectives (1 Cor. 9.19–22).

---

20 Sanneh, *Message*, p. 192.

21 Sanneh, *Message*, pp. 29, 50.

22 David J. Hesselgrave and Edward Rommen, *Contextualization: Meaning, Methods and Models*, Grand Rapids: Baker, 1989, p. 200.

23 Luzbetak, *Cultures*, p. 85.

At the Lausanne Congress in 1974, René Padilla startled some listeners when he described some missionaries as exporters of 'culture Christianity' rather than the authentic gospel.[24] What he wanted his audience to begin to realize was that, on the part of missionaries, there had been a slowness to reflect on their own cultural heritage and experiences and how these impacted their understanding and interpretation of the gospel. This then had a profound effect on the Christianity they sought to communicate. Luzbetak characterizes this as 'ethnocentrism', a tendency to regard one's own culture as normal and right, stretching from very mild forms of paternalism to xenophobia and racism. He sees it as paternalistic, triumphalist and leaving the receiving church dependent on its Western benefactors, who have provided everything with a 'Made in USA' stamp.[25]

Irrelevance, syncretism and the Holy Spirit

Historically, the degree to which contextualization may be adopted has been seen as a continuum, where authentic and legitimate expression sits somewhere between the poles of cultural isolation and irrelevance at one end and cultural syncretism and assimilation at the other. Herein lies a dilemma: 'In the attempt to be relevant one may fall into syncretism, and in the effort to avoid syncretism one may become irrelevant.'[26] These options are stark: compromise or obscurantism, a comfortable and familiar message or one that is veiled and hidden and makes no sense – the dangers of contextualization or failing to contextualize. For those committed to contextualization, the danger is always at the syncretism end of the spectrum. This is the accommodation to premises and values that are incongruent to the gospel. The safeguard has to be to allow the gospel itself to control and arbitrate its penetration of a culture. Patrick Sookhdeo writes:

> The process of contextualisation recognises that all cultures contain elements which oppose or compromise the gospel. Contextualisation is therefore committed to the gospel controlling its forms of expression. Syncretism reverses this priority.[27]

Syncretism, then, is the inappropriate baptizing of elements of a culture that compromise the gospel. But what is inappropriate? Too often, in a

---

24 'Willowbank Report', p. vii.
25 Luzbetak, *Church and Cultures*, pp. 65–6.
26 Newbigin, *Foolishness to the Greeks*, p. 7.
27 Patrick Sookhdeo, 'Issues in Contextualisation', *World Evangelization* 80 (September–October 1997), p. 4.

genuine desire to keep the gospel pure, elements of culture can be rejected not for inherent evil, but only because of their association with evil. The Willowbank Report recognized that not everything associated with evil was inherently evil itself and therefore recommended redemption and baptism for those things that are not intrinsically evil.[28]

However, all attempts at contextualization need to be regularly submitted to the gospel, and preferably by those who have a different cultural background. Only in this way will the danger of syncretism be minimized. Yet Luzbetak makes a sobering observation: 'A syncretism-free church is an eschatological hope, not a reality.'[29]

Keen to establish the role of the Holy Spirit in this process of contextualization lest it become merely a technique for cross-cultural communication, Newbigin points out:

> While it is the work of the Spirit to convert in this gospel-culture encounter, the 'missionary' character of the church is not ruled out ... The Spirit always converts by an embodied form of the gospel, never by some 'distilled, pure, unadulterated' gospel ... The crucial insight here is that the embodied form which is involved in the encounter is that formed primarily in terms of the receptor culture, not the missionaries' culture.[30]

This has been so from the very beginning as the role of the Holy Spirit has been to drive church into mission. The encounter between the wholly Jewish early Church with the Spirit-inspired 'Gentile mission' created the first occasion to wrestle with issues of contextualization, ultimately leading to the Council of Jerusalem in Acts 15 and the question of whether new Gentile converts needed to be circumcised.

For Newbigin, then, it is vital to recognize the role of the Holy Spirit in cross-cultural communication. He is the one who converts through his secret working, and he is never under the control of the evangelist. 'The wind blows freely.' Yet the Spirit does not accept a receptor culture as a mere necessity to which there must be a grudging capitulation, but rather positively embraces it. All this is not to rule out the responsibility of the Church to communicate effectively in any cross-cultural situation. When it does so it works with the Spirit in his mission, albeit in a secondary role.[31]

---

28 'Willowbank Report', p. 334.
29 Luzbetak, *Church and Cultures*, p. 369.
30 Hunsberger, *Witness*, p. 241.
31 Newbigin, *Pluralist Society*, p. 153; Hunsberger, *Witness*, pp. 240–2.

Contextualization and the local church

All of this, then, has direct implications for a local church. As it seeks to express its missional identity, the gospel must always have a cultural form. The question will be, 'Which culture?' Right from the beginning of the conversation about contextualization, the premise has been that this must always be determined 'locally and situationally'. So a first question to be asked for a congregation is, 'Who are we trying to reach?' Then, following in quick succession, are questions about culture. How do we learn their culture from a missionary perspective? How far does the culture of our church match or reflect those with whom we are seeking to serve or share the gospel? How do we steer the path between uncritical accommodation and irrelevance, keeping our contextualization authentic and appropriately prophetic? All of this should make us very wary of 'off-the-shelf' programmes and cloning successful initiatives from elsewhere.

A second series of questions for a local congregation to engage with revolve around the area of language and concepts. Now, in contemporary Britain, with a shared common language, this would seem not to be a problem; however, appearances may be deceptive here for a number of reasons. Accepting that in many of our larger cities there will be first-generation churches for those who have come to Britain from overseas and have English as a second language, our use of English in the churches poses us with a series of challenges. Words are important in Christianity, and we have spent centuries finding the right ones to use theologically as precision instruments. We are an articulate faith, and even singing many hymns and songs requires a level of literacy that will exclude many. Or again, because of the very issues highlighted by the concept of contextualization regarding the Bible, an increasingly biblically illiterate culture will have no comprehension of the ideas behind concepts such as the 'Lamb of God', 'Zion, city of our God' or 'justification by faith'. Just translating these into English is wholly inadequate. Then again, because Christianity is a 'received faith' with historical roots, linguistically our communication will always have a historical tug that will make it seem dated. In a culture where language is fluid, with usage and nuance changing rapidly, it will be hard to keep up. In its evangelism, worship and wider communication, a local church will need to work hard at how it voices its life in the context of which it is a part. It will be all too easy to become a community's eccentric maiden aunt!

A third area of concern for a local church goes to the very nature of its wider community. How does it understand itself? For example, a rural village may have a great deal of cohesion and a clear sense of identity, whereas a more anonymous suburb does not. Foundational truths, shared values and owned priorities, or the lack of them, are determinative of the way in which a congregation might be or become a part of that community and the role they might play within it. A community's perceived needs can be a helpful starting point. However, the gospel remains the arbiter of engagement. Is this in harmony with the gospel, and might it be embraced? Is it at odds with the gospel and the appropriate response is more prophetic? Or is it neither one nor the other but may be helpful purely on the basis of building genuine relationships of friendship and trust?

Mutual transformation is then the fourth element to be highlighted, noting that it flows out of a mutual dialogue between a church and its wider community. As a community of discipleship, the church is fundamentally an institution of lifelong learning. As it contextualizes with its locality, it learns what it means to live life as Christians 'right here, right now'. Then, as it engages, builds relationships and becomes involved, it helps to shape that wider community with the values of the gospel. Authentic contextualization results in mutual transformation.

It is highly likely that contextualized mission will take a local congregation well outside its comfort zone. It is therefore encouraging to understand that this is done under guidance, and in the power, of the Holy Spirit. But then, after all, contextualized mission is always about adopting 'an attitude of risk-taking' for the sake of the gospel.

20

Mission and the Cultural Landscape

Culture is all around us, like the air we breathe. It has many expressions and is far from uniform: high culture, low culture, popular culture, niche culture all have their place. Life without culture is an impossibility. We inhabit a culture, and it inhabits us, shaping how we perceive the world, how we understand what is going on around us and how we live within it. Most of the time, this all goes on unconsciously and intuitively, but it is a lived reality nonetheless. As someone once blithely commented, 'Culture is the way we do things around here.'

We live at a time in history that is experiencing unparalleled changes in culture. Old-time stability has given way to a brave new world of accelerated development, not only in technological advances but in the re-sculpting of social mores. The interrelated action and effect of consumerism, communications technology and glocalization is probably the most powerful driver of change.

While we have always been consumers, economic, political and social developments over the last half-century have given it a supreme hegemony in the West. For psychologist and commentator Oliver James, this selfish form of capitalism has led to the social disease of 'affluenza'.[1] The ease with which Christians can slip into expressing their commitment through consuming a local church's programmes rather than through missionary discipleship, is clear and much observed.

Communications technology has mushroomed exponentially since the 1990s. From the mobile phone, through the massive amounts of information published online, to the rapid emergence of social media, these developments have radically changed how people connect and relate to one another. A website has been a must for all but the smallest churches for years, and now the development of social media policies and the recognition of real issues the phenomenon is raising are indicative of

---

1 Oliver James, *Affluenza*, London: Vermilion, 2007; Oliver James, *The Selfish Capitalist*, London: Vermilion, 2008.

how the new technology has been enthusiastically taken up by those congregations with vibrant youth ministries.

'Glocalization' has only more recently come of age and is best described by the sociologist Zygmunt Bauman as where 'geographical distances no longer matter ... Stimuli travel independently of their causes: causes may be local, but the reach of their inspiration is global; causes may be global, but their impacts are shaped and targeted locally.'[2] The Church has always been internationalist in its vision, but the connections between the world Church no longer necessarily need to be mediated through denominational, missionary or para-church organizations.

Culture is a dynamic, multi-dimensional, multi-faceted and intercon-nected whole. Understanding it is an art and not a science. It is only through observation and interpretation that we begin to come to grips with it and its implications. While it is clearly an impossible task even to begin to have a comprehensive and up-to-date understanding of what is going on around us, it is a missional imperative that we seek to compre-hend it to the best of our ability. In this sense, it is a direct implication of seeking to contextualize the gospel.

From social phenomena like the Arab Spring and the Occupy Movement to more general trends like the rise of celebrity culture or the increasing disengagement with the political process in the UK, most cultural phenom-ena possess an accompanying narrative of received wisdom that explains and embeds them in the public consciousness. With the latter, for exam-ple, it is often portrayed as the mature fruit of the public's disenchantment with spin doctors, hypocrisy, self-interest and sleaze.

While there are any number of the elements of contemporary culture that would reward exploration and reflection, there are few that, along with the narrative that accompanies them, have a direct bearing on a church's missional life in the UK. The decline in church attendance, the secularization of British life, the postmodern direction of culture and the arrival of the post-Christendom era of society have all been variously cast as negative or world-changing narratives for the Church. While the signifi-cance of each of these is clear, they are often oversimplified, misinterpreted or misrepresented as inadequate attention is paid to what is really being said, alternative perspectives are neglected and the flourish of rhetorical arguments that are made are more about the 'tickling of the ear' than the scrutiny of the eye.

---

2 Zygmunt Bauman, *On Education*, London: Polity, 2012, p. 139.

Christianity in decline and growing churches

There can be no doubting the state of Christianity in contemporary Britain – it is in decline. At least this is the accepted narrative that is consistently portrayed within the media and appears to have ample supporting evidence. It does not take too prolonged a search to discover redundant churches and poorly attended services of worship from across the historic denominations. Sociologists like Steve Bruce and Callum Brown provide a theoretical commentary that accounts for this cultural turn, with the titles of their key work illustrating their theme: Bruce wrote under the heading of *God is Dead*, while Brown explored *The Death of Christian Britain*.[3]

However, it is naive in the extreme simply to chart the decline of recent decades and project them forward on a graph line to predict the demise of whole denominations. The situation is far more complex and nuanced than that. Many church leaders report that they have many growing congregations and that the present overall decline is produced by a more rapid falling away of those churches that are in difficulty. The underlying health of the growing churches means that at some point in the future a different scenario will become apparent. Researcher Peter Brierley thought that he had begun to see the first signs of this with the results of the 2005 English Churches Census, the report of which he optimistically entitled *Pulling Out of the Nosedive*.[4]

An array of research data is regularly produced from a range of sources that attempts to map the present state of Christianity in Great Britain. While there are significant questions about how such research is framed and the affect such framing can have on its outcomes, an overview of the most significant work provides a consistent, insightful and helpful account to inform contemporary mission.

Investigations into the present position of Christianity tend to follow one of two lines of enquiry: behaviour regarding church attendance and personal attitudes with regard to belief. Perhaps the most comprehensive survey of individual religious identity is the National Census. Figures from the 2011 Census are yet to be fully analysed and published, but those from 2001 revealed a surprisingly high level of self-identification as Christian at 72 per cent of the population. This percentage consistently grows as age increases with, for example, those aged 54 registering as 80.1 per cent Christian, while 36-years-olds were much lower at 69.7 per cent

---

3 Steve Bruce, *God is Dead*, Oxford: Blackwell, 2002; Callum Brown, *The Death of Christian Britain*, London: Routledge, 2009.

4 Peter Brierley, *Pulling Out of the Nosedive*, London: Christian Research, 2006.

Christian.[5] More recently, the Integrated Household Survey of 2010–11 established the present figure at 68.5 per cent.[6] What these statistics demonstrate is an abiding cultural identification with Christianity. While it appears to be slowly diminishing at this point in history, it is still part of the self-identity of the overwhelming majority of the population. Beyond the headline figure, what it actually represents will vary from individual to individual, but it is clear that it is a present reality rather than a historic memory. Indeed, a fascinating piece of research by YouGov reveals that while 76 per cent of those polled did not consider themselves to be religious, 56 per cent believed that Britain *was* a Christian country, and 61 per cent thought that it *should* be.

When examining church attendance, published research is normally either based on actually counting worshippers or relying on the self-disclosure of respondents. The fourth English Church Census was held on 8 May 2005 and was primarily based on statistics gathered from churches throughout the country. It produced a snapshot that revealed 3.2 million adults and children were present in church on that Sunday, amounting to 6.3 per cent of the population. Comparison with the results from earlier research revealed that this figure had declined from 5.4 million when the first census was held in 1979. More encouragingly, it also demonstrated that the number of churches whose attendance was declining had reduced between 1998 and 2005 from 65 to 50 per cent, whereas the number of growing churches had increased over the same period from 21 to 34 per cent.[7] In a follow-up report covering 2005–10, Peter Brierley noted a 2 per cent increase in the number of congregations to 50,700 and a corresponding 4 per cent increase in the number of ministers to 36,600, with church membership mostly static.[8]

The 2005 Census revealed that underneath the national trends were some very interesting phenomena. For example, 10 per cent of all churchgoers were black, and within inner London this figure rose to 44 per cent of worshippers. Or again, while the Roman Catholic, Anglican and Methodist churches had the largest fall in attendance, independent churches held their own, and Pentecostals saw significant growth. Another more recent observation that is counter to the narrative of decline is the growth in

---

5 Roger Standing, *Re-emerging Church*, Abingdon: BRF, 2008, p. 163.

6 http://www.ons.gov.uk/ons/rel/integrated-household-survey/integrated-household-survey/april-2010-to-march-2011/stb---integrated-household-survey-april-2010-to-march-2011.html.

7 Brierley, *Nosedive*, pp. 12, 192.

8 Peter Brierley, *UK Church Statistics, 2005–2015*, Tonbridge: ADBC Publishers, 2011, pp. 5–6.

numbers attending worship in cathedrals, with a steady increase of 3 per cent year on year being recorded since 2000.[9] Statistics gathered by the major Christian denominations and collated in 2010 also indicated a stabilizing of the numbers of people attending worship. Benita Hewitt, Director of Christian Research, commented: 'At long last it looks as if we may be reaching the end of the decline for church attendance in the UK.'[10]

The Christian relief agency Tear Fund carried out extensive research into patterns of church attendance over several years. In 2007 they published their results, which indicated that 7.6 million attend church each month (including 4.9 million weekly), which, when added to fringe and occasional churchgoers (5 million), meant that one in four UK adults (26 per cent) or 12.6 million attend church at least once a year. This annual figure is broadly corroborated by the British Social Attitudes survey, which, while examining the question 'Losing faith?' in their 2012 report, noted that across the whole population around 30 per cent of people affiliate to and actively practise a religion where this is defined as at least an annual attendance at a meeting.[11]

The Tear Fund research also sought to explore further the categories suggested by Richter and Francis to help understand the differing profiles of non-worshippers. They had suggested that those individuals who did not attend worship services could be divided into those who previously belonged to a church but had left, the 'de-churched', and those who had never belonged to the Church, the 'non-churched'. Further, each group could also be subdivided by their attitude towards the Church and the possibility of connecting to it: they could be 'open' or 'closed' to such a possibility. In seeking to reach those outside of its immediate network with the good news of the gospel, clearly a different style of approach is appropriate to each. The *Churchgoing in the UK* report identified the various cohorts in the following proportions:

- Open de-churched, 5 per cent (2.3 million)
- Closed de-churched, 28 per cent (13.7 million)
- Open non-churched, 1 per cent (0.6 million)
- Closed non-churched, 32 per cent (15.6 million)[12]

---

9 'Surge in cathedral congregations shows enduring appeal of religion says Church', *Daily Telegraph*, 3 April 2012.

10 'Churchgoing numbers more stable', *Quadrant* 23 (November 2010), pp. 1–2.

11 *Churchgoing in the UK*, Tear Fund, 2007; *British Social Attitudes* 28, Office of National Statistics, 2011, p. 178. To some degree the higher figure is offset by the inclusion of non-Christian religions.

12 Tear Fund, *Churchgoing*, p. 6. For the original designations see Philip Richter

Hidden under the aggregate figures of national trends charted by opinion polls and attendance data are the many stories of church growth that run counter to received wisdom. David Goodhew, for example, points to the 70 per cent growth experienced in the Anglican Diocese of London since 1990.[13] In a volume of essays exploring the phenomenon he observes:

> church growth in contemporary Britain is most common in areas of migration, population growth and economic dynamism. Corridors of church growth have developed alongside major economic arteries such as the A1 and the east coast mainline and the growing cities to be found on these arteries ...
>
> Such growth crosses the denominations but there are two particular strands of vitality; black, Asian and minority ethnic Christianity and new churches. There is significant growth amongst the indigenous British population and amongst established denominations ... Such church growth has been happening across the last 30 years and beyond – and shows no signs of slowing down. The notion that all British churches are in inexorable decline is a myth.[14]

The narrative of the decline of Christianity, the closing of churches and the ageing of believers is true, but only in part. Christianity remains deeply embedded within the population at large. How deep this 'cultural Christianity' might go and what it really expresses is clearly a question that will bear further scrutiny; that it exists cannot be denied and must be taken into account by a missionally orientated church. That the number of people attending services of worship may appear to be stabilizing after many years of decline is encouraging, as is the evidence of numerous growing congregations. Herein lies the opportunity for congregations to mentor and disciple one another as missional communities. To be hostage to the narrative of decline and irrelevance leads to an embattled and dispirited mindset that saps energy and quenches creativity. But this would involve being hostage to a lie.

---

and Leslie Francis, *Gone But Not Forgotten*, London: Darton, Longman & Todd, 1998.

13 David Goodhew (ed.), *Church Growth in Britain: 1980 to the Present*, Farnham: Ashgate, 2012, p. 3.

14 Goodhew, *Church Growth*, pp. 8, 253.

Post-Christendom and the next Christendom

Another dimension of the perceived decline of Christianity is its connection to and defining relationship with wider culture in general and the state in particular. This role is commonly recognized as first emerging following the conversion of the Roman Emperor Constantine in 312 and the Edict of Milan a year later, which guaranteed Christian freedom from persecution throughout the Empire. However, the roots of its British expression lay elsewhere in the conversion of the Germanic peoples of Northern and Western Europe, following a pattern where the conversion of a chieftain or ruler was followed swiftly by the mass conversion of their tribe or subjects. In Britain it was the arrival in 597 of a group of monks who had been sent by Pope Gregory I to convert the pagan Anglo-Saxons and the subsequent conversion of King Æthelberht that marked the arrival of Christendom. The Venerable Bede records what followed: 'Every day more and more began to flock to hear the Word, to forsake their heathen worship, and, through faith, to join the unity of Christ's holy Church.'[15] While Æthelberht reputedly did not compel conversion, this chapter of the progress of Christianity was far more about tribal identity and allegiance embodied in communal life and custom than it was in a personal assent to a new belief system.

If this was the birth of the British expression of Christendom, this relationship between Christianity, the state/rulers and wider culture has seen many different phases where it has successfully adapted its way through absolute monarchy, the emergence of parliamentary democracy and empire into the post-colonial reconstruction of national identity in the latter part of the twentieth century. However, many commentators have identified the beginning of the end as the decline in church attendance and the practice of faith combining with other social forces to erode this long-standing cultural consensus.

> Post-Christendom is the culture that emerges as the Christian faith loses coherence within a society that has been definitively shaped by the Christian story and as the institutions that have been developed to express Christian convictions decline in influence.[16]

Post-Christendom does not, of course, mean that every evidence of Christendom has disappeared, only that it is passing as received ways of

---

15 Andrew F. Walls, 'Ecumenical Missiology in Anabaptist Perspective', *Mission Focus: Annual Review* 13 (2005), p. 192; Jehu J. Hanciles, *Beyond Christendom*, Maryknoll: Orbis Books, 2008, pp. 86–7.

16 Stuart Murray, *Post-Christendom*, Carlisle: Paternoster, 2004, p. 19.

thinking and doing are dissolved or replaced by new ones that are no longer rooted within the Christian tradition. Indeed, Britain will always have a cultural heritage that is thoroughly Christian, and, in that sense, however small the believing community becomes, the country will never return to a pre-Christian state. Christianity, for good or ill, will always be in its past.

The operative question for a local church now is about understanding the cultural context in which we are presently living. That Christendom is still a present reality in contemporary Britain is undeniable. An established Church with the monarch as its 'Supreme Governor' is the highest-profile example of its institutional expression, while the deeply embedded and widely held expression of a cultural form of Christianity is the most popular expression.

Some see the major shifts that have taken place within British culture over the last half-century as the fruit of a gradual and inexorable demise that 'led to a headlong collapse in the late twentieth century. [That is] ... surely terminal and irreversible.'[17] Others see these changes as Christianity redefining once more what 'Christian Britain' means, with ideas of the good life and the common good still drawing heavily on the Christian tradition.[18] This was evidenced in Danny Boyle's use of Christian imagery and the 'idea of building Jerusalem' in the opening ceremony of the 2012 Olympic Games in London, as it was five months earlier in a speech given by the Queen at Lambeth Palace to mark her Diamond Jubilee on 15 February 2012. What she said clearly illustrates that a redefining process of the role of the established Church and the expression of Christendom it embodies is at work. She began by expressing the desire to

> pay tribute to the particular mission of Christianity and the general value of faith in this country.
>
> ... Our religions provide critical guidance for the way we live our lives, and for the way in which we treat each other. Many of the values and ideas we take for granted in this and other countries originate in the ancient wisdom of our traditions. Even the concept of a Jubilee is rooted in the Bible.
>
> Here at Lambeth Palace we should remind ourselves of the significant position of the Church of England in our nation's life. The concept of our established Church is occasionally misunderstood and, I believe, commonly under-appreciated. Its role is not to defend Anglicanism to

---

17 Murray, *Post-Christendom*, p. 178.

18 Jane Garnett et al. (eds), *Redefining Christian Britain: Post 1945 Perspectives*, London: SCM Press, 2006.

the exclusion of other religions. Instead, the Church has a duty to protect the free practice of all faiths in this country.

It certainly provides an identity and spiritual dimension for its own many adherents. But also, gently and assuredly, the Church of England has created an environment for other faith communities and indeed people of no faith to live freely. Woven into the fabric of this country, the Church has helped to build a better society – more and more in active co-operation for the common good with those of other faiths.[19]

Recognizing the growth of Christianity in the global South and the impact on countries like Great Britain of large numbers of economic and political migrants, Philip Jenkins suggests the emergence of a 'new Christendom', not in the sense of a rebirth of a political entity of the past, but rather in the identity of being 'Christian' that expresses a primary allegiance that surpasses nationality. The growth of black and minority ethnic churches has already been noted above. Jehu Hanciles explores this phenomenon further and suggests that Jenkins is imprisoned by unhelpful Western categories and constructs that do not provide a secure basis for properly understanding non-Western Christian realities. Global Christianity is very different from the West yet, through migration, will affect Western societies like the UK. He argues that Christianity from the South embodies a complex interplay between the global and the local, domination and weakness, paternalism and marginalization, with dynamics that make its organizational 'margins' and 'centre' fluid and interchangeable. With every migrant seen as a missionary it is clear that mission is church-based, while relative economic poverty and political powerlessness set them apart from the structures of social dominance or control. He sees the emergence of this non-Western missionary movement in the context of global migratory flow as 'a major turning point in the history of Christianity'.[20]

While inward migration from the global South disproportionately affects urban areas, there are few parts of present-day Britain that are not touched by it in some way or another. Welcoming migrants and establishing relationships with minority ethnic congregations are key factors in local churches responding to this continuing cultural shift. Developing patterns of co-working with culturally different congregations is a challenge to be risen to, as will be the issue of British-born children in

---

19 http://www.royal.gov.uk/LatestNewsandDiary/Speechesandarticles/2012/TheQueensspeechatLambethpalace15February2012.aspx.

20 Philip Jenkins, *The Next Christendom*, Oxford: Oxford University Press, 2007; Hanciles, *Beyond Christendom*, pp. 383–6, 391.

ethnically mono-cultural congregations raised in a multi-cultural context with developing expectations that are different from their parents'.

Secular Britain

The place of Christian faith in public life has increasingly become a contentious issue in contemporary Britain. Should the state fund 'faith-based' schools, especially those that are perceived to have a theologically conservative foundation that calls into question the integrity of the teaching of science, the children's integration into wider society or the proselytizing of vulnerable young people? Or again, in the workplace can Christians wear a cross at an airline check-in desk, be required as a registrar to officiate at civil partnerships or as a sex therapist be required to work with gay or lesbian couples experiencing sexual dysfunction?[21]

The present situation in the UK is not straightforward for a number of reasons. However, to understand the situation accurately is to be in a better position to engage with it positively and appropriately. At its core much of the present situation centres on what is meant by the idea of 'secular Britain', however this might be expressed. In essence, this seemingly simple term emerges from several different cultural narratives where it is variously deployed as a loose descriptor to aid contemporary social commentary, as a rhetorical totem around which to marshal support or a precise academic concept that seeks to analyse and interpret cultural trends and realities. Common for each of these narratives is the uncoupling of the relationship of the Church and Christian faith with wider society.

The most common encounter with ideas of 'secular Britain' is through the media. In many ways Britain is among the most secularized societies,[22] and the media, understanding itself as secular, seeks to embody this. Yet this is only part of the story, and the media is not so proficient at properly

---

21 'Two thirds oppose state aided faith schools', *Guardian*, 23 August 2005; Nadia Eweida was sent home from her job as a BA check-in clerk at Heathrow, 'BA "wrong" to ban Christian from wearing cross because it "plays into extremists' hands"', *Daily Telegraph*, 10 January 2010; Registrar Lilian Ladele was disciplined by Islington Borough Council for refusing to conduct civil partnership ceremonies, 'Christian registrar to appeal over same-sex ceremonies', *Guardian*, 2 November 2009; Gary McFarlane was sacked by Relate for refusing to give sex therapy counselling to practising homosexuals, 'Counsellor's bid to appeal sacking over refusal to help homosexuals dismissed', *Daily Telegraph*, 29 April 2010.

22 Philip S. Gorski et al. (eds), *The Post-Secular in Question*, New York: New York University Press, 2012, p. 256.

reflecting this other dimension of the nation's life. The country still has an established Church, presided over by the head of state, which provides the symbolic, liturgical backdrop that affirms the place and cultural influence of religion on the nation at large. For example, the wedding of Prince William and Kate Middleton at Westminster Abbey in April 2011 was one of the most watched UK TV broadcasts of all time, and, across all platforms globally, is reputed to be one of the most viewed religious services in history. Rowan Williams, when Archbishop of Canterbury, indicated that while the disestablishment of the Church of England would be 'by no means the end of the world', if pressed to consider it by those wanting to push Christianity into a purely private sphere he admitted, 'I think I'd be bloody-minded and say, "Well, not on that basis."'[23] The present situation is further complicated by an ongoing revision of the role by the royal family themselves. This began with Prince Charles' expressed intention to reinterpret the papal designation of Henry VIII as 'Defender of the Faith', still present on coinage in the form of the 'DF', as 'defender of faiths'.[24] The speech of the Queen at her Diamond Jubilee cited above extends this to the Church of England itself as she places upon it 'a duty to protect the free practice of all faiths in this country'.

Theological and ecclesiological illiteracy within the media also further confuses the situation. The uncritical importation of American ideas of the separation of church and state betrays little understanding of British history and culture, while the portrayal of mainstream conservative or bizarre fundamentalist churches from the United States is not helpful in educating a UK audience about the nature of the churches within these shores.

Media portrayal of any issue is always enhanced if it can be presented according to a pre-established template with protagonists and antagonists. In regard to 'secular Britain', such characters are readily available and can be variously deployed according to the story being told. On the one side are those believers who want the state to continue to embody and uphold the inherited values and morality of our shared Christian tradition. Deviation from these is a form of moral slippage that is to be resisted. 'Secular Britain' is viewed in a predominantly negative light. On the other side are the secularists, who, as a matter of principle, want faith in general and Christianity in particular to be actively removed and barred from the public square. The organization *Christian Voice* would be an

---

23 'Interview: Rowan Williams', *New Statesman*, 18 December 2008.
24 'Prince Charles to be known as Defender of Faith', *Daily Telegraph*, 13 November 2008.

example of the former, with its stated mission to 'uphold Christianity as the Faith of the United Kingdom, to be a voice for Biblical values in law and public policy, and to defend and support traditional family life',[25] while the Richard Dawkins Foundation for Reason and Science would be illustrative of the latter, with its objective to 'support scientific education, critical thinking and evidence-based understanding of the natural world in the quest to overcome religious fundamentalism, superstition, intolerance and suffering'.[26] In this adversarial representation of the struggle around the nature of British society, it is important to recognize how this excludes more moderate voices as the intensity of conflict makes for a better story. Consciously or unconsciously the media's own secular nature most often also provides the framework of meaning through which this is viewed.

Sitting behind and informing more popular portrayals of the relationship between faith and wider society is the sociology of religion. Under the influence of key nineteenth-century thinkers such as Émile Durkheim, Max Weber and Karl Marx, the gradual decline and death of religion has been anticipated. In summary form, as societies modernized, life became more secure and a rational understanding and appreciation of life spread through education, so, successively, religion would lose its functions in wider society and ultimately wither away as the privatized preoccupation of a dwindling remnant of believers. Classic secularization theory was further developed in the 1960s–70s and became the predominant narrative by which to interpret the decline of the churches in the Western world.

More recently the hegemony of this understanding has come under question. A long-time proponent of secularization, Peter Berger, revised his position and wrote in his book *Desecularization*, 'My point is that the assumption that we live in a secularized world is false.'[27] In his revised understanding he argued that secularization as a concept was only partially true in Western Europe and westernized countries, while in the rest of the world it appears wholly inaccurate. The 'American exception' had long been identified by sociologists, but increasingly they highlight the resilient nature of religion, while more popular treatments like that of journalists John Micklethwait and Adrian Wooldridge can proclaim that *God is Back*.[28] This is not to say that some form of secularization of British society has not happened; only that the situation is far from being as

---

25 www.christianvoice.org.uk.

26 www.richarddawkinsfoundation.org.

27 Peter Berger (ed.), *Desecularization: Resurgent Religion and World Politics*, Grand Rapids: Eerdmans, 1999, p. 2.

28 John Micklethwait and Adrian Wooldridge, *God is Back: How the Global Rise of Faith is Changing the World*, London: Allen Lane, 2009.

simple as had previously been maintained, and a revision of the theory of secularization is necessary to account for this.[29]

The ideas of German sociologist and atheist Jürgen Habermas with regard to what he terms a 'post-secular society' are also worth noting, not least because of the flurry of writing they have initiated within the sociology of religion, but also because of their implications for Christian engagement in the public square. Having previously followed the line of classic secularization theory, in the immediate aftermath of the terrorist atrocities of 9/11 Habermas argued for a vision of 'democratically enlightened common sense' that enabled the full engagement of religious believers in the life of a liberal and secular state.

> [T]he expression 'post-secular' is not a genealogical but a sociological predicate. I use this expression to describe modern societies that have to reckon with the continuing existence of religious groups and the continuing relevance of the different religious traditions, even if the societies themselves are largely secularized.[30]

For the religious believer this implies a recognition and acceptance of a liberal, pluralistic society, while secularists 'must be able to meet their religious fellow citizens as equals'.[31]

As Habermas has developed his ideas, he argues that inclusive democracies have to discover ways in which both secular and religious voices can contribute to civic and political life. More than mere participation, he explores the potential for a positive and constructive contribution. A dialogue with the then Cardinal Ratzinger in 2004 led Habermas to his observation of how the Enlightenment project of modernization had 'gone somewhat awry' in its globalized economic markets and to look at how religious values might provide a potential pathway to reorientate society towards economic and social justice.[32] Then, in a 2007 debate with the Jesuit School for Philosophy in Munich, he explored the relationship between faith and reason in a post-secular age and where secular society

---

29 For examples of neo-secularization theory, see Pippa Norris and Ronald Inglehart, *Sacred and Secular: Religion and Politics Worldwide*, New York: Oxford University Press, 2011; David Martin, *On Secularization: Towards a Revised General Theory*, Aldershot: Ashgate, 2005; and Rob Warner, *Secularization and Its Discontents*, London: Continuum, 2010.

30 Eduardo Mendieta, *A Postsecular World Society? An Interview with Jürgen Habermas*, http://www.csudh.edu/dearhabermas/habermas11.htm.

31 Jürgen Habermas, 'Secularism's Crisis of Faith', *New Perspectives Quarterly* 25 (2008), p. 29.

32 Gorski, *Post-Secular*, pp. 254–5.

is lacking, under the title *An Awareness of What is Missing*.[33] In the post-secular society advocated by Habermas, the democratic state must beware of pre-emptively cutting itself off from those religious voices that share the scarce resources that enable it to generate meaning, shape identity and articulate moral sensitivity.[34]

Missiologically speaking it is vitally important properly to understand the nature of 'secular Britain'. To accept the narratives frequently repeated within the media or in classic secularization theory would be to become variously subject to a world-view that is inappropriately imposed from the United States, ideologically driven by anti-religionists or is based on a sociological analysis and understanding that is out of date. While there is important mission work to be conducted on the margins of society, the insights of Berger and Habermas provide significant support for the confident reframing of a Christian missional engagement with the centre and core of our shared life in secular Britain. This is not to seek a resurrection of a position of privileged access, but rather a participation as equals on the basis of the recognition of what Christian communities have to contribute to the life of wider society.

Zygmunt Bauman and 'liquid modernity'

In looking to understand the wider cultural context within which all of these changes are occurring, the almost universally accepted point of reference for a generation has been the commentary of postmodernism. This has proven to be a fruitful engagement as Christian thinkers and practitioners alike have been forced to engage with postmodern themes such as pluralism, relativism and subjectivism, as they have grappled with issues of deconstruction, power and metanarratives. However, the engagement has often been little more than at the level of 'bumper sticker' sloganeering, with the notion of postmodernism, as James Smith shrewdly observes, 'invoked as both poison and cure within the contemporary church'.[35] Unfortunately this engagement has frequently led to postmodern theorists being misunderstood and their ideas misapplied to Christian thinking, as Smith illustrates with Lyotard's oft-quoted stance of 'incredulity towards metanarratives'. This is frequently applied to all 'big stories' on the basis

---

33 Jürgen Habermas et al., *An Awareness of What is Missing*, Cambridge: Polity, 2010.

34 Habermas, 'Crisis of Faith', p. 29.

35 James K. A. Smith, *Who's Afraid of Postmodernism? Taking Derrida, Lyotard and Foucault to Church*, Grand Rapids: Baker, 2006, p. 18.

of their scope and the grand claims and universal pretensions they express. Christianity is then identified as falling prey to this postmodern expression of scepticism. However, this is to fail to understand the kind of 'modern' metanarratives that Lyotard has in view. It is those that are the product of the Enlightenment and depend upon an appeal to universal reason that he has in mind. The subject of Lyotard's incredulity is the modern rationalism and scientific naturalism, which claim to be demonstrable by reason alone, not a pre-modern proclamation of good news, which requires a response of faith.[36]

In looking to understand the dynamics at work in contemporary British culture, the time has come to move on from talking about postmodernism, as its usefulness is increasingly limited. Over-use alongside the misapplication of its insights and misattribution of any 'new' cultural phenomenon as 'postmodern' have significantly compromised its ability to communicate ideas through the confusing cacophony that surrounds it. More serious critiques also question whether it remains 'fit for purpose'. Terry Eagleton, for example, explores its fallacies and contradictions in his *Illusions of Postmodernism*,[37] while key sociological thinkers like Zygmunt Bauman have chosen to distance themselves from the subject for which they were previously formative thinkers.[38] Bauman identifies three reasons for this. First, that 'postmodern' was only a stop-gap choice of concept that signalled things were changing and were quite unlike what had gone before, but, while pointing in the right direction had quickly outlived its usefulness. Second, the concept was flawed from the beginning in that, despite a number of attempts to qualify it, if something is 'postX' it means the state of things after X has gone, and patently modernity has not been consigned to history. Alternative terms like 'late modernity' are equally flawed in that they presume a closure that remains in the future. Third, as a concept it was limiting, not least because it unhelpfully defined itself against modernity and was prone to restricting itself to rearranging plus and minus signs while undermining the effort to grasp the novelty of the present situation; 'the umbilical cord had to be cut. Symbolically this

---

36 Smith, *Postmodernism*, pp. 64–5.

37 Terry Eagleton, *The Illusions of Postmodernism*, Oxford: Blackwell, 2007, pp. 93–135.

38 Milena Yakimova, 'A Postmodern Grid of the Worldmap? An Interview with Zygmunt Bauman', *Eurozine*, 8 November 2002. Bauman had previously written *Intimations of Postmodernity* (London: Routledge, 1992), *Postmodern Ethics* (Cambridge, MA: Blackwell, 1993), *Life in Fragment: Essays in Postmodern Morality* (Cambridge, MA: Blackwell, 1995), and *Postmodernity and its Discontents* (New York: New York University Press, 1997).

meant the need to abandon the terminology ... that limited the freedom of thought necessary to have it done.'[39]

Bauman's metaphor of choice to help understand the present-day state of affairs is 'liquid modernity'.

> Fluids travel easily. They 'flow', 'spill', 'run out', 'splash', 'pour over', 'leak', 'flood', 'spray', 'drip', 'seep', 'ooze'; unlike solids, they are not easily stopped – they pass around some obstacles, dissolve some others and bore or soak their way through others still. From the meeting with solids they emerge unscathed, while the solids they have met, if they stay solid, are changed – get moist or drenched.[40]

He notes that liquids are constantly ready or prone to change shape under the weakest of stresses and that the notion of flow is a defining characteristic. As a consequence, any description of a fluid has to be understood as merely a snapshot.[41]

> Liquid modern is a society in which the conditions under which members act change faster than it takes the ways of acting to consolidate into habits and routines ... Liquid life ... cannot keep its shape or stay on course for long ... Extrapolating from past events to predict future trends becomes ever more risky.[42]

Lives lived in this liquid modern world are increasingly precarious, with jobs no longer being for life, communities lacking cohesion and human relationships rarely resulting in permanent bonds between family, friends, neighbours or lovers. Bauman believes that this unprecedented context presents individuals in the 'developed' world with five challenges that have never previously been encountered:

1 Social forms can no longer keep their shape for long and serve as points of reference and provide a framework for life.
2 Power and politics are separating, leaving the nation-state often impotent to act on behalf of its citizens.
3 A loss of community as society moves from structured relationships to a random network of connections and disconnections and an infinite number of potential permutations.

---

39 Yakimova, 'Postmodern Grid', p. 2.
40 Zygmunt Bauman, *Liquid Modernity*, London: Polity, 2000, p. 2.
41 Yakimova, 'Postmodern Grid', p. 3.
42 Zygmunt Bauman, *Liquid Life*, London: Polity, 2005, p. 1.

4 A collapse of long-term thinking, planning and acting as the speed of change leads to a swift forgetting of outdated information and fast ageing habits.

5 Individuals having responsibility for resolving the quandaries generated by their own life choices in volatile and changing circumstances.[43]

Bauman's exploration of the changing face of human relationships is illustrative of the impact of the fluid nature of contemporary life. While romance and relationship pepper the mass culture through the movies, pop music, TV and paperback fiction, the explosion of online dating, relationship counselling and agony aunts seems to indicate a hunger for relationship and a compulsion to pursue it. It is easy to conclude from empirical data that people are strongly seeking friendships, bonds, togetherness and community. Bauman, however, questions whether the evidence points in another direction: 'Are they indeed after relationships that hold, as they say they are, or do they, more than anything else, desire relationships to be light and loose ...?'[44] He observes that changes in the language that is used and the means of pursuing relationships beg some interesting questions. So it is that relating and relationships morph to connecting and being connected, kinship and partnership to networks and being in touch. 'Those who stay apart, mobiles allow to get in touch. Those who get in touch, mobiles permit to stay apart ... Virtual proximity defuses the pressure that non-virtual closeness is in the habit of exerting.'[45] Virtual relationships are just that, not quite the real thing. Easy to enter into, easy to dispose of by pressing the delete button, they become another object of consumption.

In an era experiencing such a momentous cultural shift, how we understand the nature of church is vitally important to inform how culture is engaged with, and the extent to which its external forces should be allowed to shape the Christian community and when they should be resisted. An early speculative attempt to imagine what such a church might look like is Pete Ward's *Liquid Church*.[46] He argued unashamedly that the Church should take consumer society more seriously and transition itself from a twentieth-century focus on meeting people's needs, which has its roots in the therapeutic disciplines and self-help movement, to stimulating their desires, as choice in a consumer society is always driven by desire. Regulated by the Word of God and exercised with integrity and authenticity,

---

43 Zygmunt Bauman, *Liquid Times*, London: Polity, 2007, pp. 1–4.

44 Zygmunt Bauman, *Liquid Love*, London: Polity, 2003, p. ix.

45 Bauman, *Liquid Love*, pp. 60–4.

46 Pete Ward, *Liquid Church*, Carlisle: Paternoster, 2002.

a *liquid church* inhabits a new way of being where congregations are supplanted by networks of connection, community is built around social media, and an altogether more fluid expression of church emerges.[47] While accepting that *solid church* will also remain in a liquid culture, albeit in a modified form, he explores the idea of *perichoresis* (mutual indwelling and participation) and wonders whether the flow of relationship within a *Liquid Trinity* might be an empowering and inspirational idea for worship and mission that indwells and participates in the life of God.[48]

For all the strengths and stimulating insights of Ward's ecclesiological dream, the question to be asked is whether it is a *liquid church* or a *church for a liquid world* that is the most appropriate response. A church for a liquid world would be no less a paradigm shift, just a different one. At the heart of the Christian faith is something abiding, unchanging and eternal, rooted in a saviour who is the same 'yesterday, today and for ever'. Indeed, the metaphors used of the church in the New Testament have substance and physicality in them. Pre-eminently the Church is the 'body of Christ'. This re-incarnation is about fleshly, coherent substance, physically connected together into one body. Or again, Paul's vision in Ephesians 2.21–22 of believers being built together into a temple in which God lives by his Spirit is structured, solid and robust. Bauman's exposition of his metaphor is helpful here. Solids can exist in liquid culture though they will not remain unaffected by it as it reshapes by flowing around them or dissolving, boring or soaking its way through them. Presumably, a body can also be immersed in this liquid culture; it might also then learn to swim.

In a fluid world, a church that has substance and physicality faces new challenges. It must not fear or resist the reshaping action of the culture on its life and practice. Fidelity to the gospel does not demand an immovably conservative attitude that seeks to preserve at any cost the institutions and patterns of corporate life that express it. Rather, what is required is an openness to discover appropriate patterns of life and organization that enable Christians to live the Christian life together with authenticity and integrity. Openness to continual change, to creatively shaping and reshaping the life of a congregation or the forms of church then become the hallmarks of a church fit for purpose in liquid modernity.

---

47 Ward, *Liquid Church*, pp. 86–98.
48 Ward, *Liquid Church*, pp. 25, 53–4.

21

Mission and Evangelism

Around eighty members of the congregation had turned out, midweek, for a special evening looking at their mission and evangelism. I was acting as an outside consultant-cum-facilitator, and, in small groups, they were looking at different mission activities and seeking to establish how important they were as priorities and how effective they were as a church at engaging in them. The larger the discrepancy that they identified between these two perspectives, the greater was their perceived weakness in the area. Their response mirrored that which I had frequently seen before: the biggest gap was in the area of evangelism.

If the truth be told, the very thought of evangelism strikes terror into the heart as visions of door-knocking, handing out tracts on the high street or intense, fiery-eyed preachers come to mind. If Christian 'witness' is hard enough on its own – living lives in conformity with Christ and embracing spontaneous conversational opportunities to share one's faith – then the altogether more planned and deliberate activity of evangelism stands little chance. It is no surprise therefore that volunteers for a church's outreach programme can be even smaller than the numbers attending the weekly prayer meeting.

Evangelism as intentional activity

So what is evangelism? It is important to know what we are talking about, and the following definitions are helpful. The landmark Church of England report, *Towards the Conversion of England*, stated in 1945:

> To evangelise is so to present Jesus Christ in the power of the Holy Spirit, that men shall come to put their trust in God through him, to accept him as their Saviour, and serve him as their King in the fellowship of his church.[1]

---

1 William Temple, *Towards the Conversion of England*, London: Press and Publication Dept. of the Church of England, 1945, p. 1.

While the South African missiologist David Bosch presents a rather fuller statement:

> Evangelism is the core, heart, or center of mission; it consists in the proclamation of salvation in Christ to nonbelievers, in announcing forgiveness of sins, in calling people to repentance and faith in Christ, in inviting them to become living members of Christ's earthly community and to begin a life in the power of the Holy Spirit.[2]

Evangelism is, then, that intentional activity that has the aim of bringing people into a living relationship with God through the saving work of Jesus Christ, in the power of the Holy Spirit.

It is no surprise therefore that when local churches in Britain have mobilized themselves for evangelism over the last fifty years, it has been the more benign initiatives that have been most fully embraced. The stadium evangelism of a Billy Graham or a Luis Palau has enabled church members to take their friends and family, who are not believers, to hear a great preacher and be presented with an invitation to make a commitment; while courses like Alpha and Christianity Explored have provided the opportunity for those on the fringe of a church's list of contacts to have the space to look more closely at what believing in Jesus is all about over an extended period of time.

In the twenty-first century, things are not what they were. Stadiums are much harder to fill these days, and when they are, the focus is more on gatherings to inspire the committed rather than to reach the lost. Alpha too appears to have 'peaked' as a strategy, with many churches reporting how difficult it has become to recruit a new group of participants. As for the keen believers on the evangelism committee, they are finding that many shopping centres won't allow them inside any more, alongside which 'door to door' work is increasingly unwelcome as home owners don't want their personal space and time invaded.

All this is hardly surprising. The mid-twentieth century saw the Church still riding the high-water mark of Christianity in these shores. The evangelical revival of the eighteenth century and the expansion of the Church during the Victorian years meant that the total number of worshippers in Britain only started to begin to decline in the 1930s. Christianity was a central part of the fabric of our society from the pomp of state occasions through to the grassroots of every local community.

---

2 David Bosch, 'Evangelism: Theological Currents and Cross-currents', *International Bulletin of Missionary Research* 11.3 (July 1987), pp. 98–103.

Times change. Where a third of children were in Sunday school then, only one in twenty-five had anything to do with church at the turn of the century. Rather than the Church being portrayed as a pillar of society, the fundamentalist atheists have set a very different tone. Theological illiteracy in the media has only compounded this to leave many deeply suspicious of the Church and its motives.

Understanding this present context is vitally important for us as, in evangelism, context is everything. As the context changes, so our received patterns of evangelism have become less fruitful. We need to look again at what we do in the light of this, if we are to have any chance of understanding what it means to evangelize in the twenty-first century. The place to start is paying attention to the context around us. Leonard Sweet makes the observation that Jesus taught his disciples the importance of reading the signs of the times, and concludes, 'evangelism is the art and science of "paying attention". Evangelism is more pay attention than attract attention. The best evangelists are not the attention-getters, but attention givers.'[3]

An evangelistically engaged church needs to be alive to the culture around them. How is it changing? What are its expressed needs, its fears and anxieties? What does it invest in as of value? Where does it locate hope and aspiration, and in what does it find fulfilment? What is longed after and why? If God loves people and his omniscience is not aloof, detached or remote, then he is not unmoved by the experience of life that both challenges and enriches those he has created. It is no coincidence, then, that the apostle Paul should express his conviction to the church in Rome that it should 'rejoice with those who rejoice, [and] weep with those who weep' (Rom. 12.15–16, NRSV). Such contextual intelligence is at the heart of authentic Christian discipleship. Some have even understood this to imply a sacramental dimension to the churches' evangelism. In empathetically participating in the life of the community of which it is a part, a congregation discovers the omnipresent God already there and sharing the joy and sorrow of their neighbours. As relationships are built, Kingdom values embodied and gospel truth shared, grace is active – the sacrament of evangelism.[4]

---

3 Leonard Sweet, 'Pay Attention: Every Bush is Burning! The Semiotics of Evangelism', *Review and Expositor* 105 (Fall 2008), pp. 595–605.

4 See Jerry Root and Stan Guthrie, *The Sacrament of Evangelism*, Chicago: Moody Press, 2011, pp. 14–16, for another brief exploration of this idea.

Evangelism locally

All of this has implications for a local congregation, and there are issues that it would be wise to address. First, we need to dispel the myth that evangelism is the responsibility of just a few in each congregation. Walking by Lake Galilee, Jesus called out to Simon Peter and Andrew, 'Come, follow me and I will send you out to fish for people' (Matt. 4.19, TNIV). Throughout his ministry, it is clear that, for Jesus, this was an integral part of everyone's discipleship, climaxing in the Great Commission to go and make disciples in Matthew 28.18–20.

The London Institute of Contemporary Christianity (LICC) has it right with their Imagine project. What we need is 'whole-life disciple-making churches'. We need our congregations to be full of believers, who understand what it is to live their daily lives according to the values of the Kingdom and are confident and articulate with regard to the good news itself. This is not about learning by rote the four spiritual laws of Evangelism Explosion or by completing a course of training that enables all participants to manipulate any conversation into one about Christ. Rather, it is about being immersed in what Jesus taught: 'The Kingdom of God is to hand; you can reach out and touch it, turn your life around and believe the good news.'

We need to know for ourselves what it means to live in this new world that is animated by a generosity of life, a graciousness of attitude, a loving and valuing of people, which is typified by forgiveness, hospitality and peacefulness. When we know this for ourselves, we will have half a chance of living it and explaining it to others. 'Do you not realize that God's kindness is meant to lead you to repentance?' (Rom. 2.4–5, NRSV).

Second, we need to grasp more adequately how the Holy Spirit is at work in contemporary Britain. The landmark work of John Finney in the early 1990s, in his book *Finding Faith Today*,[5] has been corroborated more recently through the work of the Spiritual Journeys initiative.[6] Both testify to the experience of new believers, who, when they tell the story of how they came to faith, reveal that it was the influence of a friend, a family member or a colleague that was key in their journey to faith in Christ. This is why it is so important for every believer to be engaged in evangelism, living the life of the Kingdom as well as being able to articulate it.

Third, local churches need to understand how Kingdom values should inform the part they play in their local community. Through their corpor-

5 John Finney, *Finding Faith Today*, Swindon: Bible Society, 1992.
6 www.spiritualjourneys.org.uk.

ate life together, as well as through their personal lives, their neighbours need to be able to reach out and touch the reality of the Kingdom of God. Street Pastors is a great example of this, as is the work of the churches in London on gun and knife crime. Elsewhere, it might be the provision of a toddler group or a senior citizens' lunch club. Local churches must continually ask themselves, 'What does it mean to embody Kingdom values in our community?' However, it is also vital to remember that we do these things because this is being true to our faith and embodying these values in an authentic lifestyle, not as pre-evangelistic incentives for the non-believer.

Churches also need to know how to 'name the name' and proclaim the good news in ways that are appropriate for where we are. Inner-city Manchester will be different from the Fens of Cambridgeshire or the commuter communities of Surrey and Sussex. As the Micah Network's statement on Integral Mission makes clear:

> It is not simply that evangelism and social involvement are to be done alongside each other. Rather … our proclamation has social consequences as we call people to love and repentance in all areas of life. And our social involvement has evangelistic consequences as we bear witness to the transforming grace of Jesus Christ. If we ignore the world we betray the word of God which sends us out to serve the world. If we ignore the word of God we have nothing to bring to the world.[7]

Where, in the past, the vast majority of people knew and understood what Christianity is all about, this is no longer the case. How a congregation engages with the fringe members of its community will need to be different for those who used to belong to church, but don't any more; and then different again for those who have never belonged to a church; or, indeed, have their roots in a different religious tradition altogether. For most of our lifetimes we have only concentrated on our church fringe or those who have lapsed. But as these groups continue to get smaller we must learn how to extend our evangelistic reach. So what is the essence of the good news of the Kingdom that Jesus brought? What is the gospel? While there are numerous ways it could be expressed, I would express it in the following terms:

> God loves people, wants the best for us and desires to live in relationship with us. The life, death and resurrection of Jesus make this a possibility.

---

7 See www.micahnetwork.org/sites/default/files/doc/page/mn_integral_mission_declaration_en.pdf.

Jim Currin expresses this in a trinitarian form:

> God's love, forgiveness and new life is ... a framework for explaining the gospel:
>
> • God the Father: who loved and loves us
> • God the Son: Jesus who died on the cross so that we can receive forgiveness
> • God the Holy Spirit: who empowers and sustains our new life in Christ.[8]

Then, as Lesslie Newbigin argued, the reception of the gospel brings about a conversion of mind, behaviour and belonging as it impacts the believer's understanding, ethics and relationship with the body of Christ.[9]

If evangelism is an intentional activity with this trajectory in view, how we practise this activity is vitally important. Perhaps now, more than ever, the qualities of authenticity, transparency and respect need both to shape and guard how we engage in proclaiming the gospel.

• Authenticity is about 'what you see is what you get'; living the faith and proclaiming the faith are of one piece.
• Transparency means being upfront about what is being done. Evangelistic events masquerading as something else won't do. Christians live as people of the light. World Cup and Olympic events, Fun Days, BBQs and concerts that land the unsuspecting participant in the middle of an evangelistic strategy are manipulative and merely serve to confirm the world's worst fears about the Church.
• Respect for each person means giving them the space to choose to follow Jesus or to choose not to. It means that evangelism should not coerce, brow-beat or in any way play with the emotions of those who are addressed with the gospel. Freedom to choose is a God-given gift that we have no right to obstruct or take away.

Bearing these things in mind, churches will do well to be careful not to rely on 'off-the-shelf' evangelistic packages that can so easily let a congregation out of their own responsibility. Not to mention the fact that they often fall into the trap of updating the strategies of a time that is rapidly

---

8 Jim Currin, *Sharing Faith the Jesus Way*, Abingdon: BRF, 2011, pp. 64–5.

9 Gordon T. Smith, 'Conversion and Redemption', in Gerald R. McDermott (ed.), *The Oxford Handbook of Evangelical Theology*, Oxford: Oxford University Press, 2011, pp. 209–21.

passing, or that they are particularly attuned to North America rather than to our own situation.

Ethical evangelism

One of the more refreshing recent developments in discussions about evangelism has been the emergence of new thinking about ethics. How do we identify what are appropriate and inappropriate strategies? Elmer John Thiessen, a Canadian Mennonite, charts fifteen criteria to distinguish between ethical and unethical proselytizing. These range through the ruling out of all forms of coercion – physical, psychological and social – to respect for the dignity, identity and personal care of the proselytizee. He also considers the ethical character of the evangelist – truthfulness, humility, tolerance and motivation – before completing his list with the golden rule, 'So in everything, do to others what you would have them do to you, for this sums up the Law and the Prophets' (Matt 7.12, NIV).[10]

In the UK in 2009, the Christian Muslim Forum took exactly this line, as they discussed what might be considered acceptable guidelines for good practice in witnessing to one another's communities. A religiously free society, which allows individuals to convert from one religion to another, clearly would benefit from such an understanding. Not wishing to compromise the Christian commitment to evangelism or the Muslim practice of Da'wah (invitation to Islam), the Forum outlined the following guidelines:

> The Christian Muslim Forum offers the following suggestions that, we hope, will equip Christians and Muslims (and others) to share their faith with integrity and compassion for those they meet.
>
> 1 We bear witness to, and proclaim our faith not only through words but through our attitudes, actions and lifestyles.
> 2 We cannot convert people, only God can do that. In our language and methods we should recognize that people's choice of faith is primarily a matter between themselves and God.
> 3 Sharing our faith should never be coercive; this is especially important when working with children, young people and vulnerable adults. Everyone should have the choice to accept or reject the message we proclaim and we will accept people's choices without resentment.

10 Elmer John Thiessen, *The Ethics of Evangelism: A Philosophical Defence of Proselytizing and Persuasion*, Downers Grove: InterVarsity Press, 2011.

4 Whilst we might care for people in need or who are facing personal crises, we should never manipulate these situations in order to gain a convert.

5 An invitation to convert should never be linked with financial, material or other inducements. It should be a decision of the heart and mind alone.

6 We will speak of our faith without demeaning or ridiculing the faiths of others.

7 We will speak clearly and honestly about our faith, even when that is uncomfortable or controversial.

8 We will be honest about our motivations for activities, and we will inform people when events will include the sharing of faith.

9 Whilst recognizing that either community will naturally rejoice with and support those who have chosen to join them, we will be sensitive to the loss that others may feel.

10 Whilst we may feel hurt when someone we know and love chooses to leave our faith, we will respect their decision and will not force them to stay or harass them afterwards.

Some have seen these guidelines as controversial. For those committed to building a multi-faith culture that prides itself in tolerance of and respect for different faith communities, to even contemplate proselytizing from one to the other is anathema. By contrast, those who deeply value the received Christian heritage of the United Kingdom view the growth of non-Christian religions, their place in the public square and their proselytizing of British citizens as evidence of the disintegration of Britain as a Christian country. However, the Christian Church will do well to recognize that a position of religious privilege does not really facilitate genuine religious freedom. Rather, it is always best expressed and best protected if it is universally applied. To that end, an understanding of appropriate ways in which religious communities can engage in proselytizing activities is much to be welcomed.

Evangelism in twenty-first-century Britain presents us with a new challenge as the country in which we live is presenting a new face to us, a context in which we must live the gospel and proclaim the gospel that we have never seen before. We need healthy churches that disciple their congregations well in Kingdom living and embody this in their communities. Then as we make the name of Jesus known we will continue to see women, men and young people entering a living relationship with Jesus. And there is nothing quite so special as accompanying someone on that journey.

22

Worship and Mission

What is the chief end of man?
Man's chief end is to glorify God and enjoy him forever.

The Westminster Catechism

'All authority in heaven and on earth has been given to me. Therefore go and make disciples of all nations, baptizing them in the name of the Father and of the Son and of the Holy Spirit, and teaching them to obey everything I have commanded you.'

Matthew 28.18–20, NIV

The relationship between worship and mission seemingly puts Christians on the horns of a dilemma: in the life of the local church, where does the priority lie? If, in Brunner's words, 'the church exists by mission as a fire exists by burning', then mission is critically important as it is the very life of the Church. Or again, if the priorities of Jesus' personal ministry were defined by the missional content of his Nazareth sermon, and his Great Commission at the end of his time on earth to his closest friends and co-workers was about disciple-making, does this not seal the matter? As one speaker said to his congregation, 'If mission is restricted to this life, and we have all eternity to worship God, maybe this gives us a clue!' With a world to serve and individuals to be brought to faith in Christ, devoting time to worship might appear somewhat self-indulgent. The missional activist can become very impatient with the time and resources that are poured into a congregation's life of worship. But then there seems to be something intrinsically wrong with worship taking second place to anything.

A phantom fork in the road

As the relationship between worship and mission begins to be explored, it is clear that it bears far more thinking about than might at first appear. The two are inextricably linked together, but the nature of that relationship is often poorly understood and often ill-expressed. This is further complicated by centuries of tradition, where mission has been at best marginal to church life or latterly seen as an optional programme to activate at various times and seasons. The result has been an underdeveloped missional dimension of worship, which has serious implications for the discipleship of believers and their participation in the *missio Dei*. Of course, where the relationship has found a more integrated life is among those evangelicals and pentecostalists who have used the worship service as a means of evangelism. Though this is not without its own complications, not least because it begs the question of who worship is for – the believer or the non-believer?

From the earliest time in the Christian story, worship and mission were yoked in partnership together. In André Resner's memorable phrase, to try and separate them is to discover 'ecclesiology's phantom fork in the road'.[1] They belong together. Consider:

- When Jesus issued the Great Commission to his disciples, it flowed out of a context of worship (Matt. 28.17).
- The birth of the Church on the day of Pentecost that resulted in three thousand responding to Peter's sermon took place in the context of worship (Acts 2.1–41).
- When Paul and Barnabas were called to be set apart for the work of mission at Antioch, it was during a time of worship (Acts 13.1–3).
- The Philippian jailor was evangelized in the context of hymn-singing and prayer by Paul and his companions (Acts 16.25–31).
- Paul, writing to the church at Corinth, clearly expected non-Christians to be present in the worshipping community (1 Cor. 14.22–25).

Further to this, the New Testament contains a much fuller understanding of the nature of worship than purely concentrating on explicit times of focused singing, praying and studying the Scriptures. Paul appeals to the believers in Rome to be 'living sacrifices' – clearly an inclusion of the whole of life – and this he considers their 'spiritual worship' (Rom. 12.1). The theologian Miroslav Volf integrates this into an understanding of worship that has two kinds of activities, 'adoration and action'.

> The sacrifice of praise and the sacrifice of good works are two fundamental aspects of the Christian way of being-in-the-world. They are at the same time the two constitutive elements of Christian worship:

---

1 André Resner, 'To Worship or to Evangelize?', *Restoration Quarterly* 36.2 (1994), p. 66.

authentic Christian worship takes place in a rhythm of adoration and action.[2]

This is important, as it locates missional action as an act of worship at the same time as ensuring a much fuller understanding of worship and how believers give glory to God. However, it also begs the question of how mission figures in the 'adoration' dimension of worship, which comprises the core activity of most local congregations in their weekly pattern of worship service.

The worship wars

What has consumed vast tracts of the Western Church with regard to worship over the last generation has been styled as the so-called 'worship wars'. While this has been focused on the introduction of contemporary music and 'worship songs' in the evangelical and charismatic churches, a similar impetus is also to be found in the regular revisions of liturgy into more contemporary forms and language, as well as the Roman Catholic Church's move towards the Mass being said in vernacular languages and, indeed, the revision of the Mass itself at the Second Vatican Council.

Because worship is at the centre of a believer's experience and devotion, it is hardly surprising that it evokes powerful reactions. 'What is the difference between an organist and a terrorist?', goes the rather over-used piece of pulpit humour, 'You can reason with a terrorist!' Behind the gross exaggeration of the caricature lie the experiences of intense and painful conflicts in local church life that have broken relationships and split congregations. Yet whatever the motives and gloss attributed to the proponents of contemporary or traditional worship, it would be disingenuous to imply the real conviction was anything less than a desire for God-centred worship that was undertaken for its own sake. What was at stake was presumed to be relevance: relevance for the rising generation within the Church, who desired worship that was more culturally attuned to their own tastes, and relevant, too, to those outside, who were perceived to be increasingly detached and alienated from the inherited traditions of the Church and its archaic form of language, dress and ritual.

Ultimately, neither contemporary nor traditional forms of worship are inherently missional in and of themselves. Both may be at root what

---

2 Miroslav Volf, 'Worship as Adoration and Action: Reflections of a Christian Way of Being-in-the-world', in D. A. Carson (ed.), *Worship: Adoration and Action*, Grand Rapids: Baker, 1996, p. 208.

Marva Dawn identifies as 'the false idolatry of personal taste',[3] expressions of a culture of consumerism that can dress themselves in different theological and ecclesiological justifications. While it could be forcibly argued that the desire to be more contemporary is intentionally outsider-focused and has as its objective reaching new people with the gospel and involving them in worship, this is not without danger. As the missional concern that sits beneath the presenting issues of form and content in the 'worship wars' is contextualization, it should be no surprise that the twin dangers of syncretism and irrelevance face every worshipping community as it shapes its life of worship.

Contemporary-styled worship is not merely a value-free means of communication that has no impact upon the worship itself. In a culture that is, for example, informal, individualistic, consumerist, subjectivist and experientialist, it would be naive not to realize that an uncritical adoption of a contemporary style would potentially warp the nature of worship itself. Alongside personal taste and the idolatry of self, Marva Dawn identifies how God is petitioned for instant solutions, and the place of excitement, charismatic personalities, power and success are accretions from contemporary culture that cause problems for Christian worship. In fact, she warns that worship cannot be too much like the surrounding culture, or it will be impossible for it to be the alternative, yet parallel society that God calls it to be.[4] It is an alternative community because, in Christ, it offers different ways to think and speak, to be and behave. Yet it also needs to be parallel to contemporary culture so that it is not so alternative as to be completely disconnected from its neighbours.

Dawn's 'alternative' and 'parallel' mirror the dangers of irrelevance and syncretism with the concept of contextualization and Andrew Walls' categories of the need for indigenization while holding on to pilgrim values. Worship must express itself in the language, understanding and customs of a culture, while at the same time offering a pilgrim critique, where that culture contradicts God's Kingdom and frustrates his mission.[5] In this sense, it embodies a prophetic edge. The vision of God's Kingdom reveals to worshippers a 'still more excellent way'; the discernment of Spirit-filled judgement identifies that which does not conform to Christ and is therefore to be repudiated and resisted in the name of the crucified and risen one.

---

3 Marva Dawn, 'Worship to Form a Missional Community', *Direction* 28.2 (1999), p. 142.

4 Dawn, 'Missional Community', pp. 141–2.

5 Andrew Walls, *The Missionary Movement in Church History*, Maryknoll: Orbis Books, 1996, pp. 7–8.

A missional reading of worship

The heart of Christian worship services is both simple and straight-forward. The reason believers worship God is because he is infinitely worthy of praise. No other rationale stands scrutiny and no other motive is sufficient. From first to last, it must be theocentric, drawing its focus from God's revelation of himself in Christ. And, as 'God has given us a book full of stories', it will be rooted in the narrative of God's mighty acts and saving work in the Scriptures. Yet in all of this the content of worship has to be articulated in a way that unites the grand themes of the inherited faith with the lived experience of the believing community, in a manner that ensures the authenticity of both sides of the encounter. However, this theological side of our understanding is only part of the story; the other dimension of worship relates to the dynamic of the spiritual reality that is worship. Worship is the context of divine encounter. God is supremely relational in his divinity, and Jesus calls us his friends. The apostle Paul talks about the Christian community being built together into a holy temple in which God lives by his Spirit (Eph. 2.19–22). The testimony of worshippers is that, in the service of worship, they meet with God. And if God is a missionary God, this becomes defining of the whole encounter. More than that, it becomes an essential characteristic of the encounter, as Steve Holmes tellingly observes: 'if God is properly described as "missionary" … he can only be worshipped by a missionary church'.[6]

To help with this missional reading of worship, Marva Dawn emphasizes three criteria that provide the essential foundations for worship:

1 that the biblical God be the Infinite Centre of worship, that worship enable its participants to 'waste' their time immersed in all the fullness of God's splendor;

2 that worship form believers to be disciples, following Jesus and committed to God's purposes of peace, justice, and salvation in the world; and

3 that worship form the congregation to be a genuine, inclusive Christian community linked to all God's people throughout time and space in worship, doctrine, fellowship, the breaking of bread, prayers, signs and wonders, communal care, and social involvement (see Acts 2.42–47).[7]

---

6 Stephen R. Holmes, 'Trinitarian Missiology: Towards a Theology of God as Missionary', *International Journal of Systematic Theology* 8.1 (2006), p. 89.

7 Dawn, 'Missional Community', p. 149.

The conscious, corporate setting apart of time to worship God in adoration is the most easily recognized dimension of worship, yet it has a symbiotic relationship with Volf's 'worship as action' that is expressed in two ways. First, both the form of our worship services and the spiritual reality of our encounter with God have restorative and formative roles in the disciple's life. Fallen and in need of forgiveness, wounded and in need of healing, defeated and in need of new courage, weak and in need of strength – the restorative nature of worship is a multifaceted reality. Worship also allows believers to realign themselves with the Kingdom or to undergo what Gerhard Lohfink describes as the 'de-idolizing effect' of worship,[8] counteracting the effects of daily life that leave believers 'enculturated and entrapped by the world's values of materialistic and experiential consumerism, of narcissistic self-importance and personal taste, of solitary superficiality, and of ephemeral satisfaction'.[9] The songs, hymns, prayers and liturgy retell and celebrate the grand narrative of God's mighty acts, and worshippers are immersed in the character, will and purpose of God. As the Holy Spirit moves and God's presence is felt and perceived, worshippers encounter the missionary God. Then as global, local and personal stories are woven into the worship service, connections are made and pathways established between heaven and earth; between then and now and between the congregation gathered and the congregation scattered, both for the individual and the local church.

The interior life of the worshipping community therefore has within itself an outward thrust into missional living, the expression of 'worship as action' in lives lived as living sacrifices. So, second, how the transition is made between adoration and action is significant. The end of a worship service is not merely a conclusion until next week's gathering or a perfunctory dismissal that has no recognition of what follows. Rather, it should be imbued with a sense of being 'sent ones', dispersed in the power of the Spirit to join with God in his mission to the world. Indeed, Clayton Schmit underlines this by insisting that it is a liturgical misunderstanding to substitute a genuine benediction with closing prayer. One is directed to God's people, the other to God.[10] A benediction should have a declaratory quality about it, 'Go therefore …'.

The sending into 'action as worship' is deeply rooted in the practice of 'worship as adoration'. To meet with God in worship is to encounter and

---

8 Alan and Eleanor Kreider, *Worship and Mission after Christendom*, Milton Keynes: Paternoster, 2009, p. 11.

9 Dawn, 'Missional Community', p. 141.

10 Clayton J. Schmit, *Sent and Gathered: A Worship Manual for the Missional Church*, Grand Rapids: Baker, 2009, p. 53.

be shaped by the Father's character and purpose, which are expressed as the *missio Dei*. It is to praise and concentrate on Jesus, the defining focus of divine activity in God's mission and the embodiment of a life lived in relationship with the Father and in sacrificial engagement with his mission. It is to be infused with the empowering presence of the Holy Spirit, who gifts the body of Christ to continue to engage in his mission, and the fruit of whose activity is plain to see in the loving, joyful shalom-like qualities of Spirit-filled lives. It is to be caught up into the corporate solidarity of belonging to the Church of Jesus Christ and the comradeship of brothers and sisters who have been adopted into the Father's family.

Worship and evangelism

If worship is for the believer and Godward in its focus, maintaining its missional dimension in a mutually supportive cycle of adoration and action, can evangelism ever have a legitimate place in worship? Some have argued that, theologically speaking, when worship is employed for evangelistic ends it becomes people-centred and loses its correct theocentric focus.[11] Yet this is not the whole story. From 1 Corinthians 14.16–25, we know that non-believers were present in Christian worship services from the beginning and that Paul was concerned about the implications of not taking this into consideration. While contemporary evangelistic services may owe more to the nineteenth-century American Camp Meetings and the evangelistic campaigns of D. L. Moody and Billy Graham, this does seem to suggest that there is room for further exploration of the theme.

Taking the Godward focus of worship as given, non-believers come into this context for a variety of reasons, which may include friendship and family loyalties, spiritual inquisitiveness, personal need or various forms of cultural tradition. While these may be very different from the factors that caused non-believers to be present in the Corinthian congregation, the seat of Paul's expressed concern seems to centre on the ability of outsiders to comprehend and understand what is going on. If this is so, then there is a responsibility upon every local church to understand how its worship might be more accessible in language, form and ethos to its prevailing local culture. Yet as with all attempts to inculturate the Christian faith, great care must be taken not to over-contextualize. As Kreider and Kreider observe, the values of the gospel will always give indigenized Christian worship a counter-cultural 'pilgrim' quality that

---

11 Resner, 'To Worship or to Evangelize?', p. 67; Andras Lovas, 'Mission-Shaped Liturgy', *International Review of Mission* 95.378/379 (2006), p. 357.

is 'both familiar and odd; it is both culturally attuned and culturally dissonant'.[12] Recognizing that people will be attracted to different models of church worship for different reasons – domestic, table church because it is non-threatening; megachurches for the scope of their programmes and anonymity; cathedrals for their well-crafted worship in glorious settings – congregations themselves continually need to understand the experience of the outsiders who join with them in worship. This 'seeker-sensitivity' is an expression of hospitality to the outsider, but what picture of God emerges from what they 'see'? What is intuited of the church's ethos from the style, values, priorities and mood of the worship that is experienced? Do these stand scrutiny?[13]

If someone without faith is to encounter God, where is he more fully present than in an assembly of believers engaged in worship? Through hearing the truth in the songs, prayers, reading of Scripture and the sermon, through the observation of believers practising a living faith and through their own experiential participation in an act of worship, non-Christians open themselves up to potentially powerful evangelistic influences in the power of God's presence and the power of the gospel. In advocating 'worship evangelism', Sally Morgenthaler offers a number of 'rudders' to help worship leaders manoeuvre with, including the dictums to 'worship first and evangelize second' and 'never sacrifice authenticity for relevance'.[14]

Worship as gathering and sending

Theologically speaking, worship and mission are impossible to separate. By God's design, they are so interconnected as to be inseparable. Yet in the week-by-week practice of the church's pietism, consumerism and an underdeveloped Christian world-view frustrate its fullest expression in acts of Christian worship. The role of the worship leader is critical in this. It is not merely about compèring the congregation's liturgical life, selecting songs and hymns that are known, work well together and are related to the chosen theme, and ensuring a coherent expression of worship within the established timeframe of the service. Time and attention need to be given to those things that inform the detailed construction and delivery of a service of worship: questions that address what it means to be Christian disciples living here and now; the issues that are being wrestled with at work and at home; the ways in which contemporary culture

12 Kreider and Kreider, *Worship and Mission*, p. 219.
13 Kreider and Kreider, *Worship and Mission*, pp. 219–26.
14 Sally Morgenthaler, *Worship Evangelism: Inviting Unbelievers into the Presence of God*, Grand Rapids: Zondervan, 1999, p. 284.

is subverting Christian values; the translation of God's missional concerns like grace, mercy, kindness, peace and justice into the realities of everyday life and the maintaining of an outward-looking faith that seeks to discern where God is already at work are illustrative of this.

Different congregations have attempted to address this in different ways. For some, a weekly focus on 'This Time Tomorrow' gives members of the congregation the opportunity to talk about their own spheres of work or responsibility, the issues they raise and the matters of personal concern for prayer. Others mail local organizations and businesses informing them that they will be included in the church's life of prayer and inviting requests.

Creative initiatives like this need to be integrated into the overall shape of a service that is formed by an understanding of worship as 'action' and 'adoration'. One minister consciously begins every worship service with the words, 'Let us continue to worship God ...', seeking to affirm that worship of Christian action that preceded the congregational gathering. Then, looking at the dismissal, Clayton Schmit comments:

> [I]t may be useful for worship planners and leaders to think of the sequence of liturgical actions in this way: sending is not a hasty afterthought; it is the primary element of preparation for a demanding aspect of worship (action) that lasts typically from one Sunday morning to the next ... 'the living liturgy of discipleship'.[15]

Alongside the restorative and formational dimensions of worship and the evangelistic nature of Godward-focused adoration, it is clear that there is rather more contained within the leadership of worship than is often imagined. Yet properly understood, a congregation's weekly rhythm of gathering in and sending out is probably best understood as the breathing of the body of Christ, where both, in the power of the Spirit, are integral to the other.[16]

---

15 Schmit, *Sent and Gathered*, p. 52.
16 Kreider and Kreider, *Worship and Mission*, pp. 246–7.

23

Missional Disciple-Making

Jesus' parting words to the apostles in Matthew, and arguably the climax of the gospel itself, centre on the command to 'go and make disciples of all nations, baptizing them in the name of the Father and of the Son and of the Holy Spirit' (Matt. 28.16–20, NIV). Over the years, it has inspired the international missionary movement as well as evangelism initiatives closer to home. However, the ease with which this 'commission' becomes shorthand for merely seeing people come to faith is alarming. This reductionist perspective either misses completely or merely makes a passing nod to the formational corollary in Jesus' instruction, 'and teaching them to obey everything I have commanded you'. It would be disingenuous to imply from this that the Church has not taken seriously the issue of discipleship, but locating it within the Great Commission gives it missional edge. Discipleship is not purely about how individuals can live their lives, in their circumstances in a Christian way. Neither is it about producing well-balanced, moral individuals who can be good citizens and net contributors to their community and wider society. The defining centre of discipleship is participating in God's mission.

Revisiting discipleship

Over the last half-century, as missiological thinking has matured and become embedded in the wider life of the churches, it is hardly surprising that those with a concern for the day-to-day life of Christian communities have awakened to the need to revisit the issue of discipleship. As the leader of the Church of England's Fresh Expressions team, Bishop Graham Cray affirms in a DVD for the London Institute of Contemporary Christianity (LICC), 'Churches have to realize that the core of their calling is to be disciple-making communities, whatever else they do.'[1] This is indeed the focus of LICC's Imagine project, of which Director Mark Greene comments: 'The UK will never be reached until we create open, authentic,

---

1 Mark Greene, *Imagine How We Can Reach the UK*, DVD, 2007.

learning and praying communities that are focused on making whole-life disciples who live and share the Gospel wherever they relate to people in their daily lives.'[2]

In the United States, a congregational survey at the large and influential Willow Creek Community Church identified that a significant proportion of the congregation were dissatisfied with their Christian discipleship or felt that it had stalled. Senior Pastor Bill Hybels reported to their International Leadership Summit in 2007:

> We made a mistake. What we should have done when people crossed the line of faith and became Christians, we should have started telling people and teaching people that they have to take responsibility to become *self-feeders*. We should have gotten people, taught people, how to read their Bible between services, how to do the spiritual practices much more aggressively on their own.

Subsequently, the survey was rolled out in other churches belonging to the Willow Creek Association, and resources were produced to address the issues in discipleship that they had identified as being problematic.[3] Also representative of this new wave of discipleship resources are the 'life shapes' material of Mike Breen and Walt Kallestad, which has been pioneered in the UK by St Thomas, Crookes, in Sheffield,[4] and writers from the emerging church movement like Alan and Debra Hirsch, whose *Untamed: Reactivating a Missional Form of Discipleship*[5] is a passionate call for discipleship to be seen in this light and not merely as about personal morality, as important as this is. 'The fact is that you can't be a disciple without being a missionary: no mission, no discipleship. It's as simple as that.'[6]

Mainline British denominations have also ended up by adopting strategies and straplines that are not dissimilar in content to the wider

---

2 Neil Hudson, *Imagine Church: Releasing Whole-Life Disciples*, Nottingham: InterVarsity Press, 2012, p. 18.

3 Willow Creek's own account of the survey and information regarding the resource material they produced can be accessed at www.revealnow.com, which is also reported by *Christianity Today* at http://www.christianitytoday.com/ct/2008/march/11.27.html.

4 Mike Breen and Walt Kallestad, *The Passionate Church*, Eastbourne: Kingsway, 2005; and Mike Breen and Walt Kallestad, *A Passionate Life (Workbook and Leader's Guide)*, Eastbourne: Kingsway, 2005.

5 Alan and Debra Hirsch, *Untamed: Reactivating a Missional Form of Discipleship*, Grand Rapids: Baker, 2010.

6 Hirsch and Hirsch, *Untamed*, p. 29.

conversation in this area of Christian thought. The Methodist Church owns itself as 'a discipleship movement shaped for mission', while the Baptist Union understands its role as 'encouraging missionary disciples', with a strategy document maintaining that

[e]ncouraging missionary disciples in obedience to Jesus' Great Commission lies at the heart of the Baptist Union strategy. These key strategic objectives express our commitment to the encouraging of radical, life-long missionary discipleship in the belief that this needs to affect every aspect of our life together.[7]

These illustrations of the renewed interest in discipleship and in its relationship with mission underline a felt need among the churches and a perceived theological weakness in understanding that needs to be addressed. This is also evident in the work on theological education by the Australian Robert Banks. Wanting to advocate a fully missional model of ministerial formation, he, at least in part, roots it in the discipleship practice of Jesus.[8]

In many ways, discipleship is an elusive idea. At a biblical level, it is completely comprehensible, as Jesus had disciples and discipleship must be the outcome of that relationship. However, jump forward into our own time and it is easy to see that we use the word in a variety of different ways. From a programmed course for new believers or the acquisition of Bible knowledge, to the socialization of the individual into the beliefs and lifestyle of their Christian community, there are a variety of emphases that are taken in different times and different places. By contrast, when discipleship comes as pre-packaged material that is delivered over a defined period, it also runs the risk of suggesting the possibility of having 'done discipleship'.

Exploring the theological basis of discipleship

Five theological ideas properly underpin our understanding of discipleship, and the South African missiologist David Bosch is quite clear that the Lordship of Jesus is pre-eminent. He rightly observes that discipleship is determined by a believer's relationship to Christ rather than merely con-

---

7 Introduction to 'Key Strategic Objectives', Appendix of the Report of the Trustees of the Baptist Union of Great Britain, to the Baptist Union Council, 15 October 2007.

8 Robert Banks, *Reenvisioning Theological Education*, Grand Rapids: Eerdmans, 1999, pp. 94–111.

formity to an impersonal set of rules or commands, and that it involves a decisive turning towards both God and our neighbour.[9] This is important. This double turning is evocative of Jesus' distillation of the Mosaic Law, where he maintained that everything hung on loving God and your neighbour (Matt. 22.5–40). Discipleship thus begins with turning to God in Christ and, as a result, becoming caught up in the *missio Dei*, the second theological idea. Indeed, it could be said that discipleship is an integral part of the means by which God seeks to accomplish his mission in the world. As such, it is not an end in itself, merely a means towards the end of God's missional purposes. In this way, discipleship involves embodying, expressing or working for the values and principles of the Kingdom of God. As such, it is a wider and more comprehensive term than is often presumed. It not only embraces the individual's personal life and how a community of faith functions together, but also God's wider purposes of peace, truth, justice, compassion, mercy and love in the world. Of course, the individual's personal life is not unimportant, as issues of spirituality, lifestyle and morality have a vital role to play.

The Lordship of Christ presupposes lives being brought into conformity with Christ. An understanding of personal holiness is therefore a third theological idea that underpins discipleship, as believers embrace what it means to be people who are set apart for God. The LICC speak about 'whole-life discipleship' to emphasize and make clear that there must be no sacred/secular divide in this regard.[10]

The fourth idea also flows from an acknowledgement of the Lordship of Jesus, for it is that which, according to the apostle Paul, identifies those who are members of the 'body of Christ'. All too often discipleship is conceived of in primarily individualistic terms, whereas there is no escaping the fact that it is a corporate term too. Discipleship is undertaken together, and believers are formed into the likeness of Christ in community.

The fifth idea acknowledges the role of the Holy Spirit, who indwells the believing community, as they are built together, enabling them through his power and the fruit of his presence to act like Jesus.[11] As owning the Lordship of Jesus introduces disciples to the missional will and purposes of the Father and the empowering indwelling of the Spirit, discipleship can be understood both theologically and experientially in trinitarian terms.

---

9 David J. Bosch, *Transforming Mission*, Maryknoll: Orbis Books, 1996, pp. 67, 82.

10 Hudson, *Imagine Church*, p. 22.

11 Cf. Eph. 2.21–2; 1 Cor. 12.1–31; Gal. 5.22.

Discipleship with Jesus

While the term 'disciple' does not originate with the group surrounding Jesus, they must to a certain degree have fitted the classical conception that originated with Herodotus in the fifth century BCE. While the twenty-first century is clearly a very different context from the Ancient Near East, the nature of the discipleship that Jesus initiated is instructive. To begin with, perhaps the most formative element of Jesus' pattern of discipleship was the fact that he called his followers to be a travelling community with him. Metaphors of 'journeying together' aside, this meant that the context of their discipleship had of necessity to be based on the companionship of friends. At its core, it was informal, relational and shared life on every level. From the profound moments of inspiration and the in-breaking of the miraculous to the mundane elements of daily life, Jesus and his disciples developed relationships with depths and shallows. They learnt as they went with Jesus, giving public teaching and private instruction. He encouraged them to participate in his missional activity by sending them off in pairs ahead of him to do advance work and prepare the ground for him. In the wake of positive experiences, he encouraged them to focus on what really mattered rather than their immediate success, and when they were unsuccessful he used the opportunity as a learning experience. In conversation along the road, he got them to reflect theologically on their experience as well as using the dynamics of their relationships as the catalyst to help highlight issues of attitude and character. Freely commending or challenging their responses, it was clear that his was a prayerful and nurturing concern that was deeply committed to each of them.[12] For the three years during which this form of discipleship continued, Jesus wove a pattern that was intentional, structured and strategic, while at the same time giving space for informal, spontaneous learning in three-dimensional relationships grounded in the necessities of daily life.

In an excellent study that explores the significance of Jesus' educational methods for discipleship in the contemporary Church, Sylvia Wilkey Collinson identifies a number of key elements from across the Gospels, including formal teaching, modelling the life of faith, action and reflection, demonstrative acts, pastoral care and the freedom to fail.[13] Commenting on Matthew's account of Jesus' ministry, she observes:

---

12 See Matt. 4.18–20; Mark 4.1–12; Luke 10.1–16; Mark 9.14–29; Matt. 20.20–28; Matt. 16.13–16; Matt. 16.22–23; Luke 22.31–32.

13 Sylvia Wilkey Collinson, *Making Disciples*, Milton Keynes: Paternoster, 2004, pp. 11–141.

Jesus structured their lives and activities in such a way that they were constantly being challenged to question and learn from a multiplicity of informal situations. These included the new thoughts, attitudes and values which came as they left the familiarity of their homes, families, occupations and cultural norms and moved into a community composed of fellow learners, from a variety of backgrounds, moving around the provinces of Galilee and Judea.[14]

Wilkey Collinson captures well the dynamic tension of the context that Jesus creates for discipleship formation. At one and the same time, it is intentional and strategic, while maintaining a highly relational, informal and spontaneous character. It is about each disciple's own engaging with Jesus, but this is not something that can be done alone. These are important insights that need to inform and help shape our contemporary exploration of what discipleship means in our context.

Rediscovering authentic discipleship

Each new generation has to discover its own expression of authentic discipleship to Jesus, identifying the prevailing cultural norms that threaten to devour it from within like the proverbial wolf in sheep's clothing. For Britain in the twenty-first century, this is likely to be a pincer movement of individualism and consumerism. Individualism tends to isolate people from genuine communal engagement, while the heightened value it thus ascribes to subjective judgement can effectively be deployed to filter out the views and insights of others. Consumerism reinforces this world-view and produces a judgement of the value of something by 'what I get out of it'; alongside feeding the myth that we are defined by what we consume. This makes identity fluid and open to reconstruction at any point we desire. At its most perverse, an uncritical synthesis of discipleship with contemporary culture results in a gross spiritualized narcissism that exists for our personal well-being, material benefit and leisure-time entertainment. At its most benign, it seduces us with the twin myth of contentment and quest for security that leave us 'risk averse' and reluctant to take up the self-sacrificing, life-on-the-line challenges of picking up our cross and following in Jesus' footsteps.

In exploring why present-day Christian discipleship can be so ineffective, Greg Downes tellingly observes:

---

14 Wilkey Collinson, *Making Disciples*, p. 55.

Sacrifice is the missing ingredient of contemporary discipleship ... discipleship is cruciform: it is 'cross-shaped' – it means emphasising responsibilities over rights, service over pleasure, and contributing over consuming. To live this countercultural call in today's world will inevitably involve sacrifice.[15]

This, however, cannot be achieved through a programmatic approach to discipleship that is overly dependent upon short-term courses that address devotional practices, doctrinal formulations and the dos and don'ts issues of personal lifestyle. As important as these may be, they are inadequate tools to enable contemporary believers to develop a robust discipleship with Christ. What is needed is for a culture of missional discipleship to be deeply embedded in the life of a local congregation.

First, all believers need to see themselves as 'whole-life disciples'. Neil Hudson notes that if during each week of 168 hours 10 are spent in church and approximately 48 sleeping, this leaves 110 hours as each believer's primary context for mission and discipleship. The critical question for each disciple to grapple with is, 'What does it mean for me to be faithful to God's mission in Christ here?'[16] The workplace, the home, the voluntary organization, the leisure centre become the arena in which God's missional purposes are at stake. No longer is it only about the individual believer's personal holiness. Rather, it is in the way in which staff teams are managed, injustices are responded to, menial tasks undertaken and family life conducted that the values of the Kingdom of God and the *missio Dei* are affirmed and pursued or denied and neglected. Through its teaching ministry, its small groups and fellowship activity, its prayer and liturgical life, a local congregation needs to find space where these areas of its common life together can be named, explored, questioned and supported. Its mission activity is not only focused upon the more traditional expressions of missional engagement in its corporate relationships with its local neighbourhood or the overseas missionaries that it supports. Yet these frequently have a high public profile.

Second, all believers need to be 'disciple-making disciples'. Here I use the term in the evangelistic sense. While not every Christian is called to be an evangelist, all do have the responsibility to witness to their faith. A well-lived Christian life is deeply attractive. The qualities of generosity, kindness, patience, compassion and truthful dependability are highly regarded qualities. However, witness is not only the passive consequence of

15 Greg Downes, 'Deep End Discipleship', *Christianity Magazine* (October 2011), p. 43.
16 Hudson, *Imagine Church*, pp. 56–8.

faithful Christian living. There are times when faith needs to be articulated and the good news of God's love and care spoken about. 'Disciple-making disciples' are evangelistically motivated by the desire to see others discover that which has brought meaning and depth to their own lives.

Third, all believers need to be 'socially engaged disciples'. Graham Cray quickly dispels any thought that this is an inappropriate focus for Christian convictions:

> It takes only a moment's thought to see that the public life of our nation is a proper matter for Christian concern, and a proper setting for Christian discipleship. As residents we want our neighbourhoods to be secure and safe. As parents we want our children to have a good and appropriate education. As patients we want good health-care. As workers we want a fair wage ... As Christians, however, we have an additional dimension. Christian discipleship is not about self-interest. It is about looking to the interests of others. Jesus calls us to love our neighbours as ourselves.[17]

He goes on to explore how incarnational identification with our neighbours, taking responsibility for entering into public debate to 'teach' society and being prepared to count the cost of such public engagement are outworkings of this kind of socially engaged discipleship.

Fourth, the Church needs 'resilient disciples' sustained by word and sacrament. Missional discipleship is not easy. The rhythm of gathering and scattering is an important one to establish, as is an understanding of the nature of the Church, when it is together and when it is separated. It remains the Church in both forms. In this way in its gathered form a congregation can explore how more specifically to support, nourish and sustain itself when it is scattered. And then, when it is scattered, the missional discipleship of its members is better resourced and supported, establishing a virtuous cycle.

Having concluded her research into the nature of discipleship, Wilkey Collinson concluded that the practice of the early Church included six component parts: it was relational, intentional, mainly informal, typically communal, reciprocal and centrifugal in focus. She concludes her formal definition by stating, 'Christian discipleship is intended to result in each becoming an active follower of Jesus and a participant in his mission to the world.'[18]

---

17 Graham Cray, *Disciples and Citizens*, Nottingham: InterVarsity Press, 2007, p. 15.

18 Wilkey Collinson, *Making Disciples*, pp. 241–3.

In Graham Cray's memorable phrase, 'Local churches are designed by God to be crucibles of discipleship'[19] or, as a student wrote in a module assignment exploring the relationship between mission and discipleship,

Lives transformed through discipleship breathe *missio Dei* when disciples share a meal with a neighbour, make ethical decisions within their workplace, build relationships with their *Big Issue* seller, lovingly raise their children with their not-yet-Christian partner or when they maintain a healthy work–life balance in today's 24:7 society through the perspective of a Sabbath.[20]

---

19 Cray, *Disciples and Citizens*, p. 118.
20 Pete Dibdin, 7 May 2009.

24

Mission and Leadership

There is no shortage of published literature on the subject of leadership. From highly regarded authors like John Adair or Warren Bennis to more populist treatments such as the titles exploring the command style of Captain Jean-Luc Picard of the starship *Enterprise* in *Make It So: Leadership for the Next Generation* or the *Leadership Secrets of Santa Claus: How to Get Big Things Done in Your Workshop All Year Long*, there are literally thousands of books on the market at any one time.[1] Christian publishing has mirrored the more serious and reflective side of this cultural phenomenon, and where theological colleges hardly addressed the issue a generation ago, it is now unusual for the subject of leadership not to be seen as a core competency for ministry.

The evolution of Christian leadership

Darrell Guder maps out the development of leadership in the Christian community from New Testament times and charts how the apostolic age gave way to the emergence of a priestly order of leaders at the beginning of the third century, mirroring a pattern existing in the wider Roman culture. This was then further affirmed and entrenched with the conversion of the Emperor Constantine and the adoption of Christianity as the state religion under his successor Theodosius. This pattern continued until the Reformation, when for Protestants the importance of a correct understanding of Scripture and doctrine led to the elevation of the work of preaching and teaching and a more pedagogical role for Christian leaders, who were now held to be the guardians of the content of the gospel. Contemporary commentators have observed how this has morphed towards

1 John Adair, *Effective Leadership: How to be a Successful Leader*, London: Pan, 2009; Warren Bennis, *On Becoming a Leader*, New York: Basic Books, 2009; Wess Roberts and Bill Ross, *Make It So: Leadership for the Next Generation*, New York: Simon & Schuster, 1996; Steve Ventura, *Leadership Secrets of Santa Claus: How to Get Big Things Done in Your Workshop All Year Long*, Dallas: Performance Systems, 2003.

a professionalism where the minister/leader is viewed as a counsellor, manager or technician (literally, understanding the 'how to' techniques for running a church).[2] For Alan Roxburgh, this is driven by the need of Christian ministers to find new ways to reconfigure their pastoral identity and legitimize their calling in direct consequence of the Church being increasingly marginalized in wider society. Thus pastoral identity mirrors the helping professions by becoming therapeutic, or the competence of technical experts as it adopts programmes, strategies and techniques that parallel those of consumerism and entertainment from the business world. The Church is further pushed towards an inward-looking focus as faith is held to be primarily located in the highly privatized world of an individual's personal life.

> Pastors lead congregations that have little sense of a vocation as a people called to lives larger than themselves. Preaching, reflecting this cultural captivity, calls parishioners to discover a Jesus who is guarantor of inner personal happiness in a hazardous and dark world.[3]

Craig Van Gelder tellingly reflects that while some congregational leaders have developed an explicit theory of leadership out of which they minister, most do not. Rather, such leadership is an intuitive blending of their experience in the workplace, the training and mentoring they have received and their own personal reflection. It is not surprising, therefore, that church life is either consciously or unconsciously influenced by the popularity of prevailing organizational theory.

- 1970s–80s: goal attainment and strategic planning
- 1980s–now: total quality management through re-engineering and continuous improvement
- 1980s–90s: transformational leadership through vision casting
- 1990s–now: learning organization through feedback loops.[4]

---

2 Darrell L. Guder, *Missional Church*, Grand Rapids: Eerdmans, 1998, pp. 190–8. In Craig Van Gelder (ed.), *The Missional Church and Leadership Formation*, Grand Rapids: Eerdmans, 2009, pp. 12–39, Van Gelder maps this against the American experience of the minister as 'resident theologian' (1600–late 1700s), 'gentleman pastor' (late 1700s–mid-1800s), 'churchly pastor' (late 1800s–1920s), 'pastoral director' (mid 1940s–1970s), 'therapeutic pastor' (1960s–70s), 'entrepreneurial leader' (2000s).

3 Alan J. Roxburgh, *The Missionary Congregation, Leadership, and Liminality*, Harrisburg: Trinity Press, 1997, p. 21.

4 Craig Van Gelder, *The Ministry of the Missional Church*, Grand Rapids: Baker, 2007, pp. 125, 137–8.

No approach to the practice of leadership is value free; the question has to be whether those values are compatible with the gospel or adaptable to the missional purposes of the Kingdom of God. For example, the pragmatic success model of 'if it works, it's right', which undergirds consumerist capitalism and with which most of the Western world is familiar, is clearly flawed, because it embodies a philosophy of the end always justifying the means irrespective of any ethical considerations. Strategic planning is an interesting case in point too. Mark Lau Branson acknowledges that while functionalist approaches to vision, mission statements and planning can initiate important conversations, they can also provide straitjackets that thwart innovation and participation.[5] Roxburgh goes further: while accepting that planning is a crucial part of leadership, he sees the management theory of strategic planning as theologically flawed because of the presumption that leaders can predict and control their environment to accomplish their identified goals. For him, this fails to take adequate account of the nature of humanity and the unpredictability of circumstances, alongside unacceptably objectifying all who participate in a process as means towards a stated end.[6]

Those exercising Christian leadership therefore need be sufficiently self-aware to understand the theories and experiences that influence them, and self-critical enough to identify and examine the ways they contribute to or detract from God's missional purposes. Indeed, Christian leadership needs to be shaped by, and exercised out of, a missional theology. As a consequence, such leadership will then help a congregation inhabit and express their missional identity as the people of God. The insights of contemporary leadership theory and practice are only useful in so far as they are deployed within, and subject to, such a framework.

While there are many potential starting points for a theology of leadership and a vast array of emphases and nuances that could be explored and developed, at its heart it must be theocentric and, as a consequence, missional. Drawing on the trinitarian, pentecostal and eschatological dimensions of a Christian world-view, such a framework can be constructed, which explores the being, doing and orientation of Christian leadership: that is, what a leader is, what a leader does and the direction in which a leader faces.

---

5 Mark Lau Branson, 'Ecclesiology and Leadership for the Missional Church', in Craig Van Gelder (ed.), *The Missional Church in Context*, Grand Rapids: Eerdmans, 2007, p. 111.

6 Alan J. Roxburgh, *Missional Map-Making*, San Francisco: Jossey-Bass, 2010, pp. 74–82.

Trinitarian leadership – what a leader is

The theological understanding of *theosis* maintains that through a real union with God, the believer fully becomes and attains to the divine image in which she or he was created, participating in the divine nature itself (2 Pet. 1.4). This is clearly true for all believers, but is worth restating in the context of Christian leadership too, as it forms the basis of identity out of which that leadership is exercised – we do what we are. It is worth noting too that such a view is, of necessity, predicated on the basis of a life lived in union with God. Spirituality rather than gifting, eloquence or persona is the key to leadership within the body of Christ. A Christocentric, Spirit-infused discipleship will lead to an expression of that leadership that is reflective of the nature of God himself.

Our best understanding of the nature of God's being is expressed in trinitarian terms. Following the Cappadocian Fathers and Orthodox theology, we see the importance of recognizing the fundamental importance of the social and relational dimensions of the godhead. We encounter God as Trinity through his missional engagement with humanity, and from the outset this mutuality and interdependence of action is clear. It is the Holy Spirit who comes upon Mary, as she is overshadowed by the power of the most high, and she conceives. Jesus is clear, as he explains his mission is wholly dependent upon his relationship with the Father, and that the Father is only accessible through the Son. Then, as he commissions the disciples, 'As the Father has sent me, I am sending you' (John 20.21, NIV), they are also instructed to wait for the empowering of the Holy Spirit, whose creative agency was again to be integral to God's missional purposes.[7] Thus, in the classic statement, the Father sends the Son, and the Father and the Son send the Spirit. The communal nature of God's identity and the collaborative pattern of working he establishes to accomplish his purposes are patently evident.

In broad terms, the growth of leadership teams in British churches has been one of the most observable trans-denominational developments over the last generation. In terms of 'paid staff', the passing of the era of 'solo clergy' is the fruit of cash-rich, time-poor congregations with a keen desire for professional competence in those who carry responsibility for certain areas of Christian ministry. The proliferation of paid appointments for youth and children's ministers is a case in point. Such work that was serviced by an army of volunteers in the mid-twentieth century is now,

---

7 See Luke 1.35 (on Mary); Matt. 11.27/Luke 10.22, John 5.19, 5.30, 8.28, 9.4, 12.49, 14.10, 14.20 (on Jesus' understanding of his ministry); John 14.16–17 and 26, Luke 24.49 (on the coming of the Holy Spirit).

with much reduced numbers of children and young people, led by trained, qualified and competent people who are employed by the churches. Other roles ranging through the positions of associate or assistant ministers, community workers, evangelists, parish nurses and administrators, all contribute to what has been a rapid expansion of paid church leadership. Alongside this, in the wider leadership of the local church, the charismatic emphasis on 'spiritual gifts' given to the whole body of Christ has taken root, leading to a much greater level of participation, paralleling the wider cultural context, which favours team working and is far less indulgent of hierarchical or autocratic models of leadership.

In so far as these developments echo and facilitate leadership expressive of the equality, mutuality, reciprocity and outward focus of a trinitarian approach, these are positive developments. However, as at least in part the fruit of consumerism, the marketplace and a culture of individualism, their trajectory can move unhelpfully inward towards the Church, aiming to meet its own needs and service its own aspirations. A truly trinitarian approach to leadership is communal and relational rather than functional and task-orientated, and is outwardly focused on participating in God's mission rather than purely inward in its vision and constrained by the internal life of the congregation itself.

> At the heart of our faith is a divine leadership community: the Trinity ... The logic of trinitarian missional theology points toward a communal, collaborative leadership paradigm in which different persons together employ their God-given gifts to steward, shepherd, and influence the community toward deeper participation in what God is doing in the world.[8]

A real union with God draws Christian leaders, through *theosis*, into a pattern of being that conforms to the communal dynamics of the Trinity and is by nature equal, communal, reciprocal and missionally orientated.

Pentecostal leadership – what a leader does

When Jesus tells his disciples in Gethsemane, 'It is for your good that I am going away', it must have seemed almost beyond comprehension. In what circumstances would that ever be true? Yet Jesus understands the significance of the transition that Pentecost and the coming of the Holy

---

8 Craig Van Gelder and Dwight J. Zscheile, *The Missional Church in Perspective*, Grand Rapids: Baker, 2011, p. 157.

Spirit will bring. He will personally send the *parakletos* to them, the one who comes alongside to help (John 16.7). In missional terms, his coming will prove to be personally transformative, communally formational and missionally entrepreneurial.

Personally transformative

Jesus promised that the disciples would be empowered as his witnesses when the Holy Spirit came upon them, and, beginning on the day of Pentecost, this has been the experience of God's people ever since. The Spirit was not only with them, but was 'in' them, poured out and filling them. From that day, the courage to stand out and the words to articulate the good news of the Kingdom of God have been integral to this pentecostal transformation.

The Spirit's arrival has a moral and ethical dimension too, as he identifies wrong attitudes and behaviour, upholds and reinforces a vision of righteousness and continues to underline that lives lived in the world are subject to accountability and judgement. The fruit of this is lives that are transformed by his activity, embodying qualities of being that are loving, patient and kind, full of gentleness, goodness and peacefulness, demonstrating faithfulness, joyfulness and self-possession. He also gives gifts of grace to individuals to enable the Christian community to act as a continuation of the body of Christ on earth. From serving, teaching and encouraging through to faithful prophesy and diligent leadership, the Spirit gifts the community of faith with *charismata* which, while mediated through individuals, yet belong to the whole.[9]

There is nothing in the broad dynamics of personal transformation in the hands of the Holy Spirit that is uniquely the experience of Christian leaders; however, there is an expectation that they will not only embody it, but exemplify it. The list of qualifications for overseers and deacons in I Timothy 3.2–13 is illustrative of this, beginning with the clearly stated injunction, 'Now the overseer must be above reproach' and then ranging through attitudes, demeanour, behaviour, home life and reputation both within and outside of the believing community.

Spirit-formed leadership, bringing to memory the teaching and example

---

9 Acts 1.8 (Spirit-empowered witness); John 14.16–17, Acts 11.24, Eph. 5.18b (the Holy Spirit 'in' or 'filling' a believer); Luke 12.11–12 (the Spirit aiding articularity); John 16.8–11 (the Spirit identifying wrong attitudes and behaviour, exemplifying righteousness and underlining judgement); Gal. 5.22 (the fruit of the Spirit's activity); Rom 12.3–8 (Paul's preferred treatment of the gifts of the Holy Spirit).

of Jesus, results in a pattern of life that does not conform to the dynamics of power, control, authority and prestige that are more commonly associated with it. Rather, Jesus reverses these traits and envisions a Kingdom leadership, where greatness equates with servanthood and the desire to be first with the position of a slave. Acted out in his washing of the disciples' feet, Jesus epitomizes this form of self-sacrificing, servant leadership.[10]

Christian leadership therefore is grounded in the transformational activity of the Holy Spirit in the leader's own life.

> Missional leadership is first about the leader's character and formation. Leaders either form or deform the emergence of the Spirit's work among God's people ... it demands the ability to model the values and beliefs at the heart of missional transformation.[11]

Communally formational

Ephesians 4.1–13 is a key text when exploring the nature of leadership within the community of faith. The Holy Spirit's activity is central in this Pauline account, explicitly as the source of unity among believers and then by implication as the mediator of the gifts of apostles, prophets, evangelists, pastors and teachers, which Christ has given to his people. What is critical to understand here is the function that these leading roles have, 'to prepare God's people for works of service'. This is a task of formation rather than management, of growth towards spiritual maturity rather than programme development, of outward-focused service rather than inwardly directed consumption.

For the missiologist Alan Roxburgh, the task of a leader is best conceived of in terms of cultivating an environment that engages and develops the missional imagination of a congregation. This requires leaders who are formed by the Christian tradition and not contemporary culture, and yet who are able to engage with that culture rather than be separate from it. Such leaders also need to understand that a congregation is a unique organization, a social community of the Kingdom of God as opposed to a business, interest group or leisure association. In looking to reconceive congregational leadership, he proposes that pastors should develop their leadership around being poets, prophets and apostles. As poets, they listen and observe before articulating their reflections in the context of the tradition. As prophets, they address the Word of God to the specific context

---

10 Matt. 20.25–28; John 13.1–17.

11 Alan J. Roxburgh and Fred Romanuk, *The Missional Leader*, San Francisco: Jossey-Bass, 2006, pp. 126–7.

and experience of the people of God. As apostles, they are committed to the discipling and equipping of a congregation by example in a context where the old maps are no longer of any use.[12]

Through worship, discipleship and the wide array of supportive social and communal engagement within a congregation, leaders facilitate this shared exploration of life and experience with its joys and pains, its insights and dilemmas, its breakthroughs and frustrations. No pre-formulated programme or strategy can accomplish this communal formation. In fact, there is a real sense that what emerges within any congregation needs to be bespoke for its own context.

> In our view, missional imagination is fundamentally about seeing the church and the world in the light of the Triune God's presence and activity. Jesus repeatedly stresses new ways of seeing in his encounters with various people in the Gospels. Discerning the presence and possibility of the reign of God in our midst involves a fresh perspective illuminated by the Spirit.[13]

In exploring more deeply the composite elements that make up such an environment, Mark Lau Branson proposes a 'formation triad' made up of congregational, spiritual and missional dimensions. *Congregational formation* is about building a community of faith with a common memory, common life and shared intimacy, proximity and permanence. He notes that while such communities will always exhibit elements of homogeneity, the norm is for them to be intercultural and intergenerational. *Spiritual formation* is both personal and corporate, and, in New Testament terms, is always congregationally based. It is nourished by the worship, word and mission, the spiritual disciplines and the means of grace. *Missional formation* is about a local congregation's engagement with its immediate context and the wider world. It is about how it discerns the shape of a gospel life lived out in its own particular circumstances. This is not to be attempted alone but in partnership with networks of local churches and the worldwide body of Christ.[14]

A 'Leadership Triad' that addresses the interpretive, relational and implemental components of this pattern of formation then maps what

---

12 Roxburgh and Romanuk, *Leader*, pp. 16–17; Roxburgh, *Map-Making*, p. 77; Roxburgh, *Liminality*, pp. 57–66.

13 Van Gelder and Zscheile, *Perspective*, p. 148.

14 Branson, 'Ecclesiology', pp. 112–15; Mark Lau Branson and Juan F. Martinez, *Churches, Cultures and Leadership: A Practical Theology of Congregations and Ethnicities*, Downers Grove: InterVarsity Press, 2011, pp. 60–4.

missional leadership might look like in this regard. *Interpretive leadership* is about understanding and shaping meaning. This embraces the biblical and theological task as well as that of personal experience and the contemporary context. It is both formal and informal, with an objective to release new imagination, discernment and action by shaping a 'community of interpreters'. *Relational leadership* is about community building. It encompasses the traditional pastoral responsibilities and all that is involved in helping a community knit itself together in a multi-dimensional matrix of self-supporting and creative relationships. *Implemental leadership* looks to the structures, forms and resources necessary both to sustain a congregation and for experiments to be undertaken and initiatives followed through.[15]

Leadership committed to the formation of a Spirit-directed missional community has to understand that the Spirit will always blow wherever he pleases.

> One of the key assumptions of a Spirit-filled understanding of ministry in the missional church is that ministry is fundamentally uncontrollable. God's mission through the congregation cannot be tightly regulated and managed by leaders. Rather, the Spirit is constantly working to expand, deepen, provoke, and enrich that ministry. The cultivation and multiplication of leaders is necessary for the growth of the church's participation in God's mission.[16]

Pioneering and entrepreneurial

As the early Christian community grows and expands through the Roman Empire, it is the Holy Spirit who is consistently identified as the one who empowers, guides and seals its dynamic progress across geographical and cultural boundaries. As he prepared his disciples for what lay ahead, Jesus told them that the coming of the Spirit would lead to their missionary progress as his witnesses from Jerusalem and Judea to Samaria and the 'ends of the earth'. Then, beginning with the coming of the Spirit and the birth of the Church on the Day of Pentecost, his activity can be charted throughout the developing narrative. As Philip proclaimed Christ in Samaria and Peter to family and friends of the Gentile Cornelius, it was the reception of the Holy Spirit that confirmed these new cultural locations for gospel ministry. It is the Spirit who leads the congregation at Antioch

---

15 Branson, 'Ecclesiology', pp. 118–23; Branson and Martinez, *Cultures and Leadership*, pp. 54–7.

16 Van Gelder and Zscheile, *Perspective*, p. 156.

to set apart Barnabas and Paul, 'for the work to which I have called them', and who also was later to keep Paul and his team from taking their preaching ministry into the province of Asia, not allowing them to enter Bithynia either as he guided them strategically towards Europe and the port of Philippi.[17]

From the very beginning, this kind of Spirit-enabled pioneering emphasis has been integral to missional leadership. In the contemporary British church, the renaissance of church planting and the identification of those called to this ministry by the Church as 'pioneer ministers' is completely in keeping with this. It should be no surprise that the creator Spirit is constantly leading God's people to do new, innovative and creative things. Yet pioneering missional leadership has to be seen in a broader perspective than purely church planting or exploring/experimenting with fresh expressions of church. It needs to embrace the full range of a congregation's missional life. For example, as a church engages with the changing dynamics and needs of its local community, it will often find itself at the forefront of initiatives in loving service, the struggle for justice and care for the environment. In the London Borough of Croydon in 1998, an investigation into the contribution of the local churches to the borough's life was commissioned. It mapped how the 160 congregations extensively ran 1,300 community activities outside of their core religious programme, which were serviced by some 6,000 volunteers. A further 2,000 volunteers contributed to the voluntary sector outside of the church, alongside extensive donations and support for local charities. With 85 per cent of the churches having an idea about their future involvement in their local community, the report observed, 'In many ways it forms the backbone of the voluntary sector.'[18] An observation from the officers of the council during the production of this report was their surprise at the way local clergy in particular were acting as 'social entrepreneurs' within the community.

It is this entrepreneurial dimension of pioneering and innovation that is worth exploring further. As co-workers with Christ, what lessons and insights can be drawn from those who have researched and studied the practice of entrepreneurship?[19] Having done this at some depth, Bill Bolton

---

17 Acts 1.8 (Jesus on the disciples' future mission); 2.14–17 (the Samaritan Pentecost); 10.47/11.15–18 (the Gentile Pentecost); 13.1–3 (Antioch); 16.6–7 (Paul's journey to Philippi).

18 Stewart Worden, *The Church in Croydon's Community: The Role of the Church in Local Economic and Community Development*, Croydon: CTBC/London Borough of Croydon, 1998, p. 2.

19 NB: it is important to differentiate terminology here from those who form the missional church conversation in the USA, who conceive of 'entrepreneurial leader-

and John Thompson define an entrepreneur as, 'a person who habitually creates and innovates to build something of recognized value around perceived opportunities'.[20] The Skoll World Forum on Social Entrepreneurship broadens this further with the rather wordy explanation that

[t]he social entrepreneur should be understood as someone who targets an unfortunate but stable equilibrium that causes the neglect, marginalization, or suffering of a segment of humanity; who brings to bear on this situation his or her inspiration, direct action, creativity, courage, and fortitude; and who aims for and ultimately effects the establishment of a new stable equilibrium that secures permanent benefit for the targeted group and society at large.

Rather helpfully, Martin Clarke summarizes that social entrepreneurs 'see a bad situation, envisage a better one, and work out how to get from here to there'.[21] Bolton, also an Anglican Lay Reader, suggests that releasing entrepreneurial talent to build something of Kingdom worth – be it economic, social or spiritual – is the greatest task facing the Church today. He identifies such individuals as 'Kingdom Entrepreneurs'.[22]

Bolton and Thompson use the acronym FACETS to describe the six attributes of an entrepreneur that they identify from their research, the first four of which are present in all entrepreneurs.[23]

F   Focus delivers on the opportunity
A   Advantage selects the right opportunity
C   Creativity sees many opportunities
E   Ego brings motivation and courage
T   Team multiplies effectiveness
S   Social finds a cause.

Focus, advantage and creativity are self-evident talents, whereas ego is about temperament and the drive to make a difference in what is done and achieved. Experience demonstrates that most entrepreneurs are not

---

ship' as dependent upon the uncritical use of secular business models and the rise of the megachurch movement, such as Van Gelder, *Leadership Formation*, pp. 39–42.

20 Bill Bolton and John Thompson, *The Entrepreneur in Focus: Achieve your Potential*, London: Thomson, 2003, p. 49.

21 Martin Clark, *The Social Entrepreneur Revolution*, London: Marshall Cavendish, 2009, pp. 20–1.

22 Bill Bolton, *The Entrepreneur and the Church*, Cambridge: Grove, 2006, pp. 4, 23.

23 Bolton, *Entrepreneur*, pp. 15–17.

team workers. Those who are good networkers are so to multiply the team's talents and maximize its effectiveness rather than for the pleasure of building relationships. The social facet relates to social entrepreneurship, where the individual's beliefs and values are the reason a particular cause is undertaken and pursued.

When asked to identify the key qualities that enable a social entrepreneur to succeed, practitioners most frequently identified:[24]

- Perseverance
- Vision and the ability to communicate it
- Passion and commitment to the cause
- Creativity
- Optimism and belief
- Integrity and values
- Pragmatism
- Flexibility
- Self-confidence
- Thoughtfulness.

David Bornstein, however, is clear that for social entrepreneurs it is the quality of motivation that is most significant. This is because it enables them to embrace those qualities that are essential to their success, a willingness to self-correct, share credit, break free of established structures, cross disciplinary boundaries, work quietly and have a strong ethical impetus.[25] Along the way, social entrepreneurs build cohesion in their communities by developing networks of relationship that are rooted in mutuality and trust. Even economists recognize the value of this 'social capital'.

With the rapid expansion of the Fresh Expressions of church movement and the recognition of the specialized nature of pioneer ministry in church planting, alongside the ever-increasing multifaceted nature of local church engagement with the local community and inspirational movements like Hope 08 and its successor Hope UK,[26] it is increasingly important that we understand the nature of entrepreneurship from a missional perspective. This is because it has implications for our identification and training of future leaders, our deployment of staff and volunteers, the shape of the roles we expect them to fulfil, the support that we provide and the expectations we have of them.

---

24 Clark, *Revolution*, p. 107.
25 David Bornstein, *How to Change the World: Social Entrepreneurs and the Power of New Ideas*, Oxford: Oxford University Press, 2007, pp. 238–46.
26 See www.hopeuk.org.

At the heart of all this has to be the role of the Holy Spirit. Missional entrepreneurship cannot merely be a baptizing of received wisdom as, even at the most fundamental level, spiritual discernment is a necessary corollary of bringing the two words together. Alongside this, however, entrepreneurship needs to be subject to theological scrutiny. If, for example, our trinitarian understanding of Christian leadership implies that it is by nature communal and collaborative, classic entrepreneurial individualism provides a flawed basis upon which to work. Or again, the qualities of focus and passion that are transformational drivers in personal behaviour can result in impatience that is destructive of relationships and community. Bolton himself critiques his own model of entrepreneurship by highlighting that the principles of advantage and ego can easily be subverted. Over the years, many Christian leaders under the guise of working for the Kingdom have been building their own empires, taking inappropriate advantage of others and inflating their own egos. This is easily projected into a narrative of American televangelists with the high visibility of the fall from grace of preachers like Jimmy Swaggart and Jim and Tammy Bakker in the late 1980s. However, it can come much closer to home as Bolton acknowledges: 'This is a real point of difficulty for entrepreneurs who instinctively want to build empires ... I know of several who have been down that particular road.'[27] The significance of the continuing transformative work of the Spirit is abundantly clear. Yet at their best, such entrepreneurs are 'transformative forces: people with new ideas to address major problems who are relentless in the pursuit of their visions'. People who, according to Peter Drucker, change 'the performance capacity of society'.[28]

Eschatological leadership – the direction in which a leader faces

The fundamental world-view of Christians sees history as lineal and not cyclical. This is important for understanding the nature of the Church. Its life is not to be governed by the rolling seasons of the year. However attractive and helpful it is to be in harmony with the natural rhythm of life, this must not be a determining factor of its shape or direction. Such an emphasis can easily slip into a maintenance mode that is overly conservative and resistant to change. Rather, the Christian narrative views history as having a beginning and an end, with the life, death and resurrection of Jesus being the critical moment in history where the vision of the end (the

---

27 Bolton, *Entrepreneur*, pp. 23–4.
28 Bornstein, *Change the World*, pp. 1–2.

eschaton) – the final inauguration of God's rule, the unimpeded expression of the Kingdom of God, the full manifestation of God's reign – is focused in high resolution. What begins with Jesus will be brought to completion in the future, as the closing images of the book of Revelation indicate. However, because of Jesus, God's future reign breaks into the present, where it is acknowledged in believing communities and anticipated in their missional activity, giving a foretaste of God's gracious and loving intention for the whole created order. Through each local church God's future is provisionally present as their missional life is shaped by this grand eschatological revelation. In turn, this then helps to shape a congregation's vision of its life and purpose, giving direction, establishing boundaries and setting their place in the grand missional narrative of the purposes of God.

Vision for a local church is about the here and now. It is about answering the simply stated question, 'What does God want of us?' Or, more theologically, at a specific time and place, 'How is God's eschatological reign to find its present expression through us?' This is a task of spiritual discernment. Graham Cray suggests that this involves the discipline of 'triple listening' that is facilitated by a church's leaders. *Listening to God* requires a prayerful, corporate discernment that is anchored in the Scriptures and factors in the spiritual history of the church. *Listening to the church* asks the questions: Who are we? What is on our hearts? Where do we find ourselves? *Listening to the community* uses relationships and research into the context in which a congregation is located, to listen for what the Spirit is saying and discern what he is doing. Knowledge of our context comes from relational and informational sources.[29]

Van Gelder and Daubert both make the suggestion that it is far more fruitful for this vision to emerge from within a community and be corporately discerned than be strategically cast from outside by a visionary leader.[30] This would certainly ensure that such a vision was embedded and owned throughout a congregation, alongside helping to ensure that it was not unnecessarily limited to the knowledge, preferences and foibles of a given leader. It would also help to secure a long-term vision from vulnerability when a key leader or keeper of the vision departs. More importantly, it also models a practice of collaborative and communal

---

29 Graham Cray, *Discerning Leadership*, Cambridge: Grove, 2010. Dave Daubert, 'Vision-Discerning vs. Vision-Casting: How Shared Vision Can Raise Up Communities of Leaders Rather Than Mere Leaders of Community', in Van Gelder (ed.), *Leadership Formation*, p. 164.

30 Van Gelder, *Leadership Formation*, pp. 147–8; Daubert, 'Vision-Discerning', pp. 160–1.

leadership. The visionary leadership facilitates this process of discernment, acting as both a focus and conduit for the discerning process and its articulation back to the community in a biblically anchored, theologically credible and communally endorsed vision.[31]

The formation of missional leaders

In one of the earliest contributions to the missional church conversation in the late 1990s, Darrell Guder and his colleagues in the Gospel and Our Culture network reflected on the necessity for the Church to re-embrace the team-working implied in the Pauline model of leadership outlined in Ephesians 4 and thus move away from the more traditional *solus pastor* approach. While owning that the pastor-teacher remains essential in equipping and caring for a missional congregation, they pointed to the first place given to the apostolic role and the primary mark of the Church being its 'sent-ness' as a representative of the gospel. The formation of these missional leaders is vitally important, and they highlighted four key factors: first, a deep sense of vocation on the part of the leaders; second, a distinctively Christian character that is rooted in integrity and maturity; third, an academic and intellectual competency that is biblically formed and theologically grounded. If the gospel is to shape and reshape the Church in a continually changing culture, that gospel needs to be faithfully articulated, studied and explored. Fourth, because this work of shaping and forming missional communities is not simply about deploying ready-to-assemble strategies and methodologies, there are the skills of spiritual and communal formation that are essential to the success of the endeavour.[32]

Now more than ever the Church needs such leaders. Bad leadership results in malformed congregations and compromises their participation in the *missio Dei*. Properly formed missional leadership 'prepares God's people for works of service, so that the body of Christ may be built up'.

---

31 For an example of a congregation engaging in the discernment of a vision in this way, see Roger Standing, 'Rising from A Glorious Past', in Marshall Shelley (ed.), *Renewing Your Church through Vision and Planning*, Minneapolis: Bethany, 1997, pp. 117–23.

32 Guder, *Missional Church*, pp. 212–15.

25

Organizing for Mission

Given the opportunity to choose between being involved in the organizational and administrative life of a congregation or engaging directly in mission activity, most people are clear about what they would find most attractive. At best, the organizational life of a local church is often viewed as a necessary evil; at worst, it can elicit a very negative response for a variety of reasons. At one level, a church might be shackled to a cumbersome and outdated pattern of inherited structures that are resistant to change and largely irrelevant to its wider life and yet are stubbornly resistant to change. Then again, past experience may prove a disincentive to participate, with business meetings following the 'rules of debate' proving to be tedious and boring, while official reports and formal accounts cause eyes to glaze over in non-comprehension. Meetings like this can also release the manoeuvrings and bickering of 'community politics' or what by any reckoning are expressions of purely bad and unacceptable behaviour. When considered alongside living in a pressurized and time-poor world, it is no surprise that the organizational life of a congregation and the denomination or network to which it belongs is not a top priority. The result is churches can be organizationally weak and semi-detached in a kind of unconscious schismatic autonomy. However, while proper organization is no guarantee of missional effectiveness, bad organization can and will undermine it. For this reason, and this reason alone, it is a form of negligence if organizational responsibility is abdicated.

Present need and practice

Mission without organization is an impossibility. Take a new initiative, for example. As soon as it begins there are:

- decisions to be made – if they are not made, the initiative will stagnate or things will happen unhelpfully by default;
- tasks to be accomplished – no organization leads either to chaos or things not getting done;

- volunteers to be deployed – or only self-starters will get going;
- money to be raised and spent – or the initiative will be under-resourced, or the finances unaccounted for;
- a support base to be communicated with – or else other members of the congregation will be left alienated and dissatisfied. There may also be issues of the management of change that arise;
- staff to be employed – a whole range of issues need to be addressed to ensure legal compliance;
- if children or vulnerable adults are involved – child protection structures and Criminal Record Bureau checking processes need to be engaged to mitigate the risk of the vulnerable being exposed to potential abuse;
- accountability to be established – for the support and well-being of those involved in the initiative, and to protect them from becoming a law unto themselves.

Weymouth's translation of 1 Corinthians 12.28 includes, alongside the apostles, prophets and teachers that God has given to the Church, those with the 'powers of organization'. The need for organization cannot be disputed; what is open to question is its form and degree. What might it look like? 'The missionary structure of the congregation' was a concern of the World Council of Churches when it met in Delhi in 1961, yet for all of the discussion and reflection that followed, it is hard to discern any practical impact on the churches. Present-day congregational organization in Britain owes more to the emergence of nineteenth-century voluntary associations than anything else. Industrialization and urban growth demanded new forms of organization and association, and the churches spawned many of their own to work alongside the churches, before adopting the principles more fully into their own ongoing life as the century progressed. From local community associations to national and international charities, this pattern of working still defines the wider cultural landscape as well as that of the churches.

This form of organizational or associational life is a present-day inherited reality in both the Church and the wider culture. For all that activists may long for uncluttered and collaborative networks of mutual relationship, as soon as working together moves beyond the informal stage, it is unavoidable in contemporary Britain and undesirable for the long-term health of a community of believers. The critical question is how such organization might be shaped by a congregation's missional identity, rather than a congregation's identity being moulded by its organizational structure. There may be advantages in beginning afresh and allowing a structure to emerge, but this itself is a time-consuming and demanding path to take. For all of the limitations of inherited institutional life and the compelling need for it to be continually evaluated against missional criteria and present needs, it does most often have the advantage of providing a known, coherent and theologically informed infrastructure that in theory covers the important legal and ecclesial bases. There is no virtue in continually reinventing the wheel. Indeed, it could even be considered bad stewardship of limited resources.

Organization, then, provides the life-supporting environment that either enables a congregation's participation in the *missio Dei* to flourish or progressively suffocates it. In an interesting reflection on his ministry at the end of his life, the eighteenth-century evangelist George Whitfield compared his own endeavours with his more organizationally methodical friend, John Wesley: 'My brother Wesley acted wisely. The souls that were awakened under his ministry he joined in societies, and thus preserved the fruit of his labour. This I neglected, and my people are a rope of sand.'[1]

The pitfalls of uncritically adopting organizational theory

In considering the organizational expression of their corporate life, Sven-Erik Brodd[2] suggests that another issue for a congregation to bear in mind is the insight of contemporary communications theory that a community, like a church, communicates not only through its words and actions, but also through the way it exists, namely by its structures and organization. He makes the observation that frequently more time is spent on what an organization does than on what they are. He argues that the Church is primarily organic, but that organization gives expression to what it is as a church. It is therefore a misconception to consider the Church primarily or exclusively as identified with an institution. Indeed, it is a false dichotomy to pit organization and institution as in some way contrary to, or frustrating of, Kingdom-orientated mission. Brodd tellingly comments: 'Administration of the sacraments and finances (or the church organization in general) both bear witness to the Kingdom of God and can therefore not be in contradiction when communicating what the church is.'[3] Yet for as much as the Church has an organizational expression, it is

---

1 J. B. Wakeley, *Anecdotes of the Rev George Whitefield, M.A.*, London: Hodder & Stoughton, 1862, p. 220.

2 Sven-Erik Brodd, 'Church, Organisation, and Church Organisation: Some Reflections on an Ecclesiological Dilemma', *Swedish Missiological Themes* 93.2 (2005), pp. 245–63.

3 Brodd, 'Church Organisation', p. 257.

very much more than merely an organization, so real care must be taken in subjecting it to the insights of organizational theory and practice.

Few will now be familiar with Mady Thung's attempt to conceptualize a missionary church based on the theory of organization from the mid-1970s. As a contribution to the 'church for others' conversation, she proposed that every Christian should be involved in three 'cycles of activity', namely reflection on practical ends, reflection on ethical problems, and practical action for bringing about a better society.[4] However, her organizational focus on purpose and outcomes relegated the worship and sacramental life of the Church to a purely supporting role.[5] It is illustrative of how even the sympathetic importation of organizational ideas, insights and strategies from an external source can fail to understand the theological nature of the Christian community.

As with the practice of leadership, at present the organizational life of British congregations is far more at risk from the uncritical adoption of contemporary business practice. It is hardly surprising that lay leaders in a local church will bring with them the insights and practices with which they are familiar in their day-to-day lives. So, for example, in the area of recruitment, it seems to make perfect sense to adopt best practice with regard to equal opportunities and to establish a job description and person specification against which to conduct competitive interviews to identify the best person for the position. However, any set of practices embodies various assumptions and values. In this instance, while an emphasis on equal opportunities appears to correspond to ideas about the inclusivity of the Christian community, actually the policy is fundamentally based on institutional self-interest. How do we recruit the best person to do the job that we want to be done? The Church has traditionally taken another approach altogether when it has talked about discerning the call of God. In the purposes of God, the person we feel would best meet the perceived needs of our situation may be called somewhere else, as our felt needs are not paramount. Indeed, our felt needs, however they may have been determined, are potentially incomplete comprehensions of the mind of Christ and at worst compromised by our own flawed self-interest.

What is defining of the Church for its organizational life is the redemptive activity of God in the life, death and resurrection of Christ. A congregation's organizational life needs to be shaped differently, by what

4 Mady A. Thung, *The Precarious Organisation: Sociological Explorations of the Church's Mission and Structure*, The Hague: Walter De Gruyter, 1976.

5 Steven G. Mackie, Book Review, *International Review of Mission* 66.264 (1977), pp. 389–91.

is expressive of its identity as a gospel community taught by Jesus to love God and our neighbour as our selves. What is determinative of its focus is a sustained relationship with God through worship and the means of grace, alongside its participation in the *missio Dei*. Our structures and organization have to give expression to this – the Church does what it is – continually remembering that at best, to borrow Paul's image, our treasure is contained in earthen vessels.

Care needs to be taken therefore when a congregation embraces the insights, strategies and techniques from other disciplines. To do so uncritically can import into the church ideological values that do not stand gospel scrutiny. Notions of efficiency, profit, progress and growth may not be antithetical to the gospel, but neither may they best embody Kingdom values. Brodd sagely observes:

> When churches ... integrate practices that are not theologically grounded there is a danger of inner secularization ... [creating] confusions about the meaning and goal of the church. Indeed the genuine identity of the church can be pushed into the background by values that have their origin elsewhere.[6]

Modality and sodality, organizational structures of God's mission

Back in the early 1970s, the missiologist Ralph Winter wanted to clarify further how mission is organized by identifying 'The Two Structures of God's Redemptive Mission'.[7] Recognizing both as genuine and legitimate expressions of church, the first was modelled on the synagogue and is what is generally recognized as 'the New Testament church'. This was a multi-generational community based on those who comprised the faithful believers in a given place. The other was typified by Paul's missionary band, whom Winter considered to be prototypes of subsequent missionary endeavours. Joining such a group required a second commitment beyond the first structure and involved a specific missionary task or focus.

Having mapped these structures through church history, Winter uses the terms 'modality' and 'sodality' to distinguish between them (modality

---

6 Brodd, 'Church Organisation', p. 259.

7 Ralph D. Winter, *The Two Structures of God's Redemptive Mission*, Pasadena: William Carey Library, 1995. This was the title of an address he gave to the All-Asia Mission Consultation in Seoul, Korea in August 1973, though his thinking had first been outlined in Ralph D. Winter and R. Pierce Beaver, *The Warp and Woof: Organising for Christian Mission*, South Pasadena: William Carey Library, 1970, pp. 52–62.

from *mode*, the customary way things are done; sodality from the Latin *sodalis*, meaning comrade, associate or accomplice and is suggestive of close active partnership). In doing so, he wished to affirm the missionary and para-church movements as genuine and legitimate expressions of God's redemptive mission. The symbiotic relationship between the two structures is vital for the Church to fulfil its calling. This can be illustrated in various ways: sodalities provide the energy and commitment to pioneer new ground for Christ, while the stability and maturity of modalities are able to sustain and grow them; or again, the mobile flexibility of sodalities enables them to respond to new opportunities, while the stability and security of modalities can provide the resources that enable sodalities to flourish.

Winter wanted to affirm both structures as essential in God's missionary work. Modalities were not missionally second class, and sodalities were not ecclesial aberrations because of the missional failure of the modalities. What he wanted to establish was that

> God, through His Holy Spirit, has clearly and consistently used a structure other than (and sometimes instead of) the modality structure. It is our attempt here to help church leaders and others to understand the legitimacy of both structures, and the necessity for both structures not only to exist but to work together harmoniously for the fulfilment of the Great Commission.[8]

For a local congregation in contemporary Britain, besides its support of sodalities in overseas mission, what Winter's work establishes is both the legitimacy and importance of mission work in its own locality that is, or strongly resembles, a sodality. This might be an ecumenical initiative, a form of fresh expression or collaboration with a para-church organization.

Being, doing, organizing

For itself, a congregation's missional identity is expressed in what it does; and its doing determines the shape and substance of its organization – a flow from being, to doing, to organizing.[9] In the light of this, there are practical steps that an established local church can take to help improve or maintain a missional shape in the organizational dimension of its life.

First, a 'culture of spirituality' that is more than a perfunctory prayer

8 Winter, *Two Structures*, p. 15.

9 Craig Van Gelder, *The Ministry of the Missional Church*, Grand Rapids: Baker, 2007, pp. 17–18.

at the beginning of a meeting and the recitation of the grace at the end. Some meetings and committees are about 'discerning the mind of Christ' together, not just making democratically determined decisions. Others may be less grand in nature, but it is equally important that their place in the Church's participation of the *missio Dei* is owned, acknowledged and articulated.

Second, a church can audit its organizational structures against its engagement in mission and more general missional criteria. What is vital and needs to be continued? What could be done better and needs strengthening? What is peripheral or serving little or no purpose and might be discontinued, releasing time, energy and resources that might be focused elsewhere? It is particularly helpful to foster an ethos of provisionality in the organizational arrangements of a congregation's life. In an age of rapid social and technological change, this can be vital in enabling the Church to be responsive to its context.

Third, when designing, developing or revising organizational structures, make them light and flexible, paying special attention to the 'duration principle', differentiating between those functions that are a permanent requirement, those that sit with a long-term ministry function and those that are specifically task-focused and time-limited. These are important issues as they will determine who might be involved, mutual expectations and the basis upon which arrangements are put in place.

Fourth, it is important to consider how best to maintain a mission-focused functioning. 'Mission drift' can be a real danger as the original purpose is morphed by a combination of experience, personalities and external circumstances. It can be helpful to have something written down that expresses what a group or function is in place to do. Revisiting it from time to time can mitigate the tendency to drift. The larger or more fluid a congregation is the more important this becomes in helping to embed its missional functioning. Terms of reference may be too formal for some, but they do indicate the kind of base-line that establishes a missional focus that can be returned to and held accountable against. For example, it is interesting to note that Parochial Church Councils carry responsibility in 'co-operation with the minister in promoting in the parish the whole mission of the church, pastoral, evangelistic, social and ecumenical'.[10]

Ultimately, organization is unavoidable. The question for every congregation is whether theirs is fit for purpose. Is it shaped around and supportive of their participation in the *missio Dei* or not? In this way organizing for mission is of critical importance for the missional life and health of a congregation.

---

10 Parochial Church Council (Powers) Measure 1956, section 2.

26

Whose Mission?

To ask whose mission it is that a local church engages in seems pretty obvious. Does the question even need asking? Individual church mission statements aside – which owe more to importing late-twentieth-century business strategies into a congregation's life than anything else – clearly the answer is that it is God's mission. Missiological thinking over the last fifty years has firmly established the primacy of God's will and purpose in missional understanding. The existence and life of the Church is neither the source nor the goal of mission. In the oft-quoted statement that has its roots in the work of Jürgen Moltmann, 'It's not that the church of God has a mission in the world, but that the mission of God has a church in the world.'[1]

Contemporary debates may, using the Latin terms, rather tendentiously pit the *missio Dei* against the *missio ecclesiae*, but this is to run the fatal risk of creating a false dichotomy. The Church does have a mission, but this mission is wholly subsumed in its discernment of, and participation in, God's mission. Likewise, the mission of God does include the Church. It is a part of the divine plan. The Church is an integral part of God's missional intention for the world. Indeed, more than anywhere else, it is the place where the outcomes of this mission are realized; as the rule of God is embraced, the Lordship of Christ is owned and the principles of the Kingdom are acted upon in the power of the Spirit. The *missio Dei* and the *missio ecclesia*, the mission of God and the mission of the Church, belong inseparably together in an outwardly engaged church.

Understanding the locus of Christian mission, however, is only the beginning of asking the question of whose mission it is. There are different dimensions to the question that are only rarely touched upon, yet they can potentially impinge on the life of any local congregation. They relate

---

1 Moltmann's actual quote is, 'It is not the church that has a mission of salvation to fulfil in the world; it is the mission of the Son and the Spirit through the Father that includes the church, creating a church as it goes on its way.' Jürgen Moltmann, *The Church in the Power of the Spirit*, London: SCM Press, 1977, p. 64.

to those situations when a mission initiative presents an opportunity to co-operate, collaborate, partner or enter strategic alliances with others. There are clearly good reasons for countenancing such a relationship offered in the chance of making a common cause. On a practical level, the sharing of resources can better equip or further extend the reach of an initiative, alongside avoiding duplication, sharing expertise and thereby maximizing potential outcomes. Given that most such partnerships will be between Christians, theologically speaking they can also be seen to embody a biblical emphasis on unity as well as Paul's understanding of working in partnership for the sake of the gospel.[2] Indeed, it can also be said to reflect the nature of the Trinity itself, existing in, and working through, relational participation.

Collaborative missional working: a global perspective

What little missiological thinking there has been on collaborative missional working has mostly taken place in the forum of the international missionary movement, with partnership being the preferred focus. First used in a document presented to the International Missionary Council (IMC) meeting in Whitby, Canada, in 1947 entitled 'Partners in Obedience', it was part of a concerted attempt to move beyond the dominance and dependency dynamics that had evolved between the older 'sending' churches of the North and the younger 'receiving' churches of the South. Often typified as the movement from pioneer, to parent, to partner, this developing understanding shifted towards 'partnership in mission' after the meeting of the IMC in Willingen, Germany, in 1952. This was in no small part due to the emergence of the concept of *missio Dei* at Willingen and the clear relocation of missionary work from being an activity of the Western Church to the rest of the world, to a participation of all in God's one mission. However, as Max Warren was to observe in a series of lectures in March 1955, 'Partnership is an idea whose time has not yet fully come.' He believed it was the key to unlock the doors of division and disruption in society,[3] and developed an understanding of partnership as containing three commitments: to involvement, to acceptance of responsibility and to the readiness to accept liability.[4] Such partnerships are freely entered

---

2 On unity, see John 17 and Eph. 4.3–5. On partnership, see 2 Cor. 8.23; Phil. 1.5; and Philemon 1.6, 17.

3 Max Warren, *Partnership: The Study of an Idea*, London: SCM Press, 1956, p. 11.

4 Warren, *Partnership*, p. 13.

into, open to dissolution and involve a relationship of trust between the partners as they serve the purpose of their common enterprise.[5]

These themes have been echoed and developed across the theological spectrum during the late twentieth and early twenty-first centuries. The original Lausanne Covenant in 1974, for example, includes the statement: 'We urge the development of regional and functional co-operation for the furtherance of the church's mission, for strategic planning, for mutual encouragement, and for the sharing of resources and experience.' When the movement assembled in Cape Town in 2010, the development in their understanding was clear:

> Partnership in mission is not only about efficiency. It is the strategic and practical outworking of our shared submission to Jesus Christ as Lord. Too often we have engaged in mission in ways that prioritize and preserve our own identities (ethnic, denominational, theological, etc.), and have failed to submit our passions and preferences to our one Lord and Master. The supremacy and centrality of Christ in our mission must be more than a confession of faith; it must also govern our strategy, practice and unity.[6]

Partnership for a local congregation

While the context of a local congregation in the UK is vastly different from the issues that swirl around global mission, the underlying principles are still informative. The mission imperative and the impulse to Christian unity have always acted together. Whether this coming together has been through evangelistic work, such as Mission England in the 1980s and more recently the Alpha course, or through engagement with non-denominational para-church mission agencies such as Christian Aid, Tear Fund or Hope Together (Hope 08), the insights of the international missions movement are helpfully instructive.

In the light of this discussion, a primary issue for every local congregation to address must be, 'With whom might we be in partnership as we share in God's mission?' Obviously this presupposes an understanding of

---

5 For a fuller exploration of the issues of partnership in the international missions movement, see: *International Bulletin of Missionary Research* 34.3 (2010); Jonathan Y. Rowe, 'Dancing with Elephants', *Missiology: An International Review* XXXVII.2 (2009), pp. 149–63; Philip Neil Groves, 'A Model for Partnership', University of Birmingham, unpublished PhD, 2009; and Colin Marsh, 'Partnership in Mission: To Send or to Share', *International Review of Mission* XCII.366 (2003), pp. 370–81.

6 www.lausanne.org

the missional needs and opportunities that their location is presenting to them, and the answer may include another church of their denomination/ stream, an ecumenical connection or some form of para-church organization or initiative.

Second, when we enter into a missional partnership together, how do we protect it from dissolving into mere institutional or organizational empire building? If it is an expression of the *missio Dei* rather than the mission statement of our church or charity, we must be careful of where 'badges of ownership' are pinned.

Third, how do we appropriately deal with asymmetries in power and resources? If our churches and organizations reflect the issues of the wider society in which we live, we can expect issues such as wealth, education, class, ethnicity and geography all to manifest their divisive and disruptive influence. How might they be identified and the tendency towards domination and dependency averted? Of course, the answer will vary from context to context.

Fourth, what shape should such a partnership take? Is it informal and voluntary, yet with a shared understanding of the commitment and responsibilities involved, or might it be something more formal and constitutionally based? As soon as money is involved and a bank account required, some measure of formality and institutional expression is inevitable. However, whichever path is followed, there is advantage to be taken if Warren's insights into the nature of the three commitments of genuine partnerships are explicitly addressed. In the context of building relationships of trust between the prospective partners, these are:

- What is the expressed common cause of our involvement together?
- What is involved in our acceptance of responsibility in this initiative?
- What are the implications of our readiness to accept liability for this initiative?

Most of the discussion of collaborative working between Christians in the context of the international missions movement takes this form, with partnership, variously interpreted, as the starting point of choice for the exploration of the relationship. For all of the strength of the idea of partnership, not least its biblical resonances, it is not without shortcomings. In the Western context, for example, partnership is a complex term, which includes formal and informal contractual arrangements with legal implications of ownership, rights and responsibilities that may not be so helpful. Indeed, Jonathan Bonk, while acknowledging that Paul was warmly appreciative of the Philippian church's 'partnership in the gospel', notes that the apostle 'most frequently and tellingly thought of the church in organic terms, repeatedly and emphatically insisting that it is the *body of Christ*'.[7]

The cost of partnership

Account also needs to be taken of the cost of partnership. The writer of Ecclesiastes may be right that two are better than one,[8] but speaking ecclesiastically, it is a significant challenge successfully to enable congregations, denominations, special-interest groups and para-church organizations to work effectively together. As the missiologist Charles Van Engen sagely observes:

> Creating partnerships takes time and energy, is initially expensive, tends to slow the participants down, and sometimes yields less creative mission initiatives than the partners might have demonstrated by doing mission independently.[9]

Van Engen then goes on to map the increasingly complex pattern of contemporary partnerships in global mission, noting in passing the place of non-governmental organizations or NGOs. While he does not take this further, others have. Donald Mtetemala makes the observation from his experience in Tanzania that Christians cannot work in isolation, as they clearly share common concerns with non-Christians in alleviating and fighting poverty: 'we need, therefore, to find ways of working together'.[10]

Whose mission?

This adds a significant further dimension to the question, 'Whose mission?' It is one thing to collaborate or enter into a partnership with those who also owe allegiance to Jesus Christ; but what of a working relationship with those who do not share Christian faith? This has important implications for local mission initiatives when opportunities arise to partner with

---

7 Jonathan J. Bonk, 'What About Partnership', *International Bulletin of Missionary Research* 34.3 (2010), pp. 129–30.

8 Eccles. 4.9–12.

9 Charles Van Engen, 'Towards a Theology of Mission Partnerships', *Missiology: An International Review* XXIX.1 (2001), p. 12.

10 Tim Chester (ed.), *Justice, Mercy and Humility: Integral Mission and the Poor*, Milton Keynes: Paternoster, 2002, p. 148.

a local council, neighbourhood or campaigning group. Three different approaches are helpful in enabling a congregation to identify these implications and engage with them, as they seek to discern their appropriate response to any presenting need or opportunity.

First, Malcolm Duncan helpfully charts a continuum of potential responses from separation to assimilation that are open to a local congregation when they are presented by such an opportunity.[11] He advocates a position of 'distinctive faith' that enables a local congregation to face the big challenges of society without losing the distinctiveness of their commitment to Christ. Building upon ten core theological values – such as the fact that human dignity matters because it is a creation gift of God, that justice is a priority, that servant-heartedness embodies the example of Jesus and that there is always hope – he then advocates following the Faithworks Charter as a means of expressing this distinctive faith in the public square. This fifteen-point plan helpfully articulates an inclusive basis for Christian service, the valuing of individuals in a way consistent with a distinctively Christian ethos and a professional approach to management, organizational practice and funding. In doing so, it provides a detailed expression of the position of 'integral mission' that the Micah Network has advocated in international missions. Mtetemala reflects:

> It is most important, however, that as we collaborate with other agencies we do not lose sight of Jesus, the motive of our mission. Since our mission is God's mission, we must always remember that we offer something far above the material well-being of a person.[12]

The Faithworks approach is very helpful, as it encourages the Christian community to understand what it believes and why, and then seeks to identify ways in which this might be expressed in a collaborative missional engagement with wider society. However, there is necessarily a measure of assertiveness in this approach, as a distinctively Christian ethos and understanding is asserted in whatever partnerships are undertaken. A degree of control also needs to be retained, and Duncan advises caution or withdrawal when a Christian position is not appropriately ring-fenced.

Second, Nigel Wright develops a more nuanced view in his exploration of the different paradigms by which the Church can engage with the state. In a discussion of hard and soft secularism, where 'hard secularism' is an essentially atheistic world-view that seeks to banish faith from the public

---

11 Malcolm Duncan, *Kingdom Come*, Oxford: Monarch, 2007, pp. 109–27.
12 Chester, *Justice*, p. 148.

sphere, and 'soft secularism' is a political strategy to hold together a society with a plurality of ideological and religious convictions, he expresses his commitment to the latter. Recognizing that the familiarity with a position of social control is a legacy of Constantinian Christendom for the Christian Church, yet needing to resist the hard secularism of the New Atheists, who aggressively want to eject and resist faith-based initiatives in wider society, Wright argues that 'we do not need to possess the public realm to participate in it'. Rather, he maintains that Christian witness and spiritual truth are most potent when they are offered in humility from below instead of being imposed from above.[13] The question of 'Whose mission?' remains pertinent, but is now located in identity rather than possession; that is, in the self-identity of participating Christians and in the core values of the initiative to which they have committed themselves, which are commensurate with the gospel. Christians participate in wider society as Christians: this is their democratic right and responsibility. Yet as they work within civil society for the common cause of communal well-being, there is no overwhelming need for such a collaboration or project to be named as Christian. Indeed, civil and secular partners or those from other faith groups would have legitimate reservations for such an insistence.

A third consideration takes the discussion a step further by exploring this issue of identity and how far it is essential to maintain or uphold an explicitly Christian distinctiveness in missional working. Are there in fact times when our missional collaboration does not even require us to be in an informal partnership? A number of questions can be posed:

- How important is a Christian 'badge' on any missional partnership?
- Is there a point at which what we see as *Christian* mission work ceases to be purely *Christian* mission?
- Should the fruit of social, political and environmental mission work be effectively given away to the wider community as a generous gift for the benefit of all?

While Duncan might dismiss such an approach as falling into assimilation, there is some biblical warrant for considering it a legitimate expression in the range of possible options for a local congregation participating in the *missio Dei*. For example, when Jesus speaks of discipleship in terms of salt (Matt. 5.13), whether this is interpreted as seasoning or preservative,

---

13 Nigel Wright, *Free Church, Free State*, Milton Keynes: Paternoster, 2005, pp. 276–9.

it is clear that it is only as it dissolves and loses its original structural integrity that it accomplishes its purpose. Similarly, if light is contained at its point of origin, everything remains in darkness. It is only as it is dissipated that it does its work (Matt. 5.14–16). Or again, when Jesus speaks of the Kingdom as yeast, it is only as it loses itself in a great quantity of flour and water that it has its effect (Matt. 13.33). Jesus is clear: there are times when the Kingdom is like a seed growing secretly (Mark 4.26–29). Might it be that there are times when anonymous Christian participation works along this line? Rather than establishing ownership of an initiative or the rights of partnership, there are occasions when, in losing ourselves for Christ's sake, Kingdom DNA is introduced to wider society. Or again, taking a different angle, the apostle Paul observes, 'For it seems to me that God has put us ... at the end of the procession, like those condemned to die in the arena.' This is not a position of power or control. 'Blessed are the meek,' says Jesus, 'for they will inherit the earth' (Matt. 5.5, NIV).

Whose mission? There are in fact a range of legitimate responses for a congregation to consider. These stretch from a purely Christian collaboration of different churches or organizations, through a full-blown, formal partnership that upholds specific Christian values, to a more informal participating without possessing, to a voluntary sacrificial gift for the wider common good. It is always God's mission. In Christ, we know this mission to be redemptive and epitomized by the counter-intuitive self-emptying suffering of the cross. As Cathy Ross tellingly asks:

> What attitudes do we exhibit when we enter into partnership? Do we adopt a crusading mind ... or are we disciples and partners with crucified minds, giving up our rights, manifesting the courage to be weak – living the paradox of a crucified, almighty God?[14]

Street Pastors – a case study

It's a July evening, and a Street Pastor team is out on the streets in the red-light district in Plumstead, south-east London. A Street Pastor initiative was established in the Borough of Greenwich two years earlier, in September 2009, initially in response to the murder of a young man in Woolwich the previous year. A year in, the management committee was approached by the police to see whether Greenwich Street Pastors would be willing to be part of a multi-disciplinary team offering support to women involved

---

14 Cathy Ross, 'The Theology of Partnership', *International Bulletin of Missionary Research* 34.3 (2010), p. 147.

in prostitution in the area in Plumstead around St Nicholas' Church. The churchyard and adjoining park is the centre of a small but long-established sex trade in the area.

That night we talked with a number of women. One 52-year-old told us she'd been working the streets since she was fourteen. It was her mother who'd introduced her to the trade. 'What else can I do?' she said, 'It's the only thing I know.'

We engaged with one younger woman several times. In some conversations she was aggressive, in some very frightened, in all very vulnerable, born of a mix of hopelessness, alcohol and drugs. The last time we met her that night she had taken the initiative to find us. 'Please, forget about me. I'm not worth it. You're nice ladies. You're beautiful. I hope when I'm as old as you I'll be as beautiful as you. But I'll be dead.' Then she was gone. Those words, 'Forget about me. I'm not worth it', are words you often hear out on the streets.

Street Pastors began in January 2003 in response to the rising tide of gun crime and gang culture among the black communities, yet it has proved to be highly transferable and adaptable for other cultural contexts. From its first team of eighteen mainly grannies in Brixton, there are now over two hundred and fifty initiatives operating all across the country, seeking 'to listen, to help and to care'.

Street Pastors is a significant missional movement. One of its defining features is the way it works in partnership, both partnerships of local churches and in that partnership with the police and the local authority that they refer to as 'the Urban Trinity'.[15]

Seeking to understand the lived reality of this partnering more fully as a director of the Ascension Trust/Street Pastors, I set out to talk with key individuals involved in this work. Through seven semi-structured interviews, I spoke with local councillors, the police and leaders in the Street Pastors organization itself.[16] All the interviewees affirmed the fundamen-

---

15 Ray Bakke, *The Urban Christian*, MARC Europe, 1987, p. 25.

16 Interviews took place between February and April 2008. Interviewees were: Councillor Lorna Campbell, Lambeth Council Cabinet Member for Health and Care Services, formerly deputy Cabinet Member for Community Cohesion; Eustace Constance, Operations Manager for Street Pastors, formerly Co-ordinator, Lambeth Street Pastors; DC Ian Critchlow, formerly Metropolitan Police, on attachment to the Association of Chief Police Officers' National Community Tension Team; Les Isaac, Director, Ascension Trust; David Shosanya, London Baptist Association Regional Minister for Mission and Street Pastors' Co-founder; Councillor Clare Whelan, Lambeth Borough Councillor and former Mayor of Lambeth; Superintendent Paul Wilson, leading Lambeth Borough Police's Partnership and Community Safety work.

tal importance of partnership; however, through the conversations, five clearly articulated aspects of partnership emerged.

Partnership between churches

Street Pastors began as a vision of what could be achieved by partnership between churches.

> The vision for the whole thing ... was this really mad vision of getting churches working together ... and bringing them to the place where they can believe that we could impact the community. (Eustace Constance)

Partnership between churches is central to Street Pastors. It was seeing pastors of very different traditions and backgrounds working together in Jamaica that inspired Les Isaac:

> I met a group of church leaders who were able to go beyond their tradition and their theological conviction and to find common ground to work together – that inspired me.

However, David Shosanya speaks of disappointment with the slow buy-in from some major churches. When asked why that might be, he suggests that there is a model of church life that works against the possibility of community involvement, alongside personality issues being at work:

> The bigger congregations are focused on developing ... a mega-church that has the problem of losing a sense of organic engagement and credibility. Instead of the whole church being a movement for change, a particular ministry (within the church) will be charged with making a change in that community, but the church itself, the body, will be disconnected ... and there are issues around relationships ... who's perceived to be the leader within the Borough ... personality issues.

From a police perspective, Paul Wilson also recognizes the fractured nature of the Church. 'It's sporadic. It's an untapped area ... in Lambeth there are so many groups ...' Here is the issue of fragmentation, both within the Church, between churches and between church and community. However, disunity is not the end of the story. Despite this fragmentation that Street Pastors works in the middle of,

> [i]t's had the benefit of bringing a new kind of ecumenism, that's not formulaic, that's not about creed, but is about action. It's created this

black and white thing, but also across denominations. Some black denominations would never turn up together, but within Street Pastors they co-exist, almost in defiance of their ministers. (David Shosanya)

Partnership between black and white churches

Shosanya's observation, 'It's created this black and white thing', deserves further scrutiny. Street Pastors identifies its core values as

- being people of integrity
- holding the sacredness of human life
- honouring the community
- taking personal responsibility
- developing the full potential of the individual.

Isaac identifies these as Christian values; Shosanya as values of his African/African Caribbean culture: 'These were values that were a key part of our cultural identity, our cultural ecology in a sense.'

Street Pastors arose out of the black community's response to the violence in its midst. Yet Street Pastors has been remarkably transferable, operating in a wide variety of urban, suburban and rural contexts across the UK and beyond. In a sense, it can be seen as a gift from the black community to the other communities in our society.

Partnership between faith groups

The big issue for secular agencies is not partnership between churches but partnership between faith groups. There has been a strong push from some local authorities for faith groups not just to work together, but effectively to work as one.

> We don't understand faith groups. We lump them all together as if they're the same ... There's a real danger of misjudging the dynamics ... Faith communities are far more complicated things than it's generally realized. (Councillor Clare Whelan)

There is genuine tension for the Church between its identity as a community with exclusive allegiance to Christ and its involvement in a society that is unwilling to accept its distinctiveness. However, it is more an issue between a secular society and faith communities than between faith communities themselves. The issue is of common values, not common beliefs.

Partnership with the community

Street Pastors work with a strongly operant incarnational theology. When asked about the significant achievements of Lambeth Street Pastors, Constance immediately responds, 'since May 2003 ... they've been out there every week ... there's a constant presence'. This is not only a faithful committed presence, which seeks to model the faithful committed presence of God, but it is also a presence that identifies with its community:

> We need to be able to go to the homes of these children and ask Mum or Dad 'What can we do to help Johnny, he's struggling in school. How can we', and note the emphasis on 'we', because so often society blames them – and so often they're saying, 'I can't cope' ... Johnny needs to understand that even if Dad doesn't care, the church does. If Dad's not there, the church is there, God is there. So (the thing) that connects us with school, on the streets, with home, is God. (Les Isaac)

Street Pastors also seeks to be a mediating presence. This is recognized by the police:

> We need people who can speak for networks that tell us what it's really like to live in the community ... What we're finding is that things like the Police Consultative Body comprises people who really represent themselves and their point of view. (Superintendent Paul Wilson)

A significant factor in Street Pastors' credibility with the community seems to rest on the voluntary nature of the teams. In response to the question about the difference between Street Pastors and Community Safety Officers, every interviewee identified the voluntary, unpaid nature of the work:

> They're doing it in a voluntary capacity ... they're giving of their own time, and I think that makes a difference to the people they reach. They think, 'These people are here for me, and they don't have to be'. (Councillor Clare Whelan)

> Other people are doing a job. (Councillor Lorna Campbell)

This suggests that in spite of society's consumerist ethos there is a suspicion about turning caring into a commodity. There is something significant about not being paid, about the voluntary giving of time, but it is also about a perception of powerlessness in Street Pastors. Those who serve as Street Pastors are identifying with the Christ who laid aside the use of power in a conventional sense, and who gave himself sacrificially.

Practically, it seems to be the voluntary and powerless nature of the teams that makes them approachable:

> There's something about them (Community Safety Officers), maybe it's their police connection, that young people don't like them. Yet some of those PCSOs are good people ... but there's a perception that they're out there ... to report on them ... Street Pastors have no power, no power of arrest. It's relational. (Les Isaac)

Partnership with the police and the local authority

The basis upon which the Church and the police and local authorities relate is, from the standpoint of the secular authorities, primarily pragmatic. However, Street Pastors also have a strong and espoused theology of the nature of the relationship between the Church, police and the local authority.

> It's a relationship (between the church and the police, and the church and the local authorities) made in heaven ... the church has its specific role ... we're the people who're going to comfort the sick and have the conscience ... for the community. But we also forget that the whole issue of justice was also ours before it was the police's ... and taking care of the widows and the homeless, the housing associations came out of the Christian community, all of that was ours. By the nature of the fact that they've been taken on by responsible partners, that should actually encourage us to work with them ... In recent history the police and local authority have seen themselves as being totally responsible for all that ... but we can turn and say we're concerned about the health, the safety, the well-being of our community ... we have a holistic approach to life and to people ... the aims, they're the same, let's do it together. (Eustace Constance)

Common concerns, different roles

Street Pastors is clearly confident in the Church's place in public life. However, it also recognizes the Church's distinctive role. There is a strong sense in the responses that the Church does not have all the resources to solve the problems:

All of us have something unique to bring to the table ... They're all God-given institutions. The police represent law and order ... And the church is there to have the heavenly vision and the passion to ensure justice, peace and grace – whether it's education, employment – to ensure that people get their fair share of the cake. (Les Isaac)

Here is a theology of common grace, of divine providence, of God providing structures of government for the good of all. Here is also a place for a prophetic role for the Church.

When the Church and secular agencies seek to work in partnership, there is an inevitable tension and often suspicion around the place and nature of faith. The Church asks whether it can remain faithful to its identity, and the secular partners are suspicious of the Church's agenda. David Shosanya is confident about the Church's contribution:

We mustn't be ashamed to emphasize the spiritual nature of the ministry ... we're performing a spiritual function out there on the streets. We're bringing spiritual energy, we're bringing spiritual insights, even though in physical actions. When I talk (in Street Pastors training) about knowing your community, I talk about Jeremiah 29.8 ... where it says you must love the land. You can grow up in a certain physical space and dislike it ... often in my sessions we pray for a love for the land, asking God to forgive. I think that's important for somewhere like Lambeth, where people who've just come to Brixton have heard already of the riots and so on. So there's got to be a real sense of loving the land.

However, partnering with secular authority brings genuine tension:

You have to negotiate some real tensions with people who want the consequences of your faith, but not your faith itself, and that's a very tricky area to negotiate. (David Shosanya)

This is a tension secular partners also negotiate. There is suspicion about the Street Pastors' agenda. Wilson speaks from a police perspective:

I had a conversation with my colleagues in the wider partnership, and I was picking up that there was some concern about the faith-based activity of Street Pastors, and how in a diverse community such as Lambeth that was not appropriate in this day and age. (Superintendent Paul Wilson)

While this may reflect a lack of awareness of the place of the black church in its community, it is a common concern, also shared by the local authority:

> There was a worry that Street Pastors was more interested in converting people than in solving their problems ... there's still quite a suspicion about agendas. (Councillor Clare Whelan)

The crucial point about tension is that it is intrinsic to the Church's identity. The Church is called to live in the tension of being in the world but not of it; and in the tension that is also intrinsic to life between the 'now and not yet' of God's Kingdom.

If the Church's distinctive contribution is, as Shosanya says, 'spiritual', what are the distinctive contributions of the other partners? Responses touched on issues of profile, connections and funding:

> I looked around to see what I could contribute ... clearly they needed help in building better relationships ... my nagging concern was the infrastructure, they needed some pretty significant sums of money. (Superintendent Paul Wilson)

Both councillors speak of their sadness that Lambeth has not backed Street Pastors more wholeheartedly, specifically in terms of funding. Lorna Campbell's aim in relation to the initiative is 'strengthening their position within Lambeth ... my objective was to get funding for them ... to get them more recognized'. Funding, it seems, gives identity and creates relationship. The question is about the nature of the relationship created. However, Critchlow sees the police role in relation to Street Pastors somewhat differently. He identifies a role for the police in helping the Church understand the situation it is living in. Just as the Church holds a prophetic mirror to the world, so the world holds a mirror for the Church:

> There's a need for the police to have a role in bringing to the churches the reality that they might have within their membership people who may have needs and concerns that are policing issues ... I think sometimes people have their individual realities and almost park them on Sunday mornings when they come to church. (DC Ian Critchlow)

The implication is that the Church sometimes colludes in, and even exacerbates, a fragmented way of seeing and living. Secular partners may help the Church free itself from this collusion. Furthermore, as the Church demonstrates a willingness to listen to its partners, so perhaps those partners may become more ready to listen to the Church.

There were five Street Pastors out that July night in Plumstead, together with one police officer and a young woman from the local Women's Aid organization. The police insisted on a presence, out of concern for the response of some of the pimps, but the officer was un-uniform and obviously knew and cared about the women concerned. Other members of the multi-disciplinary cohort had been unable to find an available member that night.

The police's response to what the Street Pastors did that night was phenomenal. The email reports circulated to all agencies involved were fulsome in their praise. As for the Street Pastors, they were just doing what they do, being church on the streets. We couldn't have been there if it were not for the partnership that has developed. Partnership brings risk, but incredible opportunity.

27

Mission and Third-Agers

The year 2006 was a really important milestone in our cultural history, but it passed most of us by. That's hardly surprising, as there were no fanfares to herald its significance, and those who were directly affected chose mostly to live in denial. It was the year that proclaimed 'sixty is the new forty!', as the post-war Baby Boom generation began to enter their sixth decade and rewrite what it means to be an older person.

A year earlier, Gap Inc., owner of the largest chain of clothing stores in the USA, launched a new brand of store, Forth & Towne. Gap's strategy was to target the new stores at Baby Boomer women. They had made the connection that this group was responsible for 39 per cent of women's clothing purchases and yet were under-represented in the marketplace. By contrast, the traditional focus of marketing and sales towards the young meant that the 11–30 age group had nearly five times the number of retail outlets dedicated to them.

Speaking in 2009, Yael Davidowitz-Neu, of the Google Retail team, observed how 'marketers are quickly realizing that they will have to alter their traditional tactics if they hope to tap into this group's (the Boomers') collective spending power'. According to the Direct Marketing Group, by 2020 this could amount to 85–90 per cent of disposable income in the UK.

Only very slowly has any appreciation begun to dawn on how the cultural phenomenon of this ageing generation has begun to reshape our lives and experience. 'Ready or not ... the modern world is tilting steadily toward gerontocracy.'[1] Pensions, transport, access to public services and health care, the list of things that will be impacted as this generation hits retirement is almost endless.

The enormity of the social transition that will creep over Western nations during the next half-century has been styled by the United Nations as the 'quiet revolution'; by 2050 one-third of the UK population will be over 50 and the 12,000 centenarians of 2010 will have become half a

---

1 Theodore Roszak, *The Making of an Elder Culture*, Gabriola Island, CA: New Society, 2009, p. 1.

million. Indeed, Sarah Harper, Professor of Gerontology at the University of Oxford's Institute of Population Ageing, estimates that 8 million of those alive today will reach the age of 100.[2] The rapid increase in life expectancy has been one of the hallmarks of the last century, and is the fruit of everything that has been done to improve health and mitigate risk. From pioneering medical science to improvements in road safety and the implementation of health and safety strategies at work, a thousand contributory initiatives have pushed back the boundaries, not only of life expectancy, but of healthy life expectancy. Sociologists have tagged this as 'the ageing of life transitions' or 'downaging'.[3] Sixty really is the new forty!

This reframes the nature of old age. Someone in their sixties will no longer see themselves as an OAP. Their mindset is much younger and they will, by default, dissociate themselves from those things ascribed to the old. As a consequence, language, attitudes and the shape of our culture will need to adapt. Even the over-50s group SAGA may need to rename, rebrand and reinvent itself. It is no coincidence that retirement has more recently been separated by commentators into the rather useful French designations of third and fourth age, differentiating between active older life and that which has been more usually seen as old age.

Active longevity is, of course, nothing new. Methuselah aside, history is littered with those who have enjoyed a long and productive life. Churchill was 65 when the Second World War broke out, and approaching 77 when he was re-elected Prime Minister in 1951. John Wesley only admitted to starting to feel old in 1789 at the grand age of 86. However, what is different about the new social context facing the UK is the sheer number of older people in society.

The cohort effect

In the early part of the twentieth century, Karl Mannheim observed that individuals shaped by a common life experience demonstrated a 'cohort effect', a broad range of similar values that, while not universal, were generally applicable.[4] So if the Baby Boomers are the leading edge of the

---

2 Roszak, *Elder Culture*, p. 2; John T. Cacioppo, 'Lonely Planet', *RSA Journal* (Autumn 2011), p. 12; Professor Sarah Harper, speaking on the BBC Radio 4 *Today* programme on 9 July 2012.

3 Sarah Harper, '21st Century: Last Century of Youth?', 2012 Oxford London Public Lecture; Marc Freedman, *PrimeTime*, New York: Public Affairs, 1999, p. 12.

4 Karl Mannheim, *Essays on the Sociology of Knowledge*, Oxford: Oxford University Press, 1952.

ageing of society, who are they, and how are they significant for the Christian community in contemporary Britain?

'The Baby Boom' is the name that was given to the rapid increase in the birth rate on both sides of the Atlantic following the end of the Second World War. Stretching over an eighteen-year period from 1946 to 1964, the Baby Boom gave birth to a generation that has shaped and been shaped by the powerful forces at work in the second half of the twentieth century.

While the British Boomer generation is proportionately smaller than its American cousin, it still represents one in four of the population. Indeed, the Office of National Statistics projects that this generation will be responsible for swelling the number of over-65s by a massive 45 per cent between the years 2011 and 2030, as an additional 4.5 million people enter retirement.

It is commonly acknowledged that this generation is wealthier, healthier, better educated and numerically greater than any senior segment of any society in history. The 1950s, 60s and 70s were decades of rapid social change and technological advancement. As the Boomers grew up, they witnessed the birth of youth culture, the sexual revolution brought about by the contraceptive pill and the explosion in the divorce rate. Social equality became increasingly important through the work of the women's movement and those who sought to build a multi-cultural society following migration to the UK by members of the West Indian and Asian communities.

Increasing affluence, the raising of the school leaving age and much higher levels of access to higher education have all had a significant influence too. Probably the single most important contributor to the shaping of the life and experience of Baby Boomers is TV and other forms of electronic media.

Their size alone has made them a very influential group within society. Indeed, society has been forced to adjust to their needs from birth. When the boom began there were shortages of baby food, nappies and toys. Then, as they took their first steps, the footwear, photographic and sticking-plaster industries flourished. And so it has continued throughout the years.

Now, as they begin to enter retirement, they still think of themselves as younger than they are. Their attitudes and outlook are vastly different from those of their parents and grandparents. Yet, the advertising industry has already identified that roots and nostalgia are increasingly important to them.

It is their roots and view of the world that are the significant and potential connecting points with the Christian community. For example, in the mid-twentieth century, a much larger proportion of children and young people came under the influence of the Christian gospel through their attendance at Sunday school. While only one out of every twenty-five were connected to a church in 2000, back in 1964 it was one in five who were in Sunday school, and in 1946 it was one in three. Indeed, 10 million of the 13.5 million Baby Boomers born between 1946 and 1964 still identified themselves as Christian in the 2001 UK Census.

The Church has always sought to minister to the older people in its community. Pastoral visitation, day centres and luncheon clubs, midweek devotional and social meetings have been core activities within many congregations, alongside ministry to the sick and dying. However, there are a number of ways in which the ageing population and the birth of the 'third age' present the local church with both missional opportunities and challenges.

An evangelistic opportunity

However young Boomer third-agers continue to convince themselves they are, at some point they will have to face the reality of their age. Faced by their own mortality and the ultimate questions of meaning, destiny and life after death, their Christian roots will provide the spiritual framework with which to begin to engage with these questions.

On a whim, many will return to church, seeking help in making sense of the questions that are beginning to confront them. A mixture of identity and nostalgia will most likely take them back to the denomination of their childhood or adolescence. Because it is about roots and half-remembered experience, a certain degree of familiarity will be helpful. Yet the visit is only a whim. A bad or disappointing experience will easily extinguish any continuing interest. The most important question will be whether these searching visitors connect or whether the moment evaporates into the ether.

With the prospect of many within this generation seeking to reconnect with the Church, what are the potential stumbling-block issues? Here are a few that, generally speaking, resonate with those entering retirement over the coming decades and that it would serve local churches well to have an eye to.

The journey to faith

When spirituality is discussed they most frequently talk about it in the context of their whole lives and in terms of a 'journey'. This embraces the good and bad life experiences they've had in making them who they are. It also confirms the importance of their early Christian experiences in defining their own spirituality.

A lifetime of choices

In an increasingly consumerist society that has elevated choice as one of the most valued principles of life, those entering retirement have tested and broken many of the ethical boundaries they received from their parents. Homosexuality, cohabitation, divorce and abortion are perhaps some of the more controversial issues for the Church. Whatever stance is adopted, it is important to remember that this is the experience they bring with them. The corresponding value to choice is, of course, tolerance. These values are now seen as new virtues in the absence of a widespread moral consensus.

Loose organizational ties and institutional suspicion

While people are happy to participate in the life of an organization, they want to do so on their own terms, with the ability to dip in and out as they choose. Alongside this sits an intuitive dislike of more formal organizational structure and a deep mistrust of motives in the use of power. The ability to maximize inclusion, participation and belonging while minimizing the impact of institutional elements of church life is vital.

Equality, accountability and the practice of leadership

Leaders have to prove themselves through their practice of leadership. If it is seen as manipulative, bullying or self-serving, what trust there is will quickly evaporate. Ministers and church leaders must therefore be very careful not to misuse their role and dress up abusive behaviour in spiritual language. Rather, leadership should be open in style, consultative in process, transparent in practice, and accountable.

The rock 'n' roll soundtrack

With contemporary music epitomizing this generation, it would be only natural to expect that a contemporary worship style would be the most fitting. Counter-intuitively, studies seem to indicate a more nuanced approach brings a more positive response when it includes familiar hymns, albeit in a contemporary style, in the regular diet of worship. With personal roots and familiarity being significant, some have called this the need for 'new-fangled old'.

Sophisticated media consumers

Those growing up in the 1960s and 70s were weaned on TV and have developed increasingly sophisticated tastes as they consume electronic media. It has been estimated that they have averaged 30–40,000 hours each watching TV, viewing somewhere over 250,000 adverts. Any preacher stepping into the pulpit needs to be aware that the staple diet of TV is narrative. The story form heavily influences the viewing experience, from soap operas and movie blockbusters to the mini-narratives of 'news stories' and commercials.

Experience-driven understanding

The whole drift of contemporary culture in the second half of the twentieth century was towards an experiential understanding and interpretation of life. An approach to understanding Christian faith that is purely doctrinal or is heavily reliant on systematic theology will not prove easily accessible. A different starting point needs to be found, one that meets them where they are and connects with the reality of life as they live it. Faith, then, should live and take its form from the particular place and time in which it exists, just as it did for Jesus.

An inclination to social justice

The 1960s was a period of great social ferment. Civil rights marches, the advance of feminism and the birth of protest movements like those campaigning for nuclear disarmament or the end of the Vietnam War were typical of this era. What was cutting edge then became quickly embedded in popular culture, adding environmental and fair-trade issues along the way. It is no coincidence that the Make Poverty History campaign saw many ageing 1960s rock stars at its helm.

Challenging discipleship

The whole notion of 'personal growth' resonates well with the culture of self-fulfilment. Third-agers will take discipleship seriously. Yet it may present some of the most profound challenges too. How long does the Church allow for a life to be brought into 'conformity with Christ'? What issues are 'deal-breakers' for the life of faith? Which sets of circumstances can be persevered with over time and which need immediate action? Historically the Church has been very strict on what have been identified as the 'sins of the flesh', particularly sexual ones such as adultery, fornication and homosexuality; but less rigorous on the 'sins of the spirit' – pride, greed and selfishness. How does the Church walk with returning retirees as they journey with Christ? The personal lives of those coming to Christ after a lifetime away from the Church may take years to untangle.

At the leading edge of a phenomenon that could be part of the churches' experience for a generation, the portents are good. From a large suburban Baptist church that has seen significant growth in its 9.30 a.m. service on a Sunday morning, to the doubling for a village congregation in Kent from fifteen to thirty; or from a fellowship in the New Frontiers network in the home counties, to a Salvation Army citadel in a northern city, all have witnessed these prodigals from the Church re-engaging with their local congregations and finding faith.[5] However, it needs to be remembered that as the Baby Boom generation passes through retirement, Generation X that follows has a far weaker historical connection to Christianity and the Church.

From a completely different perspective, Papyrakis and Selvaretnam of the School of Economics and Finance at the University of St Andrews seek to analyse 'the greying church' from the perspective of a cost–benefit analysis. While from a sociological or theological reading, their paper and its methodology may be significantly open to question, their conclusions are fascinating in this regard. They argue that increasing life expectancy encourages individuals to postpone religious involvement as heaven and hell are pushed further into the future. Therefore they conclude that churches should anticipate attracting older members and be prepared to stress the present socio-economic benefits of believing to counter-balance this.[6]

---

5 For a fuller exploration of this evangelistic opportunity, see Roger Standing, *Re-Emerging Church: Strategies for Reaching a Returning Generation*, Abingdon: BRF, 2008.

6 Elissaios Papyrakis and Geethanjali Selvaretnam, 'The Greying Church: The Impact of Life Expectancy on Religiosity', *School of Economics and Finance Discussion Paper Series*, St Salvator's College, University of St Andrews, no. 0912 (October 2009).

An opportunity to release volunteers

Even if the age of retirement does gradually creep upwards in the coming years, it will hardly dent the leaps forward in life expectancy that are now experienced by the growing numbers of third-agers. Similarly, while diminished pension provision may require some continuation of the working life in some form, this too will not substantially undermine the retirement years of most citizens. There will still be a massive pool of experienced, well-educated, time-rich people seeking an outlet for their energies. Research published in the *Journal of Gerontological Social Work* in the United States discovered that 59 per cent of non-volunteers would like to volunteer if the right opportunity came along, leading Ken Dychtwald to predict that the 'coming years will see a proliferation of ways to bring out the power of volunteerism'.[7] Some have seen this as potentially a country's only increasing national resource in the coming decades.[8] Even back in 1956, John F. Kennedy could comment:

> Today we are wasting resources of incalculable value: the accumulated knowledge, the mature wisdom, the seasoned experience, the skilled capacities, the productivity of a great and growing number of our people – our senior citizens.[9]

If this was the case then, how much more is it so now? Yet just as the third age beckons and individuals leave work, they pay the price of the transient nature of contemporary communities and the atomization of society, as Robert Putman explored in his acclaimed study, *Bowling Alone*. The decrease in engagement in civic life and the wider activities of the local community lead to a social isolation that is only exacerbated by the loss of social networks that are centred on the workplace. It is interesting to note that the close network of family and friends and engaging in leisure activity does not offset this sense of loneliness. What does fill the gap is 'relationships with a purpose'. Interestingly, Marc Freedman observes that this probably underscores how far identity is presently drawn from the working life.[10] Volunteering will therefore potentially provide a route for individuals to help to counteract this experience of detachment and aloneness.

7 Ken Dychtwald, *Age Wave*, New York: Bantam, 1990, p. 162.
8 Roszak, *Elder Culture*, p. 90.
9 *The Gerontologist* 7.3, Part 1 (1967), p. 146.
10 Freedman, *PrimeTime*, p. viii.

Because a local congregation is potentially so well placed within its local community, it can be a key catalyst not only in releasing its members into voluntary service through its own initiatives, but also in helping to create and sustain local networks and infrastructures that enable volunteering to happen. Given the scale of what lies ahead in the coming decades, what is presently in place is likely to be very inadequate. Given the inevitable 'structural lag' in civic life, groups of local churches in particular can become effective facilitators in this area. Given the skill set and experience that many elder volunteers bring, the churches could also enable and support local entrepreneurial initiatives in the volunteer sector.

Given the importance of nostalgia and roots for third-agers, it is also highly likely that in retirement they will return to the unfinished agendas of their youth and early adulthood. As Geraldine Bedell remarked, 'What you notice about the most vital third-agers is the depth of their passions, the scope of their projects.'[11]

Engaging with coming social trends

The significance of social isolation as an experience that propels individuals to volunteering has already been noted. However, for those whose health, self-confidence or circumstances work against them in connecting to their wider community, loneliness will prove to be an increasing issue. This will be compounded by the erosion of traditional social connections by the virtual relationships of online social networking, the relationally inexpensive vicarious participation in the lives of others through reality TV, and the looser more functional nature of most face-to-face interaction. 'Densely interconnected, all-encompassing local groups are becoming less common, whereas fragmented, sparsely interconnected and less stable specialized networks are becoming more so.'[12] It is no surprise to discover that those seniors who experience the greatest sense of personal well-being are those who remain purposefully engaged with their wider community.

If social isolation is a significant issue for the third-agers themselves, the challenge facing their local community, and wider society in more general terms, is the accommodation to an 'elder culture'. This will have a multi-dimensional impact. From the design and layout of public spaces, where homes, streets, parks, shops and community facilities become increasingly 'elder sensitive', to the provision of health care, pensions and welfare benefits, society at large will move from a youth to an elder focus.

11 Geraldine Bedell, *The Observer*, 30 October 2005.
12 Cacioppo, 'Lonely Planet', p. 13.

A number of commentators have been swift in identifying the rise of inter-generational strife as the increasingly large group of retirees continues to squander the resources of the young. From the mid-1980s in the United States, former investment banker and author of *Gray Dawn*, Peter Peterson, has predicted generational warfare based on the fact that the elderly are selfish and that society cannot afford their benefits. In the UK, Conservative MP David Willetts made his position clear in the title of his 2010 treatise, *The Pinch: How the Baby Boomers Took their Children's Future – And How They Can Give it Back*. Novelist Christopher Buckley also painted a disturbing picture in his satirical *Boomsday* narrative where society pays individuals in advance to voluntarily commit suicide at the age of seventy-five for the communal good.[13]

Conflict between old and young may also be sparked by the breakdown of generational succession as status, power and resources fail to cascade down the generations, retained for increasingly longer periods of time by active and engaged elders. Such conflict, however, is predicated on a negative reading of the inevitable social transitions that lie ahead. However, this would not be the first time that Western culture has been forced to reshape itself in the wake of massive demographic shifts. No matter how any inter-generational tension and conflict may develop, as a genuinely trans-generational community the local church has the opportunity prophetically to model a whole different way of being. However strong may be the pressure for congregations to become single-generation expressions of church, this is a failure to live as a gospel community, and in such a context as this significantly compromises its ability to minister the shalom of the gospel.

An alternative, and more positive narrative can also be made. It may be that a potential solution also lies within cultural changes that are now upon us. The social contribution of volunteers, which clearly demonstrates that third-agers are net contributors to society, is clearly a significant part of this. Not unrelated to this is that phenomenon of older age that anthropologists call 'the grandmother hypothesis'. This is the significant role that post-menopausal women make to society, which is always out of proportion to their numbers. One gerontologist speaks of it in terms of 'a wave of oestrogen' washing through society to great beneficial effect.[14] Again, a

---

13 Peter G. Peterson, *Gray Dawn: How the Coming Age Wave will Transform America – and the World*, New York: Crown, 1999; David Willetts, *The Pinch: How the Baby Boomers Took their Children's Future – And How They Can Give it Back*, London: Atlantic, 2010; Christopher Buckley, *Boomsday*, Boston: Twelve, 2007.

14 Theodore Roszak, *Longevity Revolution*, Berkley: Berkley Hill, 2001, pp. 310–13.

local congregation can be a key facilitator as a community enabler, building networks of relationship and helping to unlock the untapped resources of a community and building social capital.

A significant component of local community life that a congregation may become involved with is health care. As third-agers become fourth-agers, health needs will grow rapidly with particularly intense demands on available resources. The outcome will be an opportunity for Christians to re-enter once again caring for the sick and dying, supporting private care-givers and providing a safety net for those who do not meet the criteria for state assistance. Initiatives like the development of Parish Nursing may prove to be timely indeed.[15]

Sarah Harper also calls for a more informed engagement with the third-ager debate as it touches wider society. The advances in Western society that have led to the longevity revolution also benefit the rising generation. But then, the smaller workforce and inevitable skills shortage in a globalized economy will ensure that there is far more choice and opportunity than at any other time in history. Rather than the changes caused by the growth of the third- and fourth-age cohorts being the cause of generational inequalities and an unfair burden, they can be seen as part of a global evolution that potentially has a range of benefits for all.[16] As a community of people informed by gospel values of generosity and altruism, local churches can play an important part in helping to shape the public interpretation of the cultural change going on around it.

---

15 www.parishnursing.org.uk.
16 Harper, '21st Century'

28

Mission and the Occasional Offices

What is the percentage of people who attend a Christian service of worship in any given year? Almost invariably the answer to the question is underestimated, not least because of a failure to take into account some of the most-attended services in the life of the contemporary British church, the 'occasional offices'. While technically such services are eight in number, they are normally taken as referring to infant baptism, marriage and funeral services.[1] Though exact statistics are impossible to collate, the best available analysis would suggest that attendance is somewhere between 70 and 80 per cent of the UK population in any given year.

Cultural Christianity

With such a large discrepancy between those who attend weekly worship services and those who participate in the occasional offices, it would be very easy to dismiss attendance at the latter as insubstantial and inconsequential. That someone attends a family wedding or the funeral of a friend clearly has more to do with personal relationships, family loyalty and social convention than anything else. At best, it might be viewed as a form of 'cultural Christianity' bequeathed by previous generations; at worst, it could be seen as morphing the Church into superstitious 'folk religion', with which it should not choose to collude actively.

The social forces that lie behind the durability and reach of the occasional offices warrant further investigation and scrutiny against missional criteria. Are they merely a passing legacy of the Christendom experience, which should be allowed to disappear speedily from our cultural landscape, or do they offer a present missional opportunity that it would be negligent not to embrace? Rather than beginning with theological and ecclesiological convictions, it is perhaps better, first, to hear the voice of

---

1 The Book of Common Prayer provides for Baptism, Confirmation, Matrimony, the Visitation of the Sick, the Communion of the Sick, Burial, the Churching of Women and Commination.

those who come to the Church seeking its ministry in this regard. Camilla Cavendish, associate editor of *The Times*, articulates this perspective well in a piece entitled, 'Churchgoing isn't always religious'.

> Britain is still a Christian landscape, dotted with spires. It is still a place of Christian ritual, where people go to churches to mark marriages and deaths ... I had not thought much about all of this until five years ago. My first child was a year old and my mother, who had always been a militant atheist, suggested I should start taking him to church. She thought he should 'have the option' of being part of a religious tradition. I was stunned ... Nevertheless, my mother had hit on something. I dutifully explored various churches. The first surprise was how much my son enjoyed the ritual, the kindness. The next surprise was how deeply the rhythm and the language resonated with me. The writers and composers of the best religious works can still sharpen the senses and infuse the spirit like nothing else. The hymns that we sang at school, the cadences of Bible stories, are part of my identity. What other identity can I have? I have not sent my boy to a church school, but to a school that has hymns in assembly, as well as plenty of acknowledgement of other religions. If I don't expose him to that canon, what other can he have? I suspect there are many people who would regret the passing of the Church even if they never set foot in one. The Church of England is rather like the BBC, a beloved institution, mainly mush but with flashes of inspiration ... it may be that one day we will have to contemplate paying a church licence fee. Like TV I may not use it often, but I'd pay for the option. Because it represents something precious, something that we take for granted, and which is presented as faith but is also about the national soul.[2]

The sociologist Émile Durkheim considered that there was 'something eternal in religion' that enabled a society to uphold and reaffirm its collective sentiments at regular intervals.[3] The recognition of this contribution that religion makes to the well-being of society also lay behind Alain de Botton's book *Religion for Atheists* and his call for non-believers to adopt parallel practices, stripped of the elements of faith, to help them find their place in the world. There is a very real sense in which this is exactly the role that the occasional offices play in this regard, and, as Britain will never

---

2 Camilla Cavendish, 'Churchgoing isn't always religious', *The Times*, 15 May 2008.

3 Émile Durkheim, *The Elementary Forms of the Religious Life*, London: Allen & Unwin, 1971, p. 427.

be able to return to its pre-Christian past, they will always remain deeply embedded in our national history, passed down in a form of cultural DNA that will continue to shape our national identity. To reject them is to live in denial and to attempt to initiate a kind of historical amnesia.

Before thinking about how the Church might respond to this inherited phenomenon, it is important to begin by considering what is going on within those who come to a local church requesting one of the variety of infant rites offered by the various denominations, a wedding or, through the community undertaker, a funeral. Whatever informs their action, they are coming to the church to seek its ministry.

It is no coincidence that the occasional offices are located at significant points of change and transition in people's life experience. Marking these moments with ritual expression through 'rites of passage' then becomes a way, according to Alan Billings, of both expressing and managing the feelings that are focused in that moment.[4] While the Christian content of the rite may not be fully understood, its life significance certainly is. Billings also identifies how important an individual's 'point of view' is in understanding what is happening. For the officiating minister, the service is frequently a one-off event with deep Christian symbolism and meaning. To the family celebrating a new arrival or marriage, or deep in the grief that surrounds death, the service fits in a series of narratives: the story of their own lives, the generational cycle of their wider family and the relationships and links with the wider community of which they are a part.[5] This is underlined by how frequently these services are followed by a social event, ranging from the more formal wedding reception through to the more informal christening lunch or funeral tea held in a family member's home.

While only 15 per cent of the population are considered to be regular worshippers, somewhere around 70 per cent plus self-designate themselves as Christians.[6] The difference between these two figures indicates the depth of 'cultural Christianity' in contemporary Britain. While 55 per cent of 'cultural Christians' in the population do not attend worship services, still Christianity has some place in their personal identity and world-view, however poorly it may be understood and articulated. This is more than a mere 'residual faith' in a wider culture that makes repudiation easy, if

---

4 Alan Billings, *Secular Lives, Sacred Hearts*, London: SPCK, 2004, p. 35.

5 Billings, *Secular Lives*, p. 15.

6 The 15 per cent regular-churchgoing figure was based on a pattern of at least once per month attendance. *Churchgoing in the UK*, London: Tear Fund, 2007; the 70 per cent plus self-designation as Christian is derived from the 2001 National Census (71.6 per cent) and the 2010 Integrated Household Survey (71.4 per cent).

not desirable. It may be necessary to subject it to innumerable qualifications with regard to issues of belief and lifestyle. Still, its stubborn and surprising persistence as an observable reality is increasingly saying something positive about 'cultural Christianity' rather than viewing it in purely reductionist terms before dismissing it.

How might the Church respond?

Over recent decades, the move to restrict access to the occasional offices to those within a worshipping community has been on the increase. Perceiving an erosion of the spiritual dimension of the rites and desiring to protect their integrity and keep them meaningful, all kinds of thresholds of church attendance, preparation courses and other criteria have been introduced across the denominations. However, for most clergy the occasional offices have proven to be, as Wesley Carr observes, 'a major facet of the church's pastoral ministry'.[7] Recognizing what an amazing privilege it is to be invited to share these moments of crisis and transition, the Church has the opportunity to give support, provide a framework of meaning and enable people to appropriate for themselves afresh the spiritual legacy of their cultural heritage. Carr notes, though, that the request, when it comes, is for the church to do something 'for' them, rather than 'with' them, or 'to' them.[8] It is important that a local church understand what it is that is being asked of it so that its response can be a genuine attempt to meet people where they are rather than as a pretence for something else.

For practising Christians, the occasional offices are the means whereby they express their faith in Christ at significant points of transition in their lives. For those who are not part of a worshipping community, there are other dimensions to their requests. It is these latter opportunities for ministry that should be viewed through a missional lens. However, even to begin to explore a missional understanding of the occasional offices runs the risk of their being seen merely as evangelistic opportunities. Such an understanding would warp their purpose and meaning as well as their socio-spiritual function. This is not to rule out the possibility that the spiritual dimension of the occasional offices, along with the life and witness of a local church that are expressed through them, might draw individuals to faith in Christ. Indeed, this is an ongoing and widespread experience in the Church even today. However, a missional understanding

---

7 Wesley Carr, *Brief Encounters: Pastoral Ministry through the Occasional Offices*, London: SPCK, 1985, p. 2.

8 Carr, *Brief Encounters*, p. 14.

of the occasional offices puts the emphasis in another place. It is seeking to be aligned with God's concern and interests in those seeking his blessing on their new child, their marriage or their family at a time of profound sadness. One way of seeking to explore this further is how, in its offering of the occasional offices to people beyond its own community, a congregation embodies the widely acknowledged 'five values of a missionary church'.[9] Such activity

- is focused on God the Trinity in worship
- is incarnational and meets people where they are
- is transformational and works to see the Kingdom of God made real through serving others
- makes disciples by being attentive to the call and message of Jesus
- is relational, a community epitomized by welcome and hospitality.

A missional understanding of the occasional offices is about the expression of the prevenient grace of God and a congregation embodying the kindness and generosity of the gospel. The expression of faith of those who seek the occasional offices may only be a form of 'cultural Christianity', but as one minister observed, 'A bruised reed he will not break, and a smouldering wick he will not snuff out' (Isa. 42.3, NIV). It has to be a high priority for a local church to find ways to respond positively and creatively to those who come seeking its ministry in these landmark life experiences.

Infant rites

When a young family from outside of the immediate fellowship of a local congregation seek the opportunity to bring a newborn child to church, there is a whole array of emotions, desires, pressures and drivers behind their request. At its most fundamental, there is almost something primal and instinctive about it. The birth of a child connects parents to something bigger than themselves and more mysterious than normal everyday life experiences. There is joy to be celebrated and shared and a deep desire to say 'thank you'. A service of worship makes this possible and gives the opportunity for family and friends to be invited and to participate in the festivities that are often continued back at home with food and drink. In

---

9 Originally formulated by The Anglican Consultative Council but popularized in the *Mission-Shaped Church Report*, London: Church House Publishing, 2004, pp. 81–2.

every sense, it is an event – a formal naming and first presentation to the wider world. The choice of godparents and the presence of family and friends acknowledges that no parents can accomplish this alone. Seeking to have the heart of this celebration in church recognizes that no child is brought up in a moral vacuum and that the unspoken aspirations are for this child to be aligned with the values and virtues modelled by Jesus.

There may, of course, also be darker elements that inform or cast a shadow over such a request. Maybe the child is unexpected or in some way unwanted. Or again, seeking a religious service comes under the duress of family expectations or for the expiation of guilt through an act of atonement. Those working with the family need to be sensitive in listening and understanding as they seek to respond to each approach.

Whatever ecclesiological understanding a local church has of its infant rite – baptism, dedication (of the parents or the child), thanksgiving or presentation to God – it is highly likely the parents concerned will have little theological appreciation of what they are doing. What matters is their desire to bring their child and themselves before God. The authenticity and integrity of the church's ministry is experienced in so far as it embodies a missional response that enables the family to take a step towards Christ.

Using the 'five values of a missionary church' as a helpful reference point, such a response can be embodied in various ways. The focus on God the Trinity in worship is the heart of the service itself, but further opportunities for young families to participate together in worship can be provided through direct links to family services and initiatives like Messy Church.[10] Being incarnational starts at the initial approach, meeting and seeking genuinely to understand where a family is coming from in their request. It then continues in enabling the relationship between the church and the family to carry on over time in appropriate ways. A church can be transformational in its response through its engagement with the issues of raising children within its local community. From parenting classes to the provision of children's work and engagement with local schools and uniformed organizations, a local congregation can bring substance to its missional concern. Through the provision of a candle and a book of prayers at the service itself, and specifically Christian children's ministry, either by itself or in partnership with other churches, a congregation can look to foster appropriate forms of discipleship, while in organizing mums and toddlers groups and providing playgroup facilities, opportunities are given to develop real and meaningful relationships.

---

10 www.messychurch.org.uk.

Weddings

A pincer movement between cohabitation on one side and divorce on the other has seriously eroded the institution of marriage. Figures from the Office for National Statistics indicate that the number of couples living together and remaining unmarried had jumped from 2.7 million to 4.5 million between 1992 and 2007, an increase of two-thirds or from 6 per cent to 10 per cent of the population over 16. With regard to divorce, 22 per cent of marriages in 1970 had ended by their fifteenth wedding anniversary, whereas 33 per cent of those begun in 1995 had ended after the same period of time. By contrast the annual number of weddings between 2005 and 2010 was at almost the lowest recorded figure since records began in 1895.[11] Yet this still meant that there were in excess of 275,000 marriages in the UK during 2010,[12] with over 20 per cent of these conducted in the Church of England alone.[13]

Once again, it is important to ask why, given the alternative options available, so many couples still choose to get married, and get married in church. With the traditional pattern of having a wedding before consummating the relationship and setting up home almost completely restricted to those within British faith communities, the majority now approach marriage from a different place.

At a relational level, the nature of a wedding ceremony that is formal, public and accompanied by a clear set of legal implications is central to unlocking the question why. By contrast, cohabitation is to a larger degree casual, private and easily dispensed with. Those making the choice to get married are opting for a significant transition in their relationship. 'In sickness and in health', along with 'till death us do part', express the intention of relational security and permanence. That the wedding is conducted in church underlines the seriousness of the transition and the vows that are taken. That this is done before God is made explicit by the location of the ceremony in the sacred space of a church's sanctuary. Once again, the presence of family and friends establishes the social context within which the new narrative of the couple's relationship finds meaning and support.

---

11 'Estimating the Cohabiting Population', *Population Trends* 136 (ONS, Summer 2009), pp. 21–7; 'Divorces in England and Wales 2010', *Statistical Bulletin* (ONS, 8 December 2011), p. 1; 'Marriages in England and Wales, 2010', *Statistical Bulletin* (ONS, 29 February 2012), p. 2.

12 This is a compilation of figures for England and Wales, 241,100 (ONS); Scotland, 28,480 (General Register Office for Scotland); Northern Ireland, 8,156 (Northern Ireland Statistics and Research Agency).

13 Church of England, *Church Statistics 2010/11*, London: Church House Publishing, 2012, p. 22.

From the perspective of the missional values, worship again provides the context of this occasional office within which the marriage is solemnized. Given that contact with a couple through marriage is through an expression of cultural Christianity, maintaining and developing that relationship through similar acts of worship that are expressive of cultural Christianity can prove very fruitful. Invitations to participate in worship at Christmas, Mothering Sunday, Easter and Harvest Festival are especially appropriate, as is Remembrance Sunday for those with a military background. Taking time to understand a couple seeking to be married in church, and working with them on that basis, is the essence of an incarnational approach, alongside finding ways of maintaining the relationship in a similarly sympathetic and ongoing way. Marriage preparation and providing an access point to marriage guidance counselling can be both transformational and, when provided according to Christian values, expressions of Christian discipleship in so far as they enable people to embody the values of the Kingdom of God. Indeed, where there have been prior broken marriages, identifying and owning previous faults and mistakes can be the vehicle for forgiveness, restoration and personal growth. 'The occasional services' ability to embody God's healing and empowering word even at the borders reveals their missional character.'[14]

Some churches have also experimented with wedding fayres as an opportunity to extend their expression of Christian hospitality to their wider community, which, along with a genuine commitment to remain connected to those who marry within their walls, is expressive of this particular value of the Church's missional life.

Funerals

During 2010, the clergy of the Church of England alone conducted 171,420 funerals in England. This equates to 37 per cent of the death rate for that year. In addition, some 70 per cent of the population attended one of these funerals. By any account this is a substantial contribution to the social fabric and cultural experience of contemporary life.[15] With the other Christian denominations factored in alongside other faith groups, one of the facts surrounding death and dying in contemporary Britain is the absence of any large demand for secular or humanist funerals. While this may increase over the forthcoming decades with the passing of the older

14 Robert D. Hawkins, 'Occasional Services: Border Crossings', in Thomas H. Schattauer, *Inside Out: Worship in an Age of Mission*, Minneapolis: Fortress, 1999, p. 181.

15 *Church Statistics 2010/11*, pp. 26–7.

generation whose higher incidence of Christian faith may be reflected in the funeral statistics, still the reach of this particular occasional office is deeply embedded in the life of the nation.

In the face of death, a non-religious funeral shuts the door on something beyond the end of life. Yet for many people, funerals awaken the desire for there to be something more, the hope that this is not the end. A strange combination of sources, building on a half-remembered understanding of the Christian belief of the resurrection of the dead melds together into a belief that the dead remain alive in another place and that ultimately families and friends will be reunited there. Fed by the recounting of near-death experiences with their dark tunnels, bright lights and a sense of a reassuring presence, the strong hope of paradise continues in the popular imagination. The Christian hope both informs and guides how a funeral is conducted and how the Church exercises pastoral care for those immersed in the experience of death and dying.

From the announcement of 'the comfortable words' at the beginning of a funeral service, once again the occasional office is expressed in worship of the Triune God. Indeed, engaging with the God whose empathetic love meets with compassion and understanding those who are bereaved and, in the encounter, comforts those who mourn, is integral to the whole office. The ministry to the bereaved is part of the twin emphases of the service that celebrates the life of the deceased and bears the grief of those who remain. Genuine pastoral care is thoroughly incarnational and intimately relational, as it meets the bereaved in their own home, listens to their story, shapes the funeral around the life, experience, hopes and expectations that are discerned, and then provides after-care strategically, when others may have already moved on with life, leaving the bereaved isolated with their grief. Some local churches provide follow-up pastoral visits on the anniversary of the bereavement, others offer regular services of remembrance for the bereaved. Funeral ministry can be transformational too by providing the opportunity for a life to be wholesomely drawn to a conclusion as good things are celebrated, goodbyes are said and the hurts and failures of both sides forgiven. Through the recounting of the Christian narrative in prayer and singing, the mourners are exposed once more to the Christian world-view of death and resurrection, and cultural Christianity is discipled in the way of Jesus.

Conclusion

Robert Hawkins observes that the occasional offices 'make the gospel concrete in the midst of living and dying'.[16] As such they are part of the Church's cradle-to-grave ministry to wider society. For the Church of England in 2010, this accounted for 374,300 opportunities for the gospel to be missionally expressed.[17] However half-remembered and partially understood the gospel is by many who avail themselves of the occasional offices, through the reading of Scripture, the saying of prayers and the singing of songs and hymns it is given full expression. Then through the wider ministry of the Church, its community engagement, life of service and willingness to build real relationships over time, people are brought closer to Christ and encounter him for themselves.

---

16 Hawkins, 'Occasional Services', p. 194.

17 Approximately 38 per cent baptisms, 16 per cent weddings and 46 per cent funerals. *Church Statistics 2010/11*, p. 27.

Index